P9-CER-069

Spanish
phrase book

**Berlitz Publishing / APA Publications GmbH & Co.
Verlag KG, Singapore Branch, Singapore**

TABLE OF CONTENTS

PRONUNCIATION

This section is designed to make you familiar with the sounds of Spanish using our simplified phonetic transcription. You'll find the pronunciation of the Spanish letters and sounds explained below, together with their "imitated" equivalents. This system is used throughout the phrase book: simply read the pronunciation as if it were English, noting any special rules below.

THE SPANISH LANGUAGE

There are almost 350 million speakers of Spanish worldwide – it is the third most widely spoken language after Chinese and English. These are the countries where you can expect to hear Spanish spoken (figures are approximate):

España Spain

Spanish is spoken by almost the entire population (40 million). Other languages: Catalan in northeastern Spain (6m), Galician in northwestern Spain (3m) and Basque (almost 1m).

México Mexico

Spanish is spoken by most of the 98 million population. Other languages: 6 million speak Indian languages, esp. Nahuatl (1.5 m), Maya (1m) in Yucatán.

América del Sur South America

Spanish is spoken by the great majority in **Argentina** (34 million); **Bolivia** (less than half the 7.5m population), other languages: Quechua (2m), Aymara (1.5m); **Colombia** (35m), other: Arawak, Carib; **Ecuador** (11m), other: Quechua (0.5m); **Paraguay** - three-quarters of the 5.5m population, other: Guarani (3m); **Peru** (24m) other: Quechua (5m), Aymara (0.5m); **Uruguay** (3.5m); **Venezuela** (22m), other: Arawak, Carib.

América Central Central America

Spanish is spoken in **Costa Rica** (3.5 million), **Cuba** (11m), **Dominican Republic** (8m); **Puerto Rico** (4m); **El Salvador** (6m); **Guatemala** (10m), other: Quiché (1m), Cakchiquel (0.5m); **Honduras** (5.5m), other: Lenca, Carib; **Nicaragua** (4m); **Panama** (3m).

Estados Unidos United States

Spanish is spoken by approx. 18 million people, especially in Texas, New Mexico, Arizona, California, southern Florida and New York City.

África Africa

Spanish is the official language of **Equatorial Guinea** (4.5m), other: Fang. Spanish is also spoken in the Spanish zone of **Morocco**.

The Spanish alphabet is the same as English, with the addition of the tilde on the letter **ñ**. The acute accent (´) indicates stress, not a change in sound.

Some Spanish words have been incorporated into English, for example **bonanza**, **canyon**, **patio**, **plaza**, **siesta**.

Until recently in Spanish, **ch** and **ll** were treated as separate letters, alphabetically ordered after **c** and **l** respectively. Look out for this when using old telephone directories or dictionaries.

There are some differences in vocabulary and pronunciation between the Spanish spoken in Spain and that in the Americas - although each is easily understood by the other. This phrase book and dictionary is specifically geared to travelers in Spain.

CONSONANTS

Letter	Approximate pronunciation	Symbol	Example	Pronunciation
b	1. as in English	b	**bueno**	_bw_eno
	2. between vowels as in English, but softer	b	**bebida**	be_beeda_
c	1. before **e** and **i**, like *th* in *th*in	th	**centro**	_then_tro
	2. otherwise like *k* in *k*it	k	**como**	_k_omo
ch	as in English	ch	**mucho**	_moo_cho
d	1. as in English *d*og, but less decisive	d	**donde**	_dondeh_
	2. between vowels and at the end of a word, like *th* in *th*is	th	**usted**	oos_teth_
g	1. before **e** and **i**, like *ch* in Scottish lo*ch*	kh	**urgente**	oor_khenteh_
	2. otherwise, like *g* in *g*et	g	**ninguno**	neen_goono_
h	always silent		**hombre**	_ombreh_
j	like *ch* in Scottish lo*ch*	kh	**bajo**	_bakho_
ll	like *lli* in mi*lli*on	l-y	**lleno**	_l-yeno_
ñ	like *ni* in o*ni*on	ñ	**señor**	se_ñor_
qu	like *k* in *k*ick	k	**quince**	_keentheh_
r	more strongly trilled (like a Scottish *r*), especially at the beginning of a word	r	**río**	_reeo_
rr	strongly trilled	rr	**arriba**	a_rreeba_

s	1. like s in same	s	**vista**	_vee_sta
	2. before **b**, **d**, **g**, **l**, **m**, **n**, like s in rose	z	**mismo**	_mee_zmo
v	like b in bad, but softer	b	**viejo**	_vee_yekho
z	like th in thin	th	**brazo**	_bra_tho

Letters **f, k, l, m, n, p, t, x** and **y** are pronounced as in English.

VOWELS

Letter	Approximate pronunciation	Symbol	Example	Pronunciation
a	in length, between a in English pat, and a in English bar	a	**gracias**	_gra_theeyas
e	1. like e in get	e	**puedo**	_pwe_do
	2. in a syllable ending in a vowel like e in they	eh	**me**	meh
i	like ee in feet	ee	**sí**	see
o	like o in got	o	**dos**	dos
u	1. like oo in food	oo	**una**	_oo_na
	2. silent after **g** in words like **guerra**, **guiso**, except where marked **ü**, as in **antigüedad**			
y	only a vowel when alone or at the end of a word, like ee in feet	ee	**y**	ee

Note: to aid pronunciation the phonetic transcription uses **y** where applicable between groups of vowels to indicate the sound value of y in yes.

STRESS

Stress has been indicated in the phonetic transcription: underlined letters should be pronounced with more stress (i.e. louder) than the others.

In words ending with a vowel, **-n** or **-s**, the next to last syllable is stressed, e.g. **mañana** (_ma_ñana); in words ending in a consonant, the last syllable is stressed, e.g. **señor** (se_ñor_); the acute accent (´) is used in Spanish to indicate a syllable is stressed, e.g. **río** (_ree_o).

Some Spanish words have more than one meaning; the accent mark is employed to distinguish between them, e.g.: **él** (he) and **el** (the); **sí** (yes) and **si** (if); **tú** (you) and **tu** (your).

PRONUNCIATION OF THE SPANISH ALPHABET

A	ah	**J**	_khota_	**R**	_erreh_
B	beh	**K**	ka	**S**	_ehseh_
C	theh	**L**	_ehleh_	**T**	teh
D	deh	**M**	emeh	**U**	oo
E	eh	**N**	_aynneh_	**V**	_oobheh_
F	_ehfeh_	**Ñ**	_enyeh_	**W**	_dobleh beh_
G	kheh	**O**	oh	**X**	_ekees_
H	_acheh_	**P**	peh	**Y**	ee gree_yega_
I	ee	**Q**	koo	**Z**	_theta_

Basic Expressions

ESSENTIAL	
Yes./No.	**Sí.** *see*/**No.** *no*
Okay.	**De acuerdo.** *deh akwehrdo*
Please.	**Por favor.** *por fabor*
Thank you (very much).	**(Muchas) gracias.**
	(moochas) gratheeyas

Hello./Hi!	**¡Hola!** *ola*
Good morning.	**Buenos días.** *bwenos deeyas*
Good afternoon/evening.	**Buenas tardes.** *bwenas tardes*
Good night.	**Buenas noches.** *bwenas noches*
Good-bye.	**Adiós.** *adyos*
Excuse me! *(getting attention)*	**¡Disculpe!** *deeskulpeh*
Excuse me. *(May I get past?)*	**Disculpe.** *deeskulpay*
Excuse me!/Sorry!	**¡Perdón!/¡Lo siento!** *perdon/lo seeyento*
It was an accident.	**Fue un accidente.** *fweh oon aktheedenteh*
Don't mention it.	**No hay de qué.** *no eye deh keh*
Never mind.	**No tiene importancia.** *no tyeneh eemportantheeya*

ON THE STREET

¡Hola! ¿Cómo está? *ola komo esta* (*Hi. How are you?*)
Bien gracias. ¿Y usted? *beeyen gratheeyas ee oosteth* (*Fine. And yourself?*)
Bien gracias. *beeyen gratheeyas* (*Fine. Thanks.*)

COMMUNICATION DIFFICULTIES

Do you speak English?	**¿Habla inglés?**
	abla eengles
Does anyone here speak English?	**¿Hay alguien que hable inglés?**
	eye algeeyen keh ableh eengles
I don't speak (much) Spanish.	**No hablo (mucho) español.**
	no ablo (moocho) español
Could you speak more slowly?	**¿Podría hablar más despacio?**
	podreeya ablar mas despatheeyo
Could you repeat that?	**¿Podría repetir eso?**
	podreeya repeteer eso
Excuse me? [Pardon?]	**¿Cómo?** _komo_
Sorry, I didn't catch that.	**Lo siento, no entendí eso.**
	lo seeyento, no entendee eso
What was that?	**¿Qué ha dicho?**
	keh a deecho
Could you spell it?	**¿Podría deletrearlo?**
	podreeya deletrayarlo
Please write it down.	**Escríbamelo, por favor.**
	eskreebamelo por fabor
Can you translate this for me?	**¿Podría traducirme esto?**
	podreeya tradootheermeh esto
What does this/that mean?	**¿Qué significa esto/eso?**
	keh seegneefeeku esto/eso
How do you pronounce that?	**¿Cómo se pronuncia eso?**
	komo se pronoontheeya eso
Please point to the phrase in the book.	**Por favor señáleme la frase en el libro.**
	por fabor señalemeh la fraseh en el leebro
I understand.	**Entiendo.**
	enteeyendo
I don't understand.	**No entiendo.**
	no enteeyendo
Do you understand?	**¿Entiende?**
	enteeyendeh

QUESTIONS

Questions can be formed in Spanish:

1. by a questioning intonation; often the personal pronoun is left out, both in affirmative sentences and in questions:

Hablo español.	I speak Spanish.
¿Habla español?	Do you speak Spanish?

2. by using a question word plus the inverted order:

¿Cuándo llega el tren?	When does the train arrive?

Where?

Where is it?	**¿Dónde está?** _dondeh esta_
Where are you going?	**¿Dónde vas?** _dondeh bas_
to the meeting place [point]	**en el lugar de encuentro** _en el loogar deh enkwentro_
away from me	**lejos de mí** _lekhos deh mee_
from the U.S.	**de los Estados Unidos** _deh los estados oonidos_
here	**aquí** _akee_
in the car	**en el coche** _en el kocheh_
in Spain	**en España** _en españa_
inside	**dentro** _dentro_
near the bank	**cerca del banco** _therka del banko_
next to the apples	**al lado de las manzanas** _al lado deh las manthanas_
opposite the market	**enfrente del mercado** _enfrenteh del merkado_
there	**allí** _al-yee_
to the hotel	**al hotel** _al otel_
on the left/right	**a la izquierda/derecha** _a la eethkeeyerda/derecha_
on the sidewalk	**en la acera** _en la athera_
outside the café	**fuera del café** _fwera del kafeh_
up to the traffic light	**hasta el semáforo** _asta el semaforo_

12

When?

When does the museum open?	**¿Cuándo abre el museo?** _kwando abray el moosayo_
When does the train arrive?	**¿Cuándo llega el tren?** _kwando l-yega el tren_
at 7 o'clock	**a las siete en punto** _a las seeyeteh en poonto_
after lunch	**después de comer** _despwes deh komer_
always	**siempre** _seeyempreh_
around midnight	**a eso de las doce de la noche** _a eso deh las dotheh deh la nocheh_
before Friday	**antes del viernes** _antes del beeyernes_
by tomorrow	**para mañana** _para mañana_
every week	**todas las semanas/cada semana** _todas las semanas/kada semana_
for 2 hours	**durante dos horas** _dooranteh dos oras_
from 9 a.m. to 6 p.m.	**de nueve de la mañana a seis de la tarde** _deh nwebeh deh la mañana a says deh la tardeh_
in 20 minutes	**dentro de veinte minutos** _dentro deh beynteh meenootos_
never	**nunca** _noonka_
not yet	**todavía no** _todabeeya no_
now	**ahora** _a-ora_
often	**a menudo** _a menoodo_
on March 8	**el ocho de marzo** _el ocho de martho_
on weekdays	**durante la semana** _dooranteh la semana_
sometimes	**a veces** _a bethes_
soon	**pronto** _pronto_
then	**entonces/luego** _entonthes/looego_
within 2 days	**dentro de dos días** _dentroa deh dos deeyas_
10 minutes ago	**hace diez minutos** _athay deeyeth meenootos_

What kind of ...?

I'd like something ...	**Quiero algo ...** keeyero algo
It's ...	**Es ...** es
beautiful/ugly	**bonito/feo** boneeto/fayo
better/worse	**mejor/peor** mekhor/peyor
big/small	**grande/pequeño** grandeh/pekeño
cheap/expensive	**barato/caro** barato/karo
clean/dirty	**limpio/sucio** leempeeo/sootheeo
dark/light	**oscuro/claro** oskooro/klaro
delicious/revolting	**delicioso/asqueroso** deleetheeyoso/askeroso
early/late	**temprano/tarde** temprano/tardeh
easy/difficult	**fácil/difícil** fatheel/deefeetheel
empty/full	**vacío/lleno** batheeyo/l-yeno
good/bad	**bueno/malo** bweno/malo
heavy/light	**pesado/ligero** pesado/likhehro
hot, warm/cold	**caliente/frío** kaleeyenteh/freeyo
modern/old-fashioned	**moderno/antiguo** moderno/anteegwoa
narrow/wide	**estrecho/ancho** estrecho/ancho
next/last	**próximo/último** prokseemo/oolteemo
old/new	**viejo/nuevo** beeyekho/nwebo
open/shut	**abierto/cerrado** abeeyerto/therrado
pleasant, nice/unpleasant	**agradable/desagradable** agradableh/desagradableh
quick/slow	**rápido/lento** rrapeedo/lento
quiet/noisy	**silencioso/ruidoso** seelentheeyoso/rrooeeydoso

right/wrong	**correcto/incorrecto** *korrekto/eenkorrekto*
tall/short	**alto/bajo** *alto/bakho*
thick/thin	**grueso/fino** *grooeso/feeno*
vacant/occupied	**libre/ocupado** *leebreh/okoopado*
young/old	**joven/viejo** *khoben/beeyekho*

How much/many?

How much is this/that?	**¿Cuánto es esto/eso?** *kwanto es esto/eso*
How many are there?	**¿Cuántos hay?** *kwantos eye*
1/2/3	**uno/dos/tres** *oono/dos/tres*
4/5	**cuatro/cinco** *kwatro/theenko*
none	**ninguno** *neengoono*
about 20 euros	**unos veinte euros** *oonos baynteh eh-ooros*
a little	**un poco** *oon poko*
a lot of traffic	**mucho tráfico** *moocho trafeeko*
enough	**bastante** *bastanteh*
few	**pocos(-as)** *pokos(-as)*
a few of them	**unos(-as) pocos(-as)** *oonos(-as) pokos(-as)*
many people	**mucha gente** *moocha khenteh*
more than that	**más que eso** *mas keh eso*
less than that	**menos que eso** *menos keh eso*
much more	**mucho más** *moocho mas*
nothing else	**nada más** *nada mas*
too much	**demasiado** *demaseeyado*

Why?

Why is that?	**¿Por qué?** *por keh*
Why not?	**¿Por qué no?** *por keh no*
because of the weather	**por el tiempo** *por el teeyempo*
because I'm in a hurry	**porque tengo prisa** *porkeh tengo preesa*
I don't know why.	**No sé por qué.** *no seh por keh*

Who?/Which?

Who's there?	**¿Quién es?** *keeyen es*
Who is it for?	**¿Para quién es?** *para keeyen es*
either … or …	**o … o …** *o… o*
her/him	**ella/él** *el-ya/el*
me	**mí** *mee*
you	**ti** *tee*
them	**ellos** *el-yos*
someone	**alguien** *algeeyen*
none/no one	**ninguno/nadie** *neengoono/nadeeay*
Which one do you want?	**¿Cuál quiere?** *kwal keeyereh*
that one/this one	**ése/éste** *eseh/esteh*
not that one	**ése no** *eseh no*
one like that	**uno como ése** *oono komo eseh*
something	**algo** *algo*

Whose?

Whose is that?	**¿De quién es eso?** *deh keeyehn es eso*
It's mine/ours.	**Es el mío/el nuestro.** *es el meeyo/el nwestro*
yours	**suyo/tuyo/vuestro** *sooyo/tooyo/bwestro*
his/hers/theirs	**suyo** *sooyo*
It's … turn.	**Es … turno.** *es … toorno*
my/our	**mi/nuestro** *mee/nwestro*
your	**su/tu/vuestro** *soo/too/bwestro*
his/her/their	**su** *soo*

How?

How would you like to pay?	**¿Cómo le gustaría pagar?** _komo le goostareeya pagar_
How are you getting here?	**¿Cómo va a venir aquí?** _komo bas a beneer akee_
by car	**en coche** _en kocheh_
by credit card	**con tarjeta de crédito** _kon tarkheta deh kredeeto_
by chance	**por casualidad** _por kasooalidath_
equally	**igualmente** _eegwalmenteh_
extremely	**sumamente** _soomamenteh_
on foot	**a pie** _a peeyeh_
quickly	**rápidamente** _rapeedamenteh_
slowly	**despacio** _despatheeyo_
too fast	**demasiado deprisa** _demaseeyado depreesa_
totally	**totalmente** _totalmenteh_
very	**muy** _mwee_
with a friend	**con un(a) amigo(a)** _kon un(a) ameego(a)_
without a passport	**sin pasaporte** _seen pasaporteh_

Is it …?/Are there …?

Is it …?	**¿Es/está …?** _es/esta_
Is it free of charge?	**¿Es gratis?** _es gratees_
It isn't ready.	**No está listo.** _no esta leesto_
Is/Are there …?	**¿Hay …?** _eye_
Are there any buses into town?	**¿Hay autobúses para ir a la ciudad?** _eye aootoboosses para eer a la thoooodath_
There are showers in the rooms.	**Hay duchas en las habitaciones.** _eye doochas en las abeetatheeyones_
Here it is/they are.	**Aquí tiene/los tiene.** _akee teeyeneh/los teeyeneh_
There it is/they are.	**Ahí está/están.** _ahee esta/estan_

Can ... ?

Can I have ...?	**¿Puedo tomar ...?** _pwedo tomar_
Can we have ...?	**¿Podemos tomar ...?** _podemos tomar_
Can you show me ...?	**¿Puede enseñarme ...?** _pwedeh enseñarmeh_
Can you tell me?	**¿Puede decirme?** _pwedeh detheermeh_
Can you help me?	**¿Puede ayudarme?** _pwedeh ayoodarmeh_
Can I help you?	**¿Puedo ayudarle?** _pwedo ayoodarleh_
Can you direct me to ...?	**¿Puede indicarme cómo ir a ...?** _pwede eendeekarmeh komo eer a_
I can't.	**No puedo.** _no pwedo_

What do you want?

I'd like ...	**Quiero ...** _keeyero_
Could I have ...?	**¿Podría tomar ...?** _podreeya tomar_
We'd like ...	**Queremos ...** _keremos_
Give me ...	**Déme ...** _demeh_
I'm looking for ...	**Estoy buscando ...** _estoy booskando_
I need to ...	**Necesito ...** _netheseeto_
go ...	**ir ...** _eer_
find ...	**encontrar ...** _enkontrar_
see ...	**ver ...** _behr_
speak to ...	**hablar con ...** _ablar kon_

IN THE POST OFFICE

¿De quién es este bolso? _deh keeyehn es este bolso_
(Whose handbag is that?)
Es el mío. Gracias. _es el meeyo gratheeyas_
(It's mine. Thanks.)
De nada. _de nada_ _(You're welcome.)_

OTHER USEFUL WORDS

fortunately	**afortunadamente** *afortoonadamenteh*
hopefully	**con algo de suerte** *kon algo deh swerteh*
of course	**por supuesto** *por soopwesto*
perhaps	**quizás** *keetha*
unfortunately	**desgraciadamente** *desgratheeyadamenteh*
also	**también** *tambeeyen*
and	**y** *ee*
but	**pero** *pero*
or	**o** *o*

EXCLAMATIONS

And so on.	**Etcétera, etcétera.** *etthetera etthetera*
At last!	**¡Por fin!** *por feen*
Carry on.	**Continúa.** *konteenooa*
Nonsense.	**Tonterías.** *tontereeyas*
Quite right too!	**¡Puedes estar seguro(-a)!** *pwedes estar segooro(-a)*
You're joking!	**¡No me digas!** *no moh doogas*
How are things?	**¿Cómo te va?** *komo teh ba*
great/brilliant	**estupendamente** *estoopendamenteh*
great	**muy bien** *mwee beeyen*
fine/okay	**bien** *beeyen*
not bad	**no demasiado mal** *no demaseeyado mal*
not good	**no muy bien** *no mwee beeyen*
fairly bad	**bastante mal** *bastanteh mal*
terrible	**fatal** *fatal.*

ACCOMMODATIONS

All types of accommodations, from hotels to campsites, can be found through the tourist information center (**Oficina de turismo**).

Early reservations are essential in most major tourist centers, especially during high season or special events. If you haven't booked, you're more likely to find accommodations available outside towns and city centers.

Hotel *otel*
There are five official categories of hotels: luxury, first class A, first class B, second class and third class. There may be price variations within any given category, depending on the location and the facilities offered. There are also, of course, plenty of unclassified hotels where you will find clean, simple accommodations and good food.

Refugio *refookhyo*
Small inns in remote and mountainous regions. They are often closed in winter.

Albergue de juventud *albergeh deh khoobentooth*
Youth hostel. There is usually no age limit; become a member and your **carnet de alberguista** will entitle you to a discount. There isn't an extensive network in Spain, but **casas de huéspedes** (**CH**) and **fondas** (**F**) provide budget-conscious alternatives.

Apartamento amueblado *apartamento amweblado*
A furnished apartment (flat) mainly in resorts. Available from specialized travel agents or directly from the landlord (look for the sign **se alquila** – for rent, to let).

Hostal *ostal*
Modest hotels, often family concerns, graded one to three stars; denoted by the sign **Hs**.

Parador *parador*
Palaces, country houses or castles that have been converted into hotels and are under government supervision. Their aim is to provide the chance to experience "the real Spain." The central reservation agency is **Paradores de España** ☎ 435 97 00.

Pensión *pensyon*
Boardinghouses, graded one to three stars; denoted by the sign **P**.

RESERVATIONS/BOOKING

In advance

Can you recommend a hotel in …?	**¿Puede recomendarme un hotel en …?** *pwede rekomendarmeh oon otel en*
Is it near the center (of town)?	**¿Está cerca del centro (de la ciudad)?** *esta therka del thentro (deh la theeyoodath)*
How much is it per night?	**¿Cuánto cuesta por noche?** *kwanto kwesta por nocheh*
Is there anything cheaper?	**¿Hay algo más barato?** *eye algo mas barato*
Could you reserve me a room there, please?	**¿Podría reservarme una habitación allí por favor?** *podreeya reserbarmeh oona abeetatheeyon al-yee por fabor*
How do I get there?	**¿Cómo llego allí?** *komo l-yego al-yee*

At the hotel

Do you have a room?	**¿Tienen habitaciones libres?** *teeyenen abeetatheeyones leebres*
Is there another hotel nearby?	**¿Hay otro hotel por aquí cerca?** *eye otro otel por akee therka*
I'd like a single/double room.	**Quiero una habitación individual/doble.** *keeyero oona abeetatheeyon eendeebeedooal/dobleh*
A room with …	**Una habitación con …** *oona abeetatheeyon kon*
a double bed/twin beds	**una cama de matrimonio/dos camas** *oona kama deh matreemoneeyo/dos kamas*
a bath/shower	**un baño/una ducha** *oon bano/oona doocha*

AT THE HOTEL RECEPTION

¿Tienen habitaciones libres? *teeyenen abeetatheeyones leebres (Do you have any vacancies?)*
Lo siento. *lo seeyento (I'm sorry.)*
Gracias. Adiós. *gratheeyas adyos (Thank you. Good bye.)*

RECEPTION

I have a reservation. My name is …	**Tengo una reserva. Me llamo …** *tengo oona reserba. meh l-yamo*
We've reserved a double and a single room.	**Hemos reservado una habitación doble y una individual.** *emos reserbado oona abeetatheeyon dobleh ee oona eendeebeedooal*
I confirmed my reservation by mail.	**Confirmé mi reserva por carta.** *konfeermeh mee reserba por karta*
Could we have adjoining rooms?	**¿Nos podrían dar habitaciones conjuntas?** *nos podreeyan dar abeetatheeyones konkhoontas*

Amenities and facilities

Is there (a) … in the room?	**¿Hay (un/una) … en la habitación?** *eye (oon/oona) … en la abeetatheeyon*
air conditioning	**aire acondicionado** *ayray akondeethyonado*
TV/telephone	**televisión/teléfono** *telebeeseeyon/telefono*
Does the hotel have (a)…?	**¿Tiene el hotel (un/una) …?** *teeyeneh el otel (oon/oona)*
fax facilities	**fax** *fax*
laundry service	**servicio de lavandería** *serbeetheeyo deh labandereeya*
satellite TV	**antena parabólica** *antena paraboleeka*
sauna	**sauna** *saoona*
swimming pool	**piscina** *peestheena*
Could you put … in the room?	**¿Podrían poner … en la habitación?** *podreean poner … en la abeetatheeyon*
an extra bed	**otra cama** *otra kama*
a crib/child's cot	**una cuna** *oona koona*
Do you have facilities for …?	**¿Tienen instalaciones para …?** *teeyenen eenstalatheeyones para*
the disabled/children	**los minusválidos/niños** *los meenusbaleedos/neeños*

How long?

We'll be staying …	**Nos quedaremos …**	_nos kedaremos_
overnight only	**sólo esta noche**	_solo esta nocheh_
a few days	**unos días**	_oonos deeyas_
a week (at least)	**una semana (por lo menos)**	_oona semana (por lo menos)_
I'd like to stay an extra night.	**Quiero quedarme una noche más.**	_keeyero kedarmeh oona nocheh mas_
What does this mean?	**¿Qué significa esto?**	_keh seegneefeeka esto_

IN THE STORE

¿Cómo le gustaría pagar? _komo le goostareeya pagar_
(How would you like to pay?)
En metálico, por favor. _en metaleeko por fabor_
(Cash, please.)

YOU MAY HEAR

¿Puedo ver su pasaporte?	May I see your passport?
Rellene este formulario/ firme aquí, por favor.	Please fill out this form/sign here.
¿Cuál es su número de matrícula?	What is your license plate [registration] number?

YOU MAY SEE

DESAYUNO INCLUIDO	breakfast included
SE DAN COMIDAS	meals available
SÓLO LA HABITACIÓN … EUROS	room only … euros
APELIDO/NOMBRE	name/first name
DOMICILIO/CALLE/NÚMERO	home address/street/number
NACIONALIDAD/PROFESIÓN	nationality/profession
FECHA/LUGAR DE NACIMIENTO	date/place of birth
NÚMERO DE PASAPORTE	passport number
NÚMERO DE MATRÍCULA	license plate [registration] number
LUGAR/FECHA	place/date
FIRMA	signature

Prices

How much is it …?	**¿Cuánto es …?** _kwanto es_
per night/week	**por noche/semana** _por nocheh/semana_
for bed and breakfast	**por desayuno y habitación** _por desayoono ee abeetatheeyon_
excluding meals	**excluyendo las comidas** _exklooyendo las komeedas_
for full board (American Plan [A.P.])	**por pensión completa** _por penseeyon kompleta_
for half board (Modified American Plan [M.A.P.])	**por media pensión** _por medeeya penseeyon_
Does the price include …?	**¿Incluye el precio …?** _eenklooyeh el pretheeo_
breakfast	**el desayuno** _el desayoono_
service	**el servicio** _el serbeetheeo_
sales tax [VAT]	**IVA** _eeba_
Do I have to pay a deposit?	**¿Tengo que pagar un depósito?** _tengo keh pagar oon deposeeto_
Is there a reduction for children?	**¿Hay un descuento para los niños?** _eye oon deskwento para los neeños_

Decisions

May I see the room?	**¿Puedo ver la habitación?** _pwedo behr la abeetatheeyon_
That's fine. I'll take it.	**Está bien. Me la quedo.** _esta beeyen. meh la kedo_
It's too …	**Es demasiado …** _es demaseeyado_
dark/small	**oscura/pequeña** _oskoora/pekeña_
noisy	**ruidosa** _rooeedosa_
Do you have anything …?	**¿Tiene algo …?** _teeyeneh algo_
bigger/cheaper	**más grande/más barato** _mas grandeh/mas barato_
quieter/warmer	**más tranquilo/menos frío** _mas trankeelo/menos freeyo_
No, I won't take it.	**No, no me quedo con ella.** _no, no meh kedo kon el-ya_

PROBLEMS

The … doesn't work.	**… no funciona.**	*no foontheeyona*
air conditioning	**el aire acondicionado**	*el ayreh akondeetheeyonado*
fan	**el ventilador**	*el benteelador*
heat	**la calefacción**	*la kalefaktheeyon*
light	**la luz**	*la looth*
I can't turn the heat [heating] on/off.	**No puedo encender/apagar la calefacción.**	*no pwedo enthender/ apagar la kalefaktheeyon*
There is no hot water/ toilet paper.	**No hay agua caliente/papel higiénico.**	*no eye agwa kaleeyenteh/papel eekheeyeneeko*
The faucet [tap] is dripping.	**El grifo gotea.**	*el greefo goteya*
The sink/toilet is blocked.	**El lavabo/wáter está atascado.**	*el labavo/bater esta ataskado*
The window/door is jammed.	**La ventana/puerta está atascada.**	*la bentana/pwerta esta ataskada*
My room has not been made up.	**No han hecho la habitación.**	*no an echo la abeetatheeyon*
The … is broken.	**… está roto(-a).**	*… esta roto(-a)*
blind/shutter	**la persiana**	*la perseeyana*
lamp	**la lámpara**	*la lampara*
lock	**el pestillo**	*el pesteel-yo*
There are insects in our room.	**Hay insectos en nuestra habitación.**	*eye eensektos en nwestra abeetatheeyon*

Action

Could you have that taken care of?	**¿Podrían encargarse de eso?**	*podreeyan enkargarseh deh eso*
I'd like to move to another room.	**Quiero mudarme a otra habitación.**	*keeyero moodarmeh a otra abeetatheeyon*
I'd like to speak to the manager.	**Quiero hablar con el gerente.**	*keeyero ablar kon el kherenteh*

ACCOMMODATIONS

25

REQUIREMENTS

The 220-volt, 50-cycle AC is the norm throughout Spain. If you bring your own electrical appliances, buy a Continental adapter plug (round pins, not square) before leaving home. You may also need a transformer appropriate to the wattage of the appliance.

About the hotel

Where's the …?	**¿Dónde está …?**	_dondeh esta_
bar	**el bar**	_el bar_
bathroom	**el cuarto de baño**	_el kwarto deh baño_
restroom [toilet]	**el servicio**	_el serbeetheeyo_
dining room	**el comedor**	_el komedor_
elevator	**el ascensor**	_el asthensor_
parking lot [car park]	**el aparcamiento**	_el aparkameeyento_
shower	**la ducha**	_la doocha_
swimming pool	**la piscina**	_la peestheena_
tour operator's bulletin board	**el tablón de anuncios del operador turístico**	_el tablon deh anoontheeyos del operador tooreesteeko_
Does the hotel have a garage?	**¿Tiene garaje el hotel?**	_teeyeneh garakheh el otel_
Can I use this adapter here?	**¿Puedo utilizar este adaptador aquí?**	_pwedo ooteeleethar esteh adaptador akee_

YOU MAY SEE

MARQUE … PARA HABLAR CON RECEPCIÓN	dial … for reception
MARQUE … PARA UNA LÍNEA EXTERIOR	dial … for an outside line
NO MOLESTAR	do not disturb
PROHIBIDO COMER EN LA HABITACIÓN	no food in the room
PUERTA DE INCENDIOS	fire door
SALIDA DE EMERGENCIA	emergency exit
SÓLO PARA UTILIZAR MÁQUINAS DE AFEITAR	razors [shavers] only

Personal needs

The key to room …, please.	**La llave de la habitación…, por favor.** *la l-yabeh dehla abeetatheeyon … por fabor*
I've lost my key.	**He perdido la llave.** *eh perdeedo la l-yabeh*
I've locked myself out of my room.	**No puedo entrar en mi habitación.** *no pwedo entrar en mee abeetatheeyon*
Could you wake me at …?	**¿Podría despertarme a la/las …?** *podreeya despertarmeh a la/las*
I'd like breakfast in my room.	**Quiero que me traigan el desayuno a la habitación.** *keeyero keh meh traygan el desayoono a la abeetatheeyon*
Can I leave this in the safe?	**¿Puedo dejar esto en la caja fuerte?** *pwedo dekhar esto on la kakha fwerteh*
Could I have my things from the safe?	**¿Podría darme mis cosas de la caja fuerte?** *podreeya darme mees kosas de la kakha fwerteh*
Where can I find (a) …?	**¿Dónde puedo encontrar a …?** *dondeh pwedo enkontrar a*
maid	**la chica del servicio** *la cheeka del serbeethyo*
our tour representative	**nuestro representante turístico** *nwestro representanteh tooreestiko*
Can I have (a) …?	**¿Pueden darme …?** *pweden darmeh*
bath towel	**una toalla de baño** *oona toaylya deh baño*
blanket	**una manta** *oona manta*
hangers	**perchas** *perchas*
pillow	**una almohada** *oona almoada*
soap	**jabón** *khabon*
Is there any mail for me?	**¿Hay correo para mí?** *eye korreho para mee*
Are there any messages for me?	**¿Hay algún mensaje para mí?** *eye algoon mensakheh para mee*

RENTING

We've reserved an apartment.	**Hemos reservado un apartamento.** _emos reserbado oon apartamento_
in the name of …	**a nombre de …** _a nombreh deh_
Where do we pick up the keys?	**¿Dónde recogemos las llaves?** _dondeh rekokhemos las l-yabes_
Where is the…?	**¿Dónde está …?** _dondeh esta_
electric meter	**el contador de la luz** _el kontador deh la looth_
fuse box	**la caja de fusibles** _la kakha deh fooseebles_
valve [stopcock]	**la llave de paso** _la l-yabeh deh paso_
water heater	**el calentador** _el kalentador_
Are there any spare …?	**¿Hay … de repuesto?** _eye … deh repwesto_
fuses	**fusibles** _fooseebles_
fuses/gas bottles	**bombonas de gas butano** _bombonas deh gas bootano_
sheets	**sábanas** _sabanas_
Which day does the maid come?	**¿Qué día viene la limpiadora?** _keh deeya beeyeneh la leempeeadora_
When do I put out the trash [rubbish]?	**¿Cuándo hay que sacar la basura?** _kwando eye keh sakar la basoora_

Problems?

Where can I contact you?	**¿Dónde me puedo poner en contacto con usted?** _dondeh meh pwedo poner en kontakto kon oosteth_
How does the stove [cooker]/water heater work?	**¿Cómo funciona la cocina/el calentador?** _komo foontheeyona la kotheena/el kalentador_
The … is/are dirty.	**… está/están sucios.** _esta/estan sootheeyos_
The … has broken down.	**… se ha estropeado.** _seh a estropeyado_
We accidentally broke/lost …	**Hemos roto/perdido … sin querer.** _emos roto/perdeedo … seen kerer_
That was already damaged when we arrived.	**Eso ya estaba estropeado cuando llegamos.** _eso ya estaba estropeado kwando l-yegamos_

Useful terms

dishes [crockery]	**la vajilla** la ba*kheel*-ya
freezer	**el congelador** el konkhela*dor*
frying pan	**la sartén** la sar*ten*
kettle	**el hervidor** el erbee*dor*
lamp	**la lámpara** la *lampara*
refrigerator	**el frigorífico** el freego*reefee*ko
saucepan	**el cazo** el *katho*
stove [cooker]	**la cocina** la ko*theena*
utensils [cutlery]	**los cubiertos** los koobee*yertos*
washing machine	**la lavadora** la laba*dora*

Rooms

balcony	**el balcón** el bal*kon*
bathroom	**el cuarto de baño** el *kwar*to deh *baño*
bedroom	**el dormitorio** el dormee*toreeyo*
dining room	**el comedor** el kome*dor*
kitchen	**la cocina** la ko*theena*
living room	**el salón/la sala de estar** el sa*lon*/la *sala* deh es*tar*
toilet	**el servicio** el ser*bee*theeyo

YOUTH HOSTEL

Youth hostels in Spain are few and far between, though a list is available from the Spanish National Tourist Office.

Do you have any places left for tonight?	**¿Tiene algun lugar libre para esta noche?** tee*yeneh* al*goon* loo*gar* *lee*breh *para* *esta* *no*cheh
Do you rent out bedding?	**¿Alquilan ropa de cama?** al*koo*lan *ropa* deh *kama*
What time are the doors locked?	**¿A qué hora cierran las puertas?** a keh *ora* thee*yeran* las *pwertas*
I have an International Student Card.	**Tengo el carnet internacional de estudiante.** *tengo* el kar*net* eenternatheeyo*nal* deh estoodee*anteh*

CAMPING

Spanish campsites are categorized luxury, 1st, 2nd or 3rd class. Facilities vary, but all have toilets, showers, drinking water and 24-hour surveillance. For a complete list of campsites, facilities and rates contact any Spanish National Tourist Office.

Reservations

Is there a campsite near here?	**¿Hay un cámping cerca de aquí?** *eye oon kampeen therka deh akee*
Do you have space for a tent/trailer [caravan]?	**¿Tienen una parcela para una tienda/ roulotte?** *teeyenen oona parthela para oona teeyenda/roolot*
What is the charge …?	**¿Cuánto cobran …?** *kwanto kobran*
per day/week	**por día/semana** *por deeya/semana*
for a tent/a car	**por tienda/por coche** *por teeyenda/por kocheh*
for a trailer [caravan]	**por roulotte** *por roolot*

Facilities

Are there cooking facilities on site?	**¿Tienen instalaciones para cocinar en el recinto?** *teeyenen eenstalatheeyones para kotheenar en el retheento*
Are there any electric outlets [power points]?	**¿Hay enchufes eléctricos?** *eye enshoefez elektreekos*
Where is/are the …?	**¿Dónde está/están …?** *dondeh esta/estan*
drinking water	**el agua potable** *el agwa potableh*
trash cans [dustbins]	**las papeleras** *las papeleras*
laundry facilities	**el servicio de lavandería** *el serbeetheeyo deh labandereeya*
showers	**las duchas** *las doochas*
Where can I get some butane gas?	**¿Dónde puedo comprar gas butano?** *dondeh pwedo komprar gas bootano*

YOU MAY SEE

AGUA POTABLE	drinking water
PROHIBIDO ACAMPAR	no camping
PROHIBIDO HACER HOGUERAS/BARBACOAS	no fires/barbecues

Complaints

It's too sunny here.	**Hay demasiado sol aquí.**
	eye demaseeyado sol akee
It's too shady/crowded here.	**Hay demasiada sombra/gente aquí.** *eye demaseeyada sombra/khenteh akee*
The ground's too hard/uneven.	**El suelo está demasiado duro/desnivelado.**
	el swelo esta demaseeyado dooro/ desneebelado
Do you have a more level spot?	**¿Tiene una parcela más nivelada?**
	teeyeneh oona parthela mas neebelada
You can't camp here.	**No puede acampar aquí.**
	no pwedeh akampar akee

Camping equipment

butane gas	**el gas butano** *el gas bootano*
campbed	**la cama de cámping**
	la kama deh kampeen
charcoal	**el carbón** *el karbon*
flashlight [torch]	**la linterna** *la leenterna*
groundcloth [groundsheet]	**el aislante para el suelo**
	el ayslanteh para el swelo
guy rope	**la cuerda tensora** *la kwerda tensora*
hammer	**el martillo** *el marteel-yo*
kerosene [primus] stove	**el hornillo de queroseno**
	el orneel-yo deh keroseno
knapsack	**la mochila** *la mocheela*
mallet	**el mazo** *el matho*
matches	**las cerillas** *las thereel-yas*
(air) mattress	**el colchón (inflable)**
	el kolchon (eenflableh)
sleeping bag	**el saco de dormir**
	el sako deh dormeer
tent	**la tienda** *la teeyenda*
tent pegs	**las estacas** *las estakas*
tent pole	**el mástil** *el masteel*

CHECKING OUT

What time do we need to vacate the room?	**¿A qué hora tenemos que desocupar la habitación?** *a keh _ora_ te_ne_mos keh des-okoo_par_ la abeetathee_yon*
Could we leave our baggage here until …?	**¿Podríamos dejar nuestro equipaje aquí hasta las …?** *podree_yamos de_khar _nwes_tro ekeepa_kheh a_kee _asta las …*
I'm leaving now.	**Me voy ahora.** *meh boy a-_ora*
Could you call me a taxi, please?	**¿Me podría pedir un taxi, por favor?** *meh podreeya pe_deer oon _taksee por fa_bor*
I/We've had a very enjoyable stay.	**He/Hemos disfrutado mucho nuestra estancia.** *eh/_emos deesfroo_tado _moocho _nwestra estan_theeya*

Paying

May I have my bill, please?	**¿Me da la cuenta, por favor?** *meh da la _kwenta, por fa_bor*
How much is my telephone bill?	**¿Cuánto es la cuenta de teléfono?** *_kwanto es la _kwenta deh te_lefono*
I think there's a mistake on this bill.	**Creo que hay un error en esta cuenta.** *_krayo keh eye oon _error en _esta _kwenta*
I've made … telephone calls.	**He hecho … llamadas.** *eh _echo … l-ya_madas*
I've taken … from the mini-bar.	**He tomado … del minibar.** *eh to_mado … del meenee_bar*
Can I have an itemized bill?	**¿Pueden darme una cuenta detallada?** *_pweden _darmeh _oona _kwenta detal-_yada*

Tipping

A service charge is generally included in hotel and restaurant bills. However, if the service has been particularly good, you may want to leave an extra tip. The following chart is a guide:

	Suggested tip
Bellman	€1–2
Hotel maid, for extra services	€2–3
Waiter	10% up to €10 then 5%

EATING OUT

RESTAURANTS

Bar *bar*
Bar; drinks and tapas served, sometimes hot beverages too.

Café *kafeh*
Cafés can be found on virtually every street corner. An indispensable part of
everyday life, the café is where people get together for a chat over a coffee,
soft drink or glass of wine.

Cafetería *kafetereeya*
Coffee shop; there's counter service or – for a small amount more – you can
choose a table. Fast food is generally served and the set menu is often very good.

Casa de comidas *kassa deh komeedass*
Simple inn serving cheap meals.

Heladería *eladereeya*
Ice cream parlor

Merendero *merendero*
Cheap open-air bar; you can usually eat outdoors.

Parador *parador*
A government-supervised establishment located in a historic castle, palace
or former monastery. A parador is usually noted for excellent regional dishes served in a dining room with handsome Spanish decor.

Venta *benta*
Restaurant; often specializing in regional cooking.

Pastelería/Confitería *pastelereeyu/konfootereeya*
Pastry shop; some serve coffee, tea and drinks.

Posada *possada*
A simple inn; the food is usually simple but good.

Refugio *refookhyo*
Mountain lodge serving simple meals.

Restaurante *restowranteh*
Restaurant; these are classified by the government but the official rating has
more to do with the decor than with the quality of cooking.

Salón de té *salon deh teh*
Tearoom; an upmarket cafeteria.

Taberna *taberna*
Similar to an English pub or American tavern in atmosphere; always a variety of tapas on hand as well as other snacks.

Tasca *taska*
Similar to a bar; drinks and tapas are served at the counter; standing only.

Meal times

el desayuno *el dessayoono*
Breakfast: generally from 7 to 10 a.m, traditionally toast/roll and coffee; hotels are now offering fare for tourists, serving a buffet breakfast.

la comida *la komeedah*
Lunch is generally served from around 2 or 3 p.m. The Spaniards like to linger over a meal, so service may seem on the leisurely side. In a hurry, go for fast-food outlets, pizzerias or cafés.

la merienda *la maryendah*
Light meal between 5-6pm to hold you up until dinner.

la cena *la theyna*
Dinner is served from 8.30 p.m. (10 p.m. in Madrid) to 11 p.m. However, in tourist areas you can get a meal at most places just about any time of day.

SPANISH CUISINE

The variety of Spanish cuisine comes from Celtic, Roman, Arab and New World influences, together with the profusion of Atlantic and Mediterranean seafood.

Most restaurants will offer a good value daily special (**menú del día**) – usually a three-course meal with house wine at a set price. Service and taxes are always included in the price.

ESSENTIAL	
A table for …, please.	**Una mesa para …, por favor.**
	oona mesa para …, por fabor
1/2/3/4	**uno/dos/tres/cuatro**
	oono/dos/tres/kwatro
Thank you.	**Gracias.** *gratheeyas*
The bill, please.	**La cuenta, por favor.**
	la kwenta por fabor

FINDING A PLACE TO EAT

Can you recommend a good restaurant?	**¿Puede recomendarme un buen restaurante?** *pwedeh rekomendarmeh oon bwen restawranteh*
Is there (a/an) … near here?	**¿Hay … cerca de aquí?** *eye … therka deh akee*
Chinese restaurant	**un restaurante chino** *oon restawranteh cheeno*
Greek restaurant	**un restaurante griego** *oon restawranteh greeyego*
inexpensive restaurant	**un restaurante barato** *oon restawranteh barato*
Italian restaurant	**un restaurante italiano** *oon restawranteh eetaleeyano*
traditional local restaurant	**un restaurante típico** *oon restawranteh teepeeko*
vegetarian restaurant	**un restaurante vegetariano** *oon restawranteh bekhetareeyano*
Where can I find a(n) …?	**¿Dónde puedo encontrar …?** *dondeh pwedo enkontrar*
burger stand	**una hamburguesería** *oona amboorgesereeya*
café/restaurant with a garden	**una cafetería/un restaurante con jardín** *oona kafetereeya/oon restawranteh kon khardeen*
fast food restaurant	**un restaurante de comida rápida** *oon restawranteh deh komeeda rapeeda*
ice cream parlor	**una heladería** *oona eladereeya*
pizzeria	**una pizzería** *oona peethereeya*
steak house	**una churrasquería** *oona choorraskereeya*

RESERVING A TABLE

I'd like to reserve
a table …

Quiero reservar una mesa …
keeyero reserbar oona mesa

for 2

para dos *para dos*

for this evening/
tomorrow at …

para esta noche/mañana a las …
para esta nocheh/mañana a las

We'll come at 8:00.

Llegaremos a las 8:00.
l-yegaremos a las ocho

A table for 2, please.

Una mesa para dos, por favor.
oona mesa para dos por fabor

We have a reservation.

Tenemos una reserva.
tenemos oona reserba

YOU MAY HEAR

¿Para que hora?	For what time?
Lo siento. Tenemos mucha gente/ está completo.	I'm sorry. We're very busy/full.
Tendremos una mesa libre dentro de … minutos.	We'll have a free table in … minutes.
¿Fumador o no fumador?	Smoking or non-smoking?

Where to sit

Could we sit …?

¿Podríamos sentarnos …?
podreeyamos sentarnos

over there/outside

allí/fuera *al-yee/fwera*

in a non-smoking area

en una zona de no fumadores
en oona thona deh no foomadores

by the window

al lado de la ventana
al lado deh la bentana

IN A RESTAURANT

¿Tiene una mesa fuera? *teeyeneh oona mesa fwera*
(Do you have a table outside?)
Por supuesto. *por soopwesto (Of course.)*
Muchas gracias. *moochas gratheeyas (Thank you
very much.)*

YOU MAY HEAR

¿Van a pedir ya?	Are you ready to order?
¿Qué va a tomar?	What would you like?
¿Quieren beber algo primero?	Would you like to order drinks first?
Le recomiendo …	I recommend …
Eso tardará … minutos.	That will take … minutes.
Que aproveche.	Enjoy your meal.

Ordering

Waiter/Waitress!	**¡Camarero/Camarera!** kama*re*ro/kama*re*ra
May I see the wine list?	**¿Puedo ver la carta de vinos?** *pwe*do behr la *kar*ta deh *bee*nos
Do you have a set menu?	**¿Tienen un menú del día?** teey*e*nen oon me*noo* del *dee*ya
Can you recommend some typical local dishes?	**¿Puede recomendarme algunos platos típicos de la zona?** *pwe*de rekomen*dar*meh al*goo*nos *pla*tos teep*ee*kos deh la *tho*na
Could you tell me what … is?	**¿Podría decirme lo que … es?** po*dree*ya de*theer*meh lo keh … es
What's in it?	**¿Qué lleva?** keh *l*y*e*ba
What kind of … do you have?	**¿Qué clase de … tiene?** keh *kla*seh deh … teey*e*neh
I'll have …	**Tomaré …** toma*re*h
a bottle/glass/carafe of …	**una botella/un vaso/una garrafa de …** *oo*na bo*tel*-yu/oon *ba*so/*oo*na ga*rra*fa deh

IN A RESTAURANT

La cuenta, por favor. la *kwen*ta por fa*bor* (The bill please.)
Aquí tiene. a*kee* teey*e*neh (Here you are.)
Gracias. *gra*theeyas (Thanks.)

Side dishes/Accompaniments

Could I have … without …?	**¿Podrían servirme … sin …?** *podreeyan serbeermeh … seen*
With a side order of …	**De guarnición …** *deh gwarneetheeyon*
I'd like … as a starter/ main course/side order.	**Quiero … de primero/segundo/guarnición.** *keeyero … deh preemero/segoondo/ gwarneetheeyon*
Could I have salad instead of vegetables, please?	**¿Podría tomar ensalada en lugar de verduras, por favor?** *podreeya tomar ensalada en loogar de berdooras por fabor*
Does the meal come with vegetables/potatoes?	**¿Viene la comida con verduras/patatas?** *beeyeneh la komeeda kon berdooras/patatas*
Do you have any …?	**¿Tienen …?** *teeyenen*
bread/mayonnaise	**pan/mayonesa** *pan/mayonesa*
I'd like … with that.	**Quiero … con eso.** *keeyero … kon eso*
vegetables/salad	**verduras/ensalada** *berdooras/ensalada*
potatoes/fries [chips]/rice	**patatas/patatas fritas/arroz** *patatas/patatas freetas/arroth*
sauce	**salsa** *salsa*
ice	**hielo** *eeyelo*
May I have some …?	**¿Me puede traer …?** *me pwedeh trayer*
butter	**mantequilla** *mantekeel-ya*
lemon	**limón** *leemon*
mustard	**mostaza** *mostatha*
pepper	**pimienta** *peemeeyenta*
salt	**sal** *sal*
seasoning	**aderezo** *aderetho*
sugar	**azúcar** *athookar*
artificial sweetener	**edulcorante artificial** *edoolkorante arteefeetheeyal*
blue cheese dressing	**salsa de queso azul** *salsa deh keso athool*
vinaigrette [French dressing]	**vinagreta/vinagreta francesa** *beenagreta/ beenagreta franthesa*

General questions

Could I have a(n)
(clean) …, please?

¿Podría traerme … (limpio/a), por favor?
*podreeya trayerme … (leempeeyo/a)
por fabor*

cup/glass

una taza/un vaso *oona tatha/oon baso*

fork/knife

un tenedor/cuchillo
oon tenedor/koocheelyo

napkin

una servilleta *oona serbeel-yeta*

plate/spoon

una plato/una cuchara
oona plato/oona koochara

I'd like some
more …, please.

Quiero más …, por favor.
keeyero mas … por fabor

Nothing more, thanks.

Nada más, gracias.
nada mas gratheeyas

Where are the restrooms
[toilets]?

¿Dónde están los servicios? *dondeh estan
los serbeetheeyos*

Special requirements

I mustn't eat food
containing …

No debo comer comida que tenga …
no debo komer komeeda keh tenga

salt/sugar

sal/azúcar *sal/athookar*

Do you have meals/
drinks for diabetics?

¿Tienen comidas/bebidas para diabéticos?
*teeyenen komeedas/bebeedas para
deeya beteekos*

Do you have
vegetarian meals?

¿Tienen comidas vegetarianas?
teeyenen komeedas bekhetareeyanas

For the children

Do you have children's
portions?

¿Hacen porciones para niños?
athen portheeyones para neeños

Could we have a
child's seat, please?

¿Podrían ponernos una silla para niños?
*podreeyan ponernos oona seel-ya
para neeños*

Where can I feed/
change the baby?

**¿Dónde puedo darle de comer/cambiar
al niño?** *dondeh pwedo darleh deh
komer/kambeeyar al neeño*

FAST FOOD/CAFÉ

Something to drink

I'd like (a) …	**Quiero …** *keeyero*
beer	**una cerveza** *oona therbetha*
tea/coffee/chocolate	**un té/un café/un chocolate** *oon teh/oon kafeh/oon chokolateh*
black/with milk	**solo/con leche** *solo/kon lecheh*
fruit juice/mineral water	**un zumo de fruta/un agua mineral** *oon thoomo deh froota/oon agwa meeneral*
red/white wine	**un vino tinto/blanco** *oon beeno teento/blanko*

YOU MAY HEAR

¿Qué va a tomar?	What would you like?
No tenemos …	We've run out of …
¿Algo más?	Anything else?

And to eat

I'd like two of those.	**Quiero dos de esos.** *keeyero dos deh esos*
burger/omelet	**una hamburguesa/una tortilla francesa** *oona amboorgesa/oona torteel-ya franthesa*
fries [chips]/sandwich	**patatas fritas/un bocadillo** *patatas freetas/oon bokadeel-yo*
cake *(small/large)*	**un dulce/una tarta** *oon dooltheh/oona tarta*
A … ice cream, please.	**Un helado de …, por favor.** *oon elado deh … por fabor*
chocolate/strawberry/ vanilla	**chocolate/fresa/vainilla** *chokolateh/fresa/bayneel-ya*
A … portion, please.	**Una porción …, por favor.** *oona portheeyon … por fabor*
small/medium/large	**pequeña/mediana/grande** *pekeña/medeeyana/grandeh*
It's to go [take away].	**Para llevar.** *para l-yebar*
That's all, thanks.	**Eso es todo, gracias.** *eso es todo, gratheeyas*

IN A CAFÉ

Dos cafés, por favor. *dos kafehs por fabor*
(Two coffees, please.)
¿Algo más? *algo mas (Anything else?)*
Eso es todo. Gracias. *eso es todo gratheeyas*
(That's all, thanks.)

COMPLAINTS

I have no knife/fork/spoon.	**No tengo cuchillo/tenedor/cuchara.** *no tengo koocheel-yo/tenedor/koochara*
There must be some mistake.	**Debe de haber un error.** *debeh deh aber oon error*
That's not what I ordered.	**Eso no es lo que pedí.** *eso no es lo keh pedee*
I asked for …	**Pedí …** *pedee*
I can't eat this.	**No puedo comerme esto.** *no pwedo komermeh esto*
The meat is …	**La carne está …** *la karneh esta*
overdone	**demasiado hecha** *demaseeyado echa*
underdone	**cruda** *krooda*
too tough	**demasiado dura** *demaseeyado doora*
This is too …	**Esto está demasiado …** *esto esta demaseeyado*
The food is cold.	**La comida está fría.** *la komeeda esta freeya*
This isn't fresh.	**Esto no está fresco.** *esto no esta fresko*
How much longer will our food be?	**¿Cuánto más tardará la comida?** *kwanto mas tardara la komeeda*
We can't wait any longer. We're leaving.	**No podemos esperar más. Nos vamos.** *no podemos esperar mas. nos bamos*
Have you forgotten our drinks?	**¿Se le han olvidado las bebidas?** *seh leh an olbeedado las bebeedas*
This isn't clean.	**Esto no está limpio.** *esto no esta leempeeyo*
I'd like to speak to the head waiter/manager.	**Quiero hablar con el metre/encargado.** *keeyero ablar kon el metreh/enkargado*

PAYING

Tipping: Service is generally included in the bill, but if you are happy with the service, a personal tip of €1 per person up to 10% for the waiter is appropriate and appreciated.

The bill, please.	**La cuenta, por favor.** *la kwenta por fabor*
We'd like to pay separately.	**Queremos pagar por separado.** *keremos pagar por separado*
It's all together, please.	**Póngalo todo junto, por favor.** *pongalo todo khoonto por fabor*
I think there's a mistake in this bill.	**Creo que hay un error en esta cuenta.** *kreyo keh eye oon error en esta kwenta*
What is this amount for?	**¿De qué es esta cantidad?** *deh keh es esta kanteedath*
I didn't have that. I had …	**Yo no tomé eso. Yo tomé …** *yo no tomeh eso. yo tomeh*
Is service included?	**¿Está el servicio incluido?** *esta el serbeetheeyo eenklooweedo*
Can I pay with this credit card?	**¿Puedo pagar con esta tarjeta de crédito?** *pwedo pagar kon esta tarkheta deh kredeeto*
Could I have a VAT receipt?	**¿Podría darme un recibo?** *podreeya darmeh oon retheebopor*
Can I have an itemized bill?	**¿Podría darme una cuenta detallada?** *odreeya darmeh oona kwenta detal-yada*
That was a very good meal.	**La comida estuvo muy buena.** *la komeeda estoobo mwee bwena*

COURSE BY COURSE

Breakfast

I'd like …	**Quiero …** *keeyero*
bread	**pan** *pan*
butter	**mantequilla** *mantekeel-ya*

fried eggs	**huevos fritos** _weboss freetoss_	
scrambled eggs	**huevos revueltos** _weboss rebweltoss_	
fruit juice	**un zumo de fruta**	
	oon thoomo deh froota	
jam	**mermelada** _mermelada_	
milk	**leche** _lecheh_	
roll	**panecillo** _penetheel-yo_	

Appetizers/Starters

Croquetas _kroketass_
Croquettes made with ham, fish, egg or a wide variety of other fillings.

Ensaladilla rusa _ensaladeel-ya rroossa_
Potatoes with peas, tuna, boiled eggs and olives mixed with mayonnaise.

Champiñones al ajillo _champeeñones ahl akheel-yo_
Mushrooms fried in olive oil with garlic.

Tapas _tapass_
A huge variety of snacks served in cafés and tapa bars, ranging from meat balls, cheese, smoked ham, mushrooms, fried fish plus sauces and exotic-looking specialties of the house. **Una tapa** is a mouthful, **una ración** half a plateful, and **una porción** a generous amount.

aceitunas (rellenas)	_athetoonass (rel-yenass)_	(stuffed) olives
albóndigas	_albondee-ass_	spiced meatballs
almejas	_almekhass_	clams
calamares	_kalamaress_	squid
callos	_kal-yoss_	tripe (in hot paprika sauce)
caracoles	_karakoless_	snails
chorizo	_choreetho_	spicy sausage
gambas	_gambass_	prawns (shrimps)
jamón	_khamon_	ham
mejillones	_mekheel-yoness_	mussels
pimientos	_peemyentoss_	peppers
pinchos	_peenchoss_	grilled skewered meat

¡Camarero! *kamarero* (Waiter!)
Sí, señora. *see senyohra* (Yes, m'am.)
El menú, por favor. *el menoo por fabor* (The menu, please.)
Sí, cómo no. *see komo no* (Sure.)

Soups

caldo gallego	*kaldo gal-yego*	meat and vegetable broth
consomé al jerez	*konsomeh al khereth*	chicken broth with sherry
sopa de ajo	*sopa deh akho*	garlic soup
sopa de fideos	*sopa deh feedeyoss*	noodle soup
sopa de mariscos	*sopa deh mareeskoss*	seafood soup
sopa de verduras	*sopa deh berdoorass*	vegetable soup

Ajo blanco *akho blanko*
Cold garlic and almond soup garnished with grapes (*Andalucia*).

Gazpacho *gathpacho*
A cold tomato soup with cucumber, green pepper, bread, onion, and garlic.

Sopa castellana *sopa kasteel-yana*
Baked garlic soup with chunks of ham and a poached egg,

Sopa de cocido *sopa deh kotheedo*
Broth, with beef, ham, sausage, chickpeas, cabbage, turnip, onion, and potatoes.

Egg dishes

Huevos a la flamenca *weboss a la flamenka*
Eggs baked with tomato, onion and diced ham..

Huevos al nido *weboss al needo*
"Eggs in the nest," egg yolks set in soft rolls, fried and covered in egg white.

Huevos rellenos *weboss rrel-yenos*
Boiled eggs filled with tuna fish and dressed with mayonnaise.

Tortilla *torteel-ya*
Round Spanish omelet; popular varieties include: **~ de patatas** (potato with onions), **~ de jamón** (ham), **~ paisana** (potatoes, peas, prawns or ham), **~ de queso** (cheese), **~ de setas** (mushroom).

Fish and seafood

atún	_atoon_	tuna
bacalao	_bakalao_	cod
boquerones	_bokeroness_	herring
caballa	_kabal-ya_	mackerel
chipirones	_cheepeeroness_	baby squid
langosta	_langosta_	lobster
mero	_mero_	sea bass
pez espada	_peth espada_	swordfish
pulpo	_poolpo_	octopus
trucha	_troocha_	trout

Bacalao a la catalana _bakalao a la katalana_
Salt cod in ratatouille sauce, with onions, eggplant, zucchini [courgettes], tomatoes, and pepper.

Calamares a la romana _kalamaress al la rromana_
Squid rings deep-fried in batter.

Pulpo a la gallega _poolpo a la gal-yega_
Octopus dressed with olive oil and paprika.

Lenguado a la vasca _lengwado a la baska_
Baked sole with sliced potatoes in a mushroom, red pepper, and tomato sauce.

Trucha a la navarra _troocha a la nabarra_
Grilled trout stuffed with ham.

Paella

Basically, paella is made of saffron rice garnished with meat, fish, seafood and/or vegetables. Here are four of the most popular ways of preparing paella.

Paella de verduras _pa-el-ya de berdoorass_
Artichokes, peas, broad beans, cauliflower, garlic, peppers, tomato.

Paella de marisco _pa-el-ya de mareesko_
Fish and seafood only.

Paella valenciana _pa-el-ya balenthyana_
Chicken, shrimp, mussels, prawn, squid, peas, tomato, chili pepper, garlic.

Paella zamorana _pa-el-ya thamorana_
Ham, pork loin, pig's feet, chili pepper.

Meat

carne de buey	_karneh deh bwehee_	beef
carne de cerdo	_karneh deh therdo_	pork
carne de cordero	_karneh deh kordero_	lamb
carne de ternera	_karneh deh ternera_	veal
chuletas	_chooletass_	chops
conejo	_konekho_	rabbit
filete	_feeleteh_	steak
hígado	_eegado_	liver
jamón	_khamon_	ham
pato	_pato_	duck
pavo	_pavo_	turkey
pollo	_pol-yo_	chicken
riñones	_reeñoness_	kidneys
salchichas	_salcheechass_	sausages
tocino	_totheeno_	bacon

Specialties

Asado de cordero _assado deh kordero_
Roast lamb with garlic and wine.

Cochinillo asado _kocheeneel-yo assado_
Crispy roasted suckling pig.

Cocido madrileño _kotheedo madreeleño_
Hotpot, stew.

Empanada gallega _empanada gal-yega_
Pork and onion pie.

Estofado de ternera _estofado deh ternera_
Veal stew with wine, carrots, onions, and potatoes.

Lomo de cerdo al jerez _lomo deh therdo al khereth_
Roast loin of pork with sherry.

Pollo en pepitoria _pol-yo en pepeetoreeya_
Chicken in egg and almond sauce.

Riñones al jerez _rreeñoness al khereth_
Lamb kidneys in an onion and sherry sauce.

Vegetables

arroz	*arroth*	rice
berenjena	*berekhena*	eggplant [aubergine]
cebolla	*thebol-ya*	onion
champiñones	*champeeñoness*	button mushrooms
guisantes	*qeessantes*	peas
judías verdes	*khoodecass verdess*	green beans
lechuga	*lechooga*	lettuce
patatas	*patatas*	potatoes
pimientos morrones	*peemyentoss morroness*	sweet red peppers
repollo	*repol-yo*	cabbage
setas	*setass*	mushrooms
zanahorias	*thana-oryass*	carrots

Ensalada *ensalada*
Salad; typical varieties to look out for: ~ **de atún** (tuna), ~ **de lechuga** (green); ~ **de pepino** (cucumber), ~ **del tiempo** (seasonal), ~ **valenciana** (with green peppers, lettuce, and oranges).

Lentejas estofadas *lentekhass estofadass*
Green lentils with onions, tomatoes, carrots, and garlic.

Pisto *peesto*
A stew of green peppers, onions, tomatoes, and zucchini [courgettes]; you might also see it referred to as **frito de verduras**.

Fruit

cerezas	*therethass*	cherries
ciruelas	*theerwelass*	plums
frambuesas	*frambwesass*	raspberries
fresas	*fresass*	strawberries
manzana	*manthana*	apple
melocotón	*melokoton*	peach
naranja	*narankha*	orange
plátano	*platano*	banana
pomelo	*pomelo*	grapefruit
uvas	*oovass*	grapes

Cheese

Burgos _boorgos_
A soft, creamy cheese named after the province from which it originates.

Cabrales _kabrales_
A tangy, veined goat cheese; its flavor varies, depending upon the mountain region in which it was produced.

Manchego _manchego_
Produced from ewe's milk, this hard cheese from La Mancha can vary from milky white to golden yellow. The best is said to come from Ciudad Real.

Perilla _pereel-ya_
A firm, bland cheese made from cow's milk; sometimes known as **teta**.

Roncal _rronkal_
A sharp ewe's milk cheese from northern Spain; hand-pressed, salted and smoked with leathery rind.

blue	**tipo roquefort** _teepo rrokefort_	mild		suave _swabeh_
		ripe		curado _kurado_
cream	**cremoso** _kremosso_	soft		**blando** _blando_
hard	**duro** _dooro_	strong		**fuerte** _fwerteh_

Dessert

bizcocho	_beethkocho_	sponge cake
brazo de gitano	_bratho deh geetano_	rum cream roll
canutillos	_kanooteel-yos_	custard horns with cinnamon
crema catalana	_krema katalana_	caramel pudding
flan	_flan_	crème caramel
fritos	_freetos_	fritters
galletas	_gal-yetas_	cookies [biscuits]
mantecado	_mantekado_	rich almond ice cream
pastel de queso	_pastel deh keso_	cheesecake
tarta de manzana	_tarta deh manthana_	apple tart
tortitas	_torteetas_	waffles

Helado _elado_
Ice cream; popular flavors include: ~ **de chocolate** (chocolate), ~ **de fresa** (strawberry), **de limón** (lemon), ~ **de moka** (mocha), ~ **de vainilla** (vanilla).

E A T I N G   O U T

DRINKS

Aperitifs

For most Spaniards, a before-dinner drink of vermouth or sherry is as important as our cocktail or highball. Vermouth (**vermut**) is rarely drunk neat but usually on the rocks or with seltzer water. Some Spaniards content themselves with a glass of local wine. You'll probably be given a dish of olives or nuts to nibble on. Or in a bar specializing in tapas, you can order various snacks.

Sherry (**jerez** *khereth*) is Spain's most renowned drink. It has alcohol or brandy added to "fortify" it during the fermentation process. Sherry was the first fortified wine to become popular in England – "sherry" derives from the English spelling of the town **Jerez**, where the wine originated.

Major sherry producers include Lustau, Osborne, Pedro Domecq, Antonio Barbadillo, Gonzalez Byass, Bobadilla, House of Sandeman, Valdespino, John Harvey & Sons.

Sherry can be divided into two groups:

Fino *feeno*

These are the pale, dry sherries that make good aperitifs. The Spaniards themselves are especially fond of **amontillado** and **manzanilla**. Some of the best **finos** are Tío Pepe and La Ina.

Oloroso *olorosso*

These are the heavier, darker sherries that are sweetened before being bottled. They're fine after-dinner drinks. One exception is **amoroso** which is medium dry. Brown and cream sherries are full-bodied and slightly less fragrant than **finos**.

Beer

Spanish beer, generally served cool, is good and relatively inexpensive. Try **Águila especial** or **San Miguel especial**.

A beer, please.	**Una cerveza, por favor.** *oona therbetha por ſubor*
light beer	**cerveza rubia** *therbetha roobya*
dark beer	**cerveza negra** *therbetha negra*
foreign beer	**cerveza extranjera** *therbetha ekstrankhera*
small/large beer	**cerveza pequeña/grande** *therbetha pekeña/grandeh*

Wine

Spain has the largest area under vine in the world and is the third largest producer and exporter.

Spain's best wine comes from **Rioja**, a region of Old Castile of which **Logroño** is the center. Wine makers there add **garantía de origen** to wine they feel is of above average quality.

The **Penedés** region near Barcelona is a major source of the world's best-selling white sparkling wine, **cava**.

Traditionally, white wine goes well with fish, fowl and light meats, while dark meats call for a red wine. A good rosé or dry sparkling **Cava** goes well with almost anything.

Ask for the patron's own wine "**el vino de la casa**"; you should receive a good wine, corresponding to the quality of the establishment.

I want a bottle of white/red wine.	**Quiero una botella de vino blanco/tinto.** *keeyero oona botel-ya deh beeno blanko/teento*
a carafe	**una garrafa** *oona garrafa*
a half bottle	**media botella** *medya botel-ya*
a glass	**un vaso** *oon basso*
a small glass	**un chato** *oon chato*
a liter	**un litro** *oon leetro*
a jar	**una jarra** *oona kharra*

---

añejo mature
blanco white
bodegas cellar
cava white, sparkling wine
de cuerpo full-bodied
DO (Denominación de Origen) regulated quality
DOCa superior wine (Rioja only)
dulce sweet
embotellado en bottled in
espumoso sparkling
gran reserva aged 3 years in a barrel then 3 years in the bottle (exceptional years only)

joven young
liviano light
moscatel sweet dessert wine
muy seco very dry
reserva aged over 3 years
rosado rosé
seco dry
tinto red
vino de calidad quality wine
vino de cosecha vintage wine
vino de crianza aged in oak barrels for minimum of 6 months

Wine regions

Aragón Campo de Borja, Calatayud, Cariñena, Navarra, Rioja (Alta, Alavesa, Baja), Somotano

País Vasco Chacolí de Guetaria, Rioja Alavesa

Castilla y León Bierzo, Cigales, Ribera del Duero, Rueda, Toro

Cataluña Alella, Ampurdán-Costa Brava, Conca de Barberà, Costers del Segre, Penedès (center of the Cava sparkling wine region), Priorato, Tarragona, Terra Alta

Galicia Rías Baixas, Ribeiro, Valdeorras

Central Spain Alicante, Almansa, Bullas, Jumilla, La Mancha, Levante, Méntrida, Utiel-Requena, Valdepeñas, Valencia, Vinos de Madrid, Yecla

Southern Spain Condado de Huelva, Jerez, Málaga, Manzanilla-Sanlúcar de Barrameda, Montilla-Moriles

Islands Binissalem (Balearic), Tacoronte-Acentejo (Canaries)

Spirits and liqueurs

You'll recognize: **ginebra** (gin), **ron** (rum), **oporto** (port wine), **vermut**, **vodka**, and **whisky**.

double (a double shot)	**doble** _dobleh_
straight/neat	**solo** _solo_
on the rocks	**con hielo** _kon yelo_
with soda/tonic	**con soda/tónica** _kon soda/toneeka_

Sangría _sangreea_

wine punch/cup made with red wine, fruit juice, brandy, slices of fruit, diluted with soda and ice; ideal for hot weather

Non-alcoholic drinks

I'd like a cup of coffee.	**Quiero una taza de café.** _keeyero oona tatha deh kafeh_
(hot) chocolate	**un chocolate (caliente)** _oon chokolateh (kaliyenteh)_
iced fruit juice	**un granizado** _oon graneethado_
lemonade	**una limonada** _oona leemonada_
milk	**leche** _lecheh_
milk shake	**un batido** _oon bateedo_
orangeade	**una naranjada** _oona narankhada_
(iced/mineral) water	**agua (helada/mineral)** _agwa (elada/meeneral)_

MENU READER

This Menu Reader is an alphabetical glossary of terms that you may find in a menu. Certain traditional dishes are cross-referenced to the relevant page in the *Course by course* section, where they are described in more detail.

adobado(-a)	*adobado(-a)*	marinated
ahumado(-a)	*ahoomado*	smoked
a la brasa	*a la brasa*	braised
al grill	*al greel*	grilled
al horno	*al orno*	baked
al vapor	*al bapor*	steamed
asado(-a)	*asado*	roasted
bien hecho(-a)	*beeyen echo*	well-done
con especias	*kon espetheeyas*	spicy
con nata	*kon nata*	creamed
cortado en taquitos	*kortado en takeetos*	diced
dorado(-a) al horno	*dorado(-a) al orno*	oven-browned
empanado(-a)	*empanado(-a)*	breaded
escaldado(-a)	*eskaldado(-a)*	poached
frito(-a)	*freeto(-a)*	fried
guisado(-a)	*geesado(-a)*	stewed
hervido(-a)	*erbeedo*	boiled
medio hecho(-a)	*medeeyo echo*	medium
muy poco hecho(-a)	*mwee poko echo(-a)*	rare
poco hecho(-a)	*poko echo*	medium rare
refrito(-a)	*refreeto(-a)*	sautéed
relleno(-a)	*rel-yeno(-a)*	stuffed

A

a la parrilla grilled/broiled
a la romana deep-fried
a punto medium (done)
abocado sherry made from sweet and dry wine
acedera sorrel

aceitunas (rellenas) (stuffed) olives
achicoria chicory
agua water; **~ caliente** hot water; **~ helada** iced water; **~ mineral** mineral water
aguacate avocado
aguardiente spirits (eau-de-vie)
ahumado smoked

ajo garlic; **~ blanco** garlic soup
ajoaceite garlic mayonnaise
al adobo marinated
al ajillo in garlic and oil
al horno baked
albahaca basil
albaricoques apricots
albóndigas spiced meatballs
alcachofas artichokes
alcaparra caper
alioli garlic mayonnaise
aliñado seasoned
almejas clams; **~ a la marinera** cooked in hot, pimento sauce
almendra almond; **~ garrapiñada** sugared
almuerzo lunch
almíbar syrup
alubia bean
amontillado medium-dry sherry with nutty taste
anchoas anchovies
añejo mature
anguila ahumada smoked eel
angula baby eel
Angélica Basque herb liqueur
anisado aniseed-based soft drink
anticucho beef heart grilled on skewer with green peppers
anís anisette
aperitivos aperitifs
apio celery
arándanos blueberries
arenque (ahumado) (smoked) herring

arepa pancake made of corn (maize)
arroz rice; **~ a la cubana** boiled rice served with tomato sauce and a fried egg; **~ a la valenciana** with vegetables, chicken, shellfish; **~ blanco** boiled, steamed; **~ negro** with seafood and squid ink; **~ primavera** with spring vegetables; **~ con costra** with pork meatballs; **~ con leche** rice pudding
asado roast
asturias (queso de …) strong, fermented cheese
atún tuna
avellanas hazelnuts
aves poultry
azafrán saffron
azúcar sugar

B

bacalao cod
banderillas gherkins, chile peppers and olives on a skewer
batata sweet potato, yam
batido milk shake
bebidas drinks
bebidas sin alcohol non-alcoholic drinks
becada woodcock
berberecho cockle
berenjena eggplant/aubergine
berraza parsnip
berro cress
berza cabbage
besugo (sea) bream
bien hecho well-done
biftec beef steak

bizcocho sponge cake; ~ **borracho** steeped in rum and syrup

bizcotela glazed cookie/biscuit

blanco white

blando soft; medium

Bobadilla Gran Reserva wine-distilled brandy

bocadillo sandwich

bocadillo de jamón ham sandwich

bollos cake

bonito tuna

boquerones kind of anchovy

botella bottle

brevas blue figs

(en) brocheta (on a) skewer

budín blancmange, custard

buey ox

burgos (queso de …) soft, creamy cheese

buñuelitos small fritters

C

caballa mackerel

cabra goat

cabrales (queso de …) tangy goat cheese

cabrito kid

cacahuetes peanuts

café coffee

calabacín zucchini [courgette]

calabaza pumpkin

calamares squid; ~ **a la romana** fried in batter

caldereta de cabrito kid stew

caldillo de congrio conger-eel soup with tomatoes and potatoes

caldo consommé

caldo gallego meat and vegetable broth

caliente hot

Calisay quinine-flavored liqueur

callos tripe; ~ **a la madrileña** tripe in piquant sauce with spicy pork sausage and tomatoes

camarón shrimp

canela cinnamon

cangrejo (de mar/de río) crab/crayfish

cantarela chanterelle mushroom

capón capon

caracoles snails

caramelos candy; sweets

Carlos I wine-distilled brandy

carne meat

carne a la parrilla charcoal-grilled steak

carne de buey beef

carne de cangrejo crabmeat

carne de cerdo pork

carne de cordero lamb

carne de ternera veal

carne molida chopped/minced beef

carne picada chopped/minced meat

carnero mutton

carta menu; **a la ~** a la carte

casero homemade

castanola sea perch

castañas chestnuts

catalana spicy pork sausages

caza game

(a la) cazadora with mushrooms, spring onions, herbs in wine

Cazalla aniseed liqueur

cazuela de cordero lamb stew with vegetables

cebollas onions
cebolleta spring onion
cebollinos chives
cebrero (queso de ...) blue-veined cheese
cena dinner, supper
centolla spider-crab, served cold
cerdo pork
cereales cereal
cerezas cherries
cerveza beer
chalote shallot
champiñones button mushrooms
chancho adobado pork braised with sweet potatoes, orange and lemon juice
chanfaina goat's liver and kidney stew, served in a thick sauce
chanquete herring/whitebait
chato a small glass
chile chili pepper
chilindrón sauce of tomatoes, peppers, garlic, ham and wine *(Pyr.)*
chimichurri hot parsley sauce
Chinchón aniseed liqueur
chipirones baby squid
chirivías parsnips
chocolate (caliente) (hot) chocolate
chopa type of sea bream
chorizo spicy sausage made of pork, garlic and paprika
chuletas chops
chupe de mariscos scallops served with creamy sauce and gratinéed with cheese
churro sugared tubular fritter
cigalas sea crayfish [Dublin Bay prawns]

cincho (queso de ...) hard sheep-milk cheese
ciruelas plums; **~ pasas** prunes
clavo clove
cochifrito de cordero highly seasoned stew of lamb or kid
cochinillo asado crispy roasted Castilian suckling pig
cocido boiled; beef stew with ham, fowl, chickpeas, and potatoes
cocido al vapor steamed
coco coconut
codorniz quail
cohombrillos pickles/gherkins
cola de mono blend of coffee, milk, rum, and pisco
coles de bruselas Brussels sprouts
coliflor cauliflower
comida meal
comino caraway
compota stewed fruit
con hielo on the rocks
con leche with milk
con limón with lemon
condimentos herbs
coñac brandy
conejo rabbit; **~ al ajillo** rabbit with garlic; **~ de monte** wild rabbit
confitura jam
congrio conger eel
consomé al jerez chicken broth with sherry
copa nuria egg yolk and egg white, whipped and served with jam
corazonada heart stewed in sauce
corazón heart
cordero lamb

Cordoníu brand of Catalonian sparkling wine

cortadillo small pancake with lemon

corto strong coffee

corzo deer

costilla chop

crema cream; **~ batida** whipped cream; **~ catalana** caramel pudding; **~ española** dessert of milk, eggs, and fruit jelly; **~ nieve** with beaten egg yolk, sugar, rum

cremoso cream

criadillas sweetbreads

(a la) criolla with green peppers, spices and tomatoes

croqueta fish or meat cake

crudo raw

Cuarenta y Tres egg liqueur

Cuba libre rum coke

cubierto cover charge

cuenta bill, check

curanto dish of seafood, vegetables and suckling pig

D

damasco variety of apricot

dátiles dates

de cordero lamb's

de cuerpo full-bodied

de lechuga green

de ternera calf's

del tiempo in season

desayuno breakfast

descafeinado decaffeinated

doble double (a double shot)

dulce dessert wine; sweet

dulce de naranja marmelade

durazno peach

duro hard *(egg)*

E

edulcorante sweetener

embuchado stuffed with meat

embutido spicy sausage

empanada pie or tart with meat or fish filling; **~ de horno** filled with minced meat; **~ gallega** tenderloin of pork, onions and chili peppers in a pie

empanadillas small savory pastries stuffed with meat or fish

empanado breaded

emperador swordfish

en dulce boiled

en escabeche marinated

en salazón cured

en salsa braised in casserole

en su jugo pot roasted

enchilada tortilla stuffed and served with vegetable garnish and sauce

encurtido pickled

endibia endive

eneldo dill

ensalada salad; **~ rusa** diced cold vegetables with mayonnaise

entremeses (variados) (assorted) appetizers

escabeche de gallina chicken marinated in vinegar and bay leaves

escarola escarole

espaguetis spaghetti

espalda shoulder

(a la) española with tomatoes

especialidades de la casa specialties of the house

especialidades locales local specialties
especias spices
espinacas spinach
espumoso sparkling
espárragos (puntas de) asparagus (tips)
esqueixado *(Cat.)* mixed fish salad
(al) estilo de in the style of
estofado braised; stewed
estragón tarragon

fabada (asturiana) stew of pork, beans, bacon and sausage
faisán pheasant
fiambres cold cuts
fideo thin noodle
filete steak; **~ de lenguado empanado** breaded fillet of sole; **~ de lomo** fillet steak (tenderloin); **~ de res** beef steak
fino pale, dry sherry
(a la) flamenca with onions, peas, green peppers, tomatoes and spiced sausage
flan caramel pudding
frambuesas raspberries
(a la) francesa sautéed in butter
fresas strawberries
fresco fresh, chilled
fresón large strawberry
fricandó thin slice of meat rolled in bacon and braised
frijoles beans; **~ refritos** fried mashed beans
frito fried; **~ de patata** deep-fried potato croquette

fritos fritters
fritura mixta meat, fish or vegetables deep-fried in batter
fruta fruit; **~ escarchada** candied fruit
frío cold
fuerte strong
Fundador wine-distilled brandy

galletas cookies [biscuits]; **~ de nata** cream cookies; **~ saladas** crackers
gallina hen
gallo cockerel
gambas (grandes) shrimp [prawns]; **~ a la plancha** grilled; **~ al ajillo** with garlic
ganso goose
garbanzos chickpeas
garrafa carafe
gaseosa carbonated/fizzy
gazpacho cold tomato soup
ginebra gin; **~ con limón** gin fizz; **~ con tónica** gin and tonic
(a la) gitanilla with garlic
gordo fatty, rich
granadas pomegranates
granadina pomegranate syrup mixed with wine or brandy
granizados iced drinks
gratinado gratinéed
grelos turnip greens
grosellas espinosas gooseberries
grosellas negras blackcurrants
grosellas rojas redcurrants
guacamole spicy avocado salad

guarnición garnish, trimming
guayaba guava *(fruit)*
guinda sour cherry
guindilla chili pepper
guisado stewed
guisantes peas

H

habas broad beans
habichuela verde French/green beans
hamburguesa hamburger
hayaca central cornmeal pancake, usually with minced-meat filling
helado ice cream
hervido boiled; poached
hielo ice
hierbas herbs; **~ finas** mixture of herbs
higaditos de pollo chicken livers
hígado liver
higos figs
hinojo fennel
hoja de laurel bay leaf
hongos fungi
horchata de almendra/chufa ground almond drink
(al) horno baked
hueso bone
huevos eggs; **~ a la española** stuffed with tomatoes and served with cheese sauce; **~ a la flamenca** baked with tomato, onion and diced ham; **~ al nido** "eggs in the nest"; **~ al trote** with tuna; **~ cocidos** boiled; **~ duros** hard-boiled eggs; **~ escalfados a la**

española poached egg on onions, tomatoes, peppers and zucchini; **~ fritos** fried eggs; **~ revueltos** scrambled eggs
humita boiled corn with tomatoes, green peppers, onions, and cheese

J

jabalí wild boar
jalea jelly
jamón ham; **~ en dulce** boiled and served cold; **~ y huevos** ham and eggs
(a la) jardinera with carrots, peas, and other vegetables
jengibre ginger
jerez sherry
judías blancas white beans
judías verdes green beans
jugo fresh juice; gravy, meat juice; **~ de fruta** fruit juice
jurel kind of mackerel *(fish)*

L

lacón shoulder of pork
lampreas lampreys
langosta lobster; **~ con pollo** with chicken
langostinos shrimp [prawns]
lavanco wild duck
leche milk
lechón suckling pig
lechuga lettuce
legumbres pulses
lengua tongue
lenguado sole; **~ a la vasca** baked with potatoes and vegetables
lentejas lentils

licor liqueur
liebre hare; **~ estofada** jugged
lima lime
limonada lemonade
limón lemon
lista de platos menu
lista de vinos wine list
litro a liter
liviano light
lobarro type of bass
lombarda red cabbage
lomo loin; **~ de cerdo al jerez** pork loin
loncha slice of meat
longaniza long, highly seasoned sausage
lubina bass

M

macedonia de frutas mixed fruit salad
(a la) madrileña with chorizo sausage, tomatoes and paprika
magras al estilo de Aragón cured ham in tomato sauce
Mahón (queso de ...) type of goat cheese
(a la) mallorquina highly seasoned (fish and shellfish)
maíz sweet corn
manchego (queso de ...) ewe's milk cheese
mandarina tangerine
mantecado rich almond ice cream
mantequilla butter
manzana apple

manzanilla dry, pale sherry
maní peanut
marinera fish and seafood only
(a la) marinera with mussels, onions, tomatoes, herbs, and wine
mariscos seafood
matambre rolled beef stuffed with vegetables
mazapán marzipan
media botella half bottle
medio pollo asado half a roasted chicken
mejillones mussels
melaza treacle, molasses
melocotón peach; **~ en almíbar** in syrup
melón melon
membrillo quince paste
menestra green vegetable soup; **~ de pollo** casserole of chicken and vegetables
menta mint
menudillos giblets
merengue meringue
merienda afternoon snack
merluza hake
mermelada jam; **~ amarga de naranjas** marmalade
mero sea bass
miel honey
(a la) milanese with cheese, generally baked
minuta menu
mojo picón piquant red sauce *(Can.)*
mojo verde green herb sauce served with fish *(Cat.)*

mole poblano chicken served with sauce of chili peppers, spices and chocolate

mollejas sweetbreads

moras mulberries

morcilla blood sausage *(black pudding)*

morilla morel mushroom

moros y cristianos rice and black beans with diced ham, garlic, green peppers and herbs

mostaza mustard

mújol mullet *(fish)*

muslo de pollo chicken leg

muy hecho well-done

muy seco very dry

<hr>

N

nabo turnip

naranja orange

naranjada orangeade

nata cream; ~ **batida** whipped

natillas custard

níspola medlar *(fruit)*

nopalito young cactus leaf served with salad dressing

nueces walnuts

nueces variadas assorted nuts

nuez moscada nutmeg

<hr>

O

olla stew; ~ **gitana** vegetable stew; ~ **podrida** stew made of vegetables, meat, fowl and ham

oloroso dark sherry

oporto port

ostras oysters

oveja ewe

<hr>

P

pa amb tomàquet bread with tomato and salt *(Cat.)*

pabellón criollo beef in tomato sauce, garnished with beans, rice and bananas

paella paella

paletilla shank

palitos skewered appetizer ~ **de queso** cheese sticks/straws

palmito palm heart

palta avocado

pan bread; ~ **de pueblo** plain white bread

panecillos rolls

papas potatoes; ~ **a la huancaína** with cheese and green peppers; ~ **arrugadas** new potatoes baked and rolled in rock salt *(Can.)*

parrillada grill; ~ **mixta** mixed

pasado done, cooked; ~ **por agua** soft *(egg)*

pasas raisins

pastas pastry; pasta

pastel cake; ~ **de choclo** corn [maize] with minced beef, chicken, raisins, and olives; ~ **de queso** cheesecake

pasteles cakes; pastries

patatas potatoes; ~ **(a la) leonesa** potatoes with onions; ~ **fritas** French fries [chips]; ~ **nuevas** new potatoes

pato duck/duckling

paté pâté

pavo turkey

pechuga de pollo breast of chicken

pepinillos pickles/gherkins

pepino cucumber

(en) pepitoria stewed with onions, green peppers and tomatoes

pera pear

perca perch *(fish)*

percebes goose barnacles *(seafood)*

perdiz partridge; **~ en escabeche** cooked in oil with vinegar, onions, parsley, carrots and green pepper; served cold; **~ estofada** served in a white-wine sauce

perejil parsley

perifollo chervil

perilla (queso de ...) firm cheese

pescadilla whiting *(fish)*

pescado fish **~ frito** fried fish

pez espada swordfish

picadillo minced meat, hash

picado minced

picante sharp, spicy, highly seasoned

picatoste deep-fried slice of bread

pichón pigeon

pierna leg

pimentón paprika

pimienta pepper

pimientos a la riojana sweet peppers stuffed with minced meat

pimientos morrones sweet red peppers

piña pineapple

pincho moruno grilled meat on a skewer

pintada guinea fowl

pisco grape brandy

pisto green pepper stew

(a la) plancha grilled on a griddle

plato plate, dish, portion; **~ del día** dish of the day

platos fríos cold dishes

platos típicos specialties

plátano banana

poco hecho rare

pollito spring chicken

pollo chicken; **~ a la brasa** grilled; **~ asado** roast; **~ pibil** simmered in fruit juice and spices

polvorón almond cookie [biscuit]

pomelo grapefruit

ponche crema eggnog liquor

porción small helping of tapas

postre dessert

potaje vegetable soup

puchero stew

puerros leeks

pulpitos baby octopus

pulpo octopus

punto de nieve dessert of whipped cream with beaten egg whites

puré purée; **~ de patatas** mashed potatoes

Q

queso cheese

quisquillas common shrimps

R

rábano radish; **~ picante** horseradish

rabo de buey oxtail

ración large helping
raja slice, portion
rallado grated
rape monkfish
raya ray, skate
rebanada slice
rebozado breaded, fried in batter
recomendamos ... we recommend ...
refrescos cold drinks
regular medium
rehogada sautéed
relleno stuffed
remolacha beet [beetroot]
repollo cabbage
requesón (queso de ...) cottage cheese [fresh-curd cheese]
riñones kidneys; **~ al jerez** braised in sherry
róbalo haddock
rodaballo turbot
(a la) romana dipped in batter and fried
romero rosemary
romesco sauce of nuts, chili, tomatoes, garlic, and breadcrumbs *(Cat.)*
ron rum
roncal (queso de ...) sharp ewe's milk cheese
ropa vieja cooked, leftover meat and vegetables, covered with tomatoes and green peppers
rosado rosé
rosbif roast beef
rosquilla doughnut
rubio red mullet
ruibarbo rhubarb

sal salt
salado salted, salty
salchichas sausages
salchichón salami
salmonetes red mullet
salmón salmon; **~ ahumado** smoked salmon
salsa sauce
salsa a la catalana sauce of tomato and green peppers
salsa a la vasca parsley, peas, garlic; a delicate green dressing for fish in the Basque country
salsa alioli garlic sauce
salsa de tomate ketchup
salsa en escabeche sweet and sour sauce
salsa española brown sauce with herbs, spices, and wine
salsa mayordoma butter and parsley sauce
salsa picante hot pepper sauce
salsa romana bacon/ham and egg cream sauce
salsa romesco green peppers, pimentos, garlic; popular chilled dressing for fish on the east coast around Tarragona
salsa verde parsley sauce
salteado sautéed
salvia sage
sandía watermelon
sangrita tequila with tomato, orange, and lime juices
sangría wine punch

sardinas sardines
seco dry
sencillo plain
sepia cuttlefish
serrano cured
sesos brains
setas mushrooms
sidra cider
sobrasada salami
soda soda water
sol y sombra blend of wine-distilled brandy and aniseed liqueur
solo black *(coffee)*; straight/neat
solomillo de cerdo tenderloin of pork
sopa soup; ~ **de buey** oxtail; ~ **de ajo** garlic; ~ **de arroz** rice; ~ **de camarones** shrimp; ~ **de cangrejo** crab; ~ **castellana** baked garlic; ~ **de cebolla** onion; ~ **de cocido** a kind of broth; ~ **de espárragos** asparagus; ~ **de fideos** noodle; ~ **de mariscos** seafood; ~ **de patatas** potato; ~ **de pescado** fish; ~ **de tomate** tomato; ~ **de verduras** vegetable; ~ **juliana** bouillon of finely shredded vegetables; ~ **sevillana** highly spiced fish soup
sorbete (iced) fruit drink
suave mild
suizo bun
suplemento sobre ... ...extra
surtido assorted

T

---

taco wheat or cornflour pancake, usually with meat filling, garnished with spicy sauce

tajada slice
tallarín noodle
tamal pastry dough of coarsely ground cornmeal with meat or fruit filling, steamed in corn-husks
tapas snacks
tarta de almendras almond tart
tarta de manzana apple tart
tarta de moka mocha cake
tarta helada ice cream cake
tartaletas small open tarts filled with fish, meat, vegetables or cheese
taza de café cup of coffee
té tea
ternera veal
tinto red
Tío Pepe brand of sherry
tipo roquefort blue *(cheese)*
tocino salted fresh lard, ~ **de panceta bacon**, ~ **entreverado** streaky bacon
tocino/tocinillo de cielo dessert of whipped egg yolks and sugar
tojunto rabbit stew
tomates tomatoes
tomillo thyme
tónica tonic water
toronja type of grapefruit
tortilla omelet; ~ **al ron** rum; ~ **de alcachofa** artichoke; ~ **de cebolla** onion; ~ **de espárragos** asparagus; ~ **de jamón** ham; ~ **de patatas** potato; ~ **de queso** cheese; ~ **de setas** mushroom; ~ **gallega** potato omelet with ham, chili;

~ paisana with potatoes, peas, prawns or ham

tortitas pancakes/waffles

tostadas toast

tripas tripe

Triple Seco orange liqueur

trucha trout; **~ a la navarra** stuffed with ham; **~ frita a la asturiana** floured and fried in butter, garnished with lemon

trufas truffles

tumbet ratatouille and potato-type casserole with meat or fish *(Maj.)*

turrón nougat

U

ulloa (queso de …) soft cheese from Galicia

uvas grapes; **~ blancas** green; **~ negras** black

uvas pasas raisins

V

vaca salada corned beef

vainilla vanilla

valenciana a type of paella, the classic version

variado varied, assorted

varios sundries

vaso glass

venado venison

veneras scallops

verduras vegetables

vermut vermouth

vieira scallop

villalón (queso de …) mild cheese

vinagreta piquant vinegar dressing

vino wine; **~ de mesa** table wine; **~ del país** local wine

(a la) vizcaína with green peppers, tomatoes, garlic, and paprika

W

whisky whisky; **~ americano** bourbon; **~ con soda** whisky and soda; **~ escocés** Scotch

X

xampaña Catalonian sparkling wine

xató olive and endive salad *(Cat.)*

Y

yema egg yolk

yemas dessert of whipped egg yolks and sugar

yogur yogurt

Z

zamorana ham, pork loin, pig's feet/trotters, chili pepper

zanahorias carrots

zarzamoras blackberries

zarzuela savory stew of assorted fish and shellfish *(Cat.)*; **~ de pescado** selection of fish with highly seasoned sauce

zumo fresh juice; **~ de fruta** fruit juice

TRAVEL

ESSENTIAL	
A ticket to …	**Un billete para …** oon beel-yeteh para
Two for the museum.	**Dos para el museo.** dos para el mooseyo
one-way [single]	**de ida** deh eeda
round-trip [return]	**de ida y vuelta** deh eeda ee bwelta
How much …?	**¿Cuánto …?** kwanto

SAFETY

Spain is a relatively safe country and violent crimes against tourists are rare.

Would you accompany me to the bus stop?	**¿Me acompañaría a la parada de autobús?** meh akompañaree a la parada deh aootoboos
I don't want to … on my own.	**No quiero … solo(-a).** no keeyero …solo(-a)
stay here	**quedarme aquí** kedarmeh akee
walk home	**ir a casa andando** eer a kasa andando
I don't feel safe here.	**No me siento seguro(-a) aquí.** no meh seeyento segooro akee

ARRIVAL

Most visitors, including citizens of all EU countries, the United States, Canada, Eire, Australia and New Zealand, require only a valid passport for entry to Spain.

Import restrictions between EU countries have been relaxed on items for personal use or consumption which are bought duty-paid within the EU Suggested maximum: 90l. wine or 60l. sparkling wine; 20l. fortified wine, 10l. spirits, and 110l. beer.

Duty free into:	Cigarettes	Cigars	Tobacco	Spirits	Wine
Spain	200	50	250 g.	1 l.	2 l.
Canada	200 and	50 and	400 g.	1 l. or	1 l.
UK	200 or	50 or	250 g.	1 l. and	2 l.
U.S.	200 and	100 and	discretionary	1 l. or	1 l.

Passport control

| YOU MAY HEAR |

¿Puedo ver su pasaporte, por favor?	Can I see your passport, please?
¿Cuál es el propósito de su visita?	What's the purpose of your visit?
¿Con quién viaja?	Who are you here with?

We have a joint passport.	**Tenemos un pasaporte conjunto.** *tenemos oon pasaporteh konkhoonto*
The children are on this passport.	**Los niños están en este pasaporte.** *los neeños estan en esteh pasaporteh*
I'm here on vacation [holiday]/on business.	**Estoy aquí de vacaciones/en viaje de negocios.** *estoy akee deh bakathyones/ en beeyakheh deh negothyoss*
I'm just passing through.	**Estoy de paso ...** *estoy deh paso*
I'm going to ...	**Voy a ...** *boy a*
I won't be working here.	**No voy a trabajar aquí.** *no boy a trabakhar akee*
I'm ...	**Estoy ...** *estoy*
on my own	**solo(-a)** *solo(-a)*
with my family	**con mi familia** *kon mee fameeleeya*
with a group	**con un grupo** *kon oon groopo*

Customs

I have only the normal allowances.	**Sólo lo normal.** *solo lo normal*

66

It's a gift/for my personal use.	**Es un regalo/para uso personal.** *es oon regalo/para ooso personal*
I would like to declare …	**Quiero declarar …** *keeyero deklarar*
I don't understand.	**No entiendo.** *no enteeyendo*
Does anyone here speak English?	**¿Hay alguien aquí que hable inglés?** *eye algeeyen akee keh ableh eengles*

YOU MAY HEAR

¿Tiene algo que declarar?	Do you have anything to declare?
Tiene que pagar impuestos por por esto.	You must pay duty on this.
¿Dónde compró esto?	Where did you buy this?
Abra esta bolsa por favor.	Please open this bag.
¿Tiene más equipaje?	Do you have any more luggage?

Duty-free shopping

YOU MAY SEE

ADUANAS	customs
ARTÍCULOS LIBRES DE IMPUESTOS	duty-free goods
ARTÍCULOS QUE DECLARAR	goods to declare
NADA QUE DECLARAR	nothing to declare
CONTROL DE PASAPORTES	passport control
POLICÍA	police
PASO DE LA FRONTERA	border crossing

What currency is this in?	**¿En qué moneda/divisa está esto?** *en keh moneda/deebeesa esta esto*
Can I pay in …?	**¿Puedo pagar en …?** *pwedo pagar en*
dollars/euros/pounds	**dólares/euros/libras** *dolares/eh-ooros/leebras*

PLANE

A number of private airlines, such as Air Europa and Aviaco, offer competitive prices across the internal air network and selected international flights.

Tickets and reservations

When is the … flight to Madrid?	**¿Cuándo sale el … vuelo a Madrid?** _kwando saleh el … bwelo a madreeth_
first/next/last	**primer/próximo/último** _preemer/prokseemo/oolteemo_
I'd like 2 … tickets to Madrid.	**Quiero dos billetes … a Madrid.** _keeyero dos beel-yetehs … a madreeth_
one-way [single]	**de ida** _deh eeda_
round-trip [return]	**de ida y vuelta** _deh eeda ee bwelta_
first class	**de primera clase** _deh preemera klaseh_
business class	**de clase preferente** _deh klaseh preferenteh_
economy class	**económico** _ekonomeeko_
How much is a flight to …?	**¿Cuánto cuesta un vuelo a …?** _kwanto kwesta oon bwelo a_
Are there any supplements/ reductions?	**¿Tienen algúnos suplementos/descuentos?** _teeyenen algoonos sooplementos/deskwentos_
I'd like to … my reservation for flight number …	**Quiero … mi reserva del vuelo número …** _keeyero … mee reserba del bwelo noomero_
cancel	**cancelar** _kanthelar_
change	**cambiar** _kambeeyar_
confirm	**confirmar** _konfeermar_

Inquiries about the flight

How long is the flight?	**¿Cuánto dura el vuelo?** _kwanto doora el bwelo_
What time does the plane leave?	**¿A qué hora sale el avión?** _a keh ora saleh el abeeyon_
What time will we arrive?	**¿A qué hora llegamos?** _a keh ora l-yegamos_
What time do I have to check in?	**¿A qué hora tengo que facturar?** _a keh ora tengo keh faktoorar_

Checking in

Where is the check-in counter for flight …?	**¿Dónde está el mostrador de facturación del vuelo …?** _dondeh esta el mostrador deh faktooratheeyon del bwelo_
I have …	**Tengo …** _tengo_
three suitcases to check in	**tres maletas para facturar** _tres maletas para faktoorar_
two carry-ons	**dos bultos de mano** _dos boollos deh mano_
How much baggage is allowed free?	**¿Cuánto equipaje está permitido sin pagar?** _kwanto ekeepakeh esta permeeteedo seen pagar_

YOU MAY HEAR

¿Quiere un asiento que dé a la ventana o al pasillo?	Would you like a window or an aisle seat?
¿Fumador o no fumador?	Smoking or non-smoking?
Por favor, pase a la sala de embarque.	Please go through to the departure lounge.
¿Cuántos bultos de equipaje tiene?	How many pieces of baggage do you have?
Lleva exceso de equipaje.	You have excess baggage.
Tendrá que pagar un suplemento de … euros por kilo de equipaje en exceso.	You'll have to pay a supplement of . . . euros per kilo of excess baggage.
Eso pesa demasiado/eso es demasiado grande para pasar como equipaje de mano.	That's too heavy/large for carry-on [hand laggage].
¿Hizo las maletas usted?	Did you pack these bags yourself?
¿Contienen algún artículo punzante o eléctrico?	Do they contain any sharp or electronic items?

YOU MAY SEE

LLEGADAS	arrivals
SALIDAS	departures
NO DEJE SU EQUIPAJE DESATENDIDO	do not leave bags unattended
REVISIÓN DE SEGURIDAD	security check

Information

Is there any delay on flight …?	**¿Lleva retraso el vuelo …?** _l-yeba retraso el bwelo_
How late will it be?	**¿Cuánto tiempo lleva de retraso?** _kwanto teeyempo l-yeba deh retraso_
Has the flight from … landed?	**¿Ha aterrizado el vuelo procedente de …?** _a aterreethado el bwelo prothedenteh deh_
Which gate does flight … leave from?	**¿De qué puerta sale el vuelo …?** _deh keh pwerta saleh el bwelo_

Boarding

Your boarding card, please.	**Su tarjeta de embarque, por favor.** _soo tarkheta deh embarkeh por fabor_
Could I have a drink/ something to eat, please?	**¿Podría tomar algo de beber/comer, por favor?** _podreeya tomar algo deh beber/komer por fabor_
Please wake me for the meal.	**Por favor, despiérteme para la comida.** _por fabor despeeyertemeh para la komeeda_
What time will we arrive?	**¿A qué hora llegaremos?** _a keh ora l-yegaremos_
An airsickness bag, please.	**Una bolsa para el mareo por favor.** _oona bolsa para el mareyo por fabor_

Arrival

Where is/are the …?	**¿Dónde está/están …?** _dondeh esta/estan_
currency exchange	**la ventanilla de cambio** _la bentaneel-ya deh kambeeyo_
buses	**los autobuses** _los aootobooses_
car rental [hire]	**el alquiler de coches** _el alkeeler deh koches_
exit	**la salida** _la saleeda_
taxis	**los taxis** _los taksees_
telephones	**los teléfonos** _los telefonos_
Is there a bus into town?	**¿Hay un autobús que va a la ciudad?** _eye oon aootoboos keh ba a la theeyoodath_
How do I get to the … Hotel?	**¿Cómo se va al Hotel …?** _komo seh ba al otel_

Baggage

Tipping: €1 per bag.

Porter! Excuse me!	**¡Mozo! ¡Disculpe!** <u>mo</u>tho. dees<u>kool</u>peh
Could you take my luggage to …?	**¿Podría llevar mi equipaje a …?** po<u>dree</u>ya l-ye<u>bar</u> mee ekee<u>pa</u>kheh a
a taxi/bus	**un taxi/autobús** oon <u>tak</u>see/aooto<u>boos</u>
Where is/are (the) …?	**¿Dónde está/están …?** <u>don</u>deh es<u>ta</u>/es<u>tan</u>
luggage carts [trolleys]	**los carritos para el equipaje** los ka<u>rree</u>tos <u>pa</u>ra el ekee<u>pa</u>kheh
luggage lockers	**las taquillas** las ta<u>keel</u>-yas
baggage check	**la consigna** la kon<u>seeg</u>na
Where is the luggage from flight …?	**¿Dónde está el equipaje del vuelo …?** <u>don</u>deh es<u>ta</u> el ekee<u>pa</u>kheh del <u>bwe</u>lo

Loss, damage, and theft

My baggage has been lost/stolen.	**Han perdido/robado mi equipaje.** an per<u>dee</u>do/rro<u>ba</u>do mee ekee<u>pa</u>kheh
My suitcase was damaged in transit.	**Mi maleta se ha estropeado en el tránsito.** mee ma<u>le</u>ta seh a estrope<u>ya</u>do en el <u>tran</u>seeto
Our baggage has not arrived.	**Nuestro equipaje no ha llegado.** <u>nwes</u>tro ekee<u>pa</u>kheh no a l-ye<u>ga</u>do
Do you have claim forms?	**¿Tienen formularios para reclamaciones?** tee<u>ye</u>nen formoo<u>la</u>reeoss para rreklama<u>thee</u>oness

TRAIN

On Spain's rail network **RENFE (Red Nacional de los Ferrocarriles Españoles)** children under 4 travel free; children aged 4–12 pay half fare.

Check out the various reductions and travel cards available. Rates are cheaper on "off days" (**días azules**). Some travel cards can also be used for local buses and subway. Another way is to buy tickets in a "checkbook" from travel agents. These can be exchanged for train tickets at special rates on "off days."

Tickets can be purchased and reservations made in travel agencies or at railway stations. The purchase of a ticket usually means that you are allocated a seat. You can reserve seats in advance. For longer trips there is a smoking car, otherwise the train is non-smoking.

AVE _abeh_
High-speed train (**alta velocidad española**), operating between Madrid and Seville, and taking just two hours.

EuroCity _e-oorotheetee_
International express, first and second classes.

Talgo, Electrotren, TER _talgo, elektrotren, tehr_
Luxury diesels, first and second classes; supplementary charge over the regular fare; seats should be reserved in advance. Similar services are provided by **Intercity** and **Tren Estrella**.

Expreso, Rápido _ekspresso, rrapeedo_
Long-distance expresses; stopping at all main towns.

Omnibus, Tranvía, Automotor _omneeboos, tranbeea, awtomotor_
Local train; making frequent stops.

Auto Expreso _awto ekspresso_
Car train; you can load your car and travel in a sleeper car; reductions available on the **auto expreso** if more than one berth reserved.

Coche cama _kocheh kama_
Sleeping car; compartments with wash basins and one or two berths. A cheaper way of sleeping during your trip is to buy a **litera,** one of the berths in a compartment of six.

Coche comedor _kocheh komedor_
Dining car; generally included on overnight trips. Otherwise, there may be a buffet car; lunch served at your seats on certain trains; or simply a sandwich and drinks car on shorter trips.

Furgón de equipajes _foorgon deh ekeepakhess_
Baggage car [van]; only registered baggage permitted.

To the station

How do I get to the train station?	**¿Cómo se llega a la estación de trenes?** _komo seh lyega a la estatheeyon deh trenes_
Do trains to León leave from … Station?	**¿Salen de la estación … los trenes a León?** _salen deh la estatheeyon … los trenes a leyon_
How far is it?	**¿A qué distancia está?** _a keh deestantheeya esta_
Can I leave my car there?	**¿Puedo dejar mi coche allí?** _pwedo dekhar mee kocheh al-yee_

At the station

Where is/are …?	**¿Dónde está/están …?** _dondeh esta/estan_
currency exchange office	**la oficina de cambio de moneda** _la ofeetheena deh kambeeyo deh moneda_
information desk	**la ventanilla de información** _la bentaneel-ya deh eenformatheeyon_
baggage check	**la consigna** _la konseegna_
lost and found [lost property office]	**la oficina de objetos perdidos** _la ofeetheena deh obkhetos perdeedos_
luggage lockers	**las taquillas** _las takeel-yas_
platforms	**los andenes** _los andenes_
snack bar	**el bar** _el bar_
ticket office	**el despacho de billetes** _el despacho deh beel-yetes_
waiting room	**la sala de espera** _la sala deh espera_

YOU MAY SEE

A LOS ANDENES	to the platforms
ENTRADA	entrance
SALIDA	exit
INFORMACIÓN	information
RESERVAS	reservations
LLEGADAS	arrivals
SALIDAS	departures

Tickets

I'd like a … ticket to Toledo.	**Quiero un billete … a Toledo.** *keeyero oon beel-yeteh … a toledo*
one-way [single]	**de ida** *deh eeda*
round-trip [return]	**de ida y vuelta** *deh eeda ee bwelta*
first/second class	**de primera/segunda clase** *deh preemera/segoonda klaseh*
concessionary	**con descuento** *kon deskwento*
I'd like to reserve a seat.	**Quiero reservar una plaza.** *keeyero reserbar oona platha*
I'd like to reserve a(n) …	**Quiero reservar …** *oon aseeyento keh deh al paseel-yo*
aisle seat/window seat	**un asiento que dé al pasillo/a la ventana** *oon aseeyento keh deh al paseel-yo/ a la bentana*
I'd like to reserve a berth.	**Quiero reservar un camarote.** *keeyero reserbar oona leetera*
Is there a sleeping car?	**¿Hay coche cama?** *eye kocheh kama*
I'd like a(n) … berth.	**Quiero una litera …** *keeyero oona leetera*
upper/lower	**de arriba/abajo** *deh arreeba/abakho*
Can I buy a ticket on board?	**¿Puedo comprar un billete dentro del tren?** *pwedo komprar oon beel-yeteh dentro del tren*

Price

How much is that?	**¿Cuánto es?** *kwanto es*
Is there a discount for …?	**¿Hacen descuento a …?** *athen deskwento a*
children/families	**los niños/las familias** *los neeños/las fameeleeyas*
senior citizens	**los pensionistas** *los penseeyoneestas*
students	**los estudiantes** *los estoodeeyantes*
Do you offer a cheap same-day round-trip [return] ticket?	**¿Tienen una oferta por un billete de ida y vuelta en el mismo día?** *teeyenen oona oferta por oon beel-yeteh deh eeda ee bwelta en el meesmo deeya*

Queries

Do I have to change trains?	**¿Tengo que cambiar de trenes?** _tengo keh kambeeyar deh trenes_
Is it a direct train?	**¿Es un tren directo?** _es oon tren deerekto_
You have to change at ...	**Tiene que cambiar en ...** _teeyeneh keh kambeeyar en_
How long is this ticket valid?	**¿Para cuánto tiempo vale este billete?** _para kwanto teeyempo baleh esteh beel-yeteh_
Can I take my bicycle on the train?	**¿Puedo llevar mi bicicleta en el tren?** _pwedo l-yebar mee beetheekleta en el tren_
Can I return on the same ticket?	**¿Puedo volver con el mismo billete?** _pwedo bolber kon el meesmo beel-yeteh_
In which car [coach] is my seat?	**¿En qué compartimento está mi asiento?** _en keh komparteemento esta mee aseeyento_
Is there a dining car on the train?	**¿Hay coche restaurante en el tren?** _eye kocheh restawranteh en el tren_

Train times

Could I have a timetable, please?	**¿Podría darme un horario (de trenes), por favor?** _podreeya durmeh oon orareeyo (deh trenes) por fabor_
When is the ... train to Vigo?	**¿Cuándo sale el ... tren a Vigo?** _kwando suleh el ... tren a beego_
first/next/last	**primer/próximo/último** _preemer/prokseemo/oolteemo_

IN A TRAIN STATION

Dos billetes a Toledo, por favor. _dos beelyetehs a toledo por fabor (Two tickets to Toledo, please.)_
¿De ida o de ida y vuelta? _deh eehda o deh eehda ee bwelta (One way or round trip?)_
De ida y vuelta, por favor. _deh eehda ee bwelta por fabor (Round trip, please.)_

How frequent are trains to …?	¿Con qué frecuencia salen los trenes a …?
	kon keh frekwentheeya salen los trenes a
once/twice a day	**una/dos veces al día**
	oona/dos bethes al deeya
5 times a day	**cinco veces al día**
	theenko bethes al deeya
every hour	**cada hora** *kada ora*
What time do they leave?	¿A qué hora salen?
	a keh ora salen
on the hour	**a la hora en punto**
	a la ora en poonto
20 minutes past the hour	**a las … y veinte**
	a las … ee baynteh
What time does the train stop/arrive in …?	¿A qué hora para/llega el tren a …?
	a keh ora para/l-yega el tren a
How long is the trip [journey]?	¿Cuánto dura el viaje?
	kwanto doora el beeyakheh
Is the train on time?	¿Llega puntual el tren?
	l-yega poontoowal el tren

Departures

Which platform does the train to … leave from?	¿De qué andén sale el tren a …?
	deh keh anden saleh el tren a
Where is platform 4?	¿Dónde está el andén cuatro?
	dondeh esta el anden kwatro
over there	**allí** *al-yee*
on the left/right	**a la izquierda/derecha**
	a la eethkeeyerda/derecha
under the underpass	**debajo del pasaje subterráneo**
	debakho del pasakheh soobterraneyo
Where do I change for …?	¿Dónde tengo que cambiar para …?
	dondeh tengo keh kambeeyar para
How long will I have to wait for a connection?	¿Cuánto tiempo tengo que esperar para un enlace? *kwanto teeyempo tengo keh esperar para oon enlatheh*

Boarding

Is this the right platform for the train to …?	**¿Es éste el andén para el tren a …?** _es esteh el anden para el tren a_
Is this the train to …?	**¿Es éste el tren a …?** _es esteh el tren a_
Is this seat taken?	**¿Está ocupado este asiento?** _esta okoopado esteh aseeyento_
I think that's my seat.	**Creo que ése es mi asiento.** _kreyo keh eseh es mee aseeyento_
Here's my reservation.	**Aquí tengo la reserva.** _akee tengo la rreserba_
Are there any seats/berths available?	**¿Hay asientos/literas libres?** _eye aseeyentos/leeteras leebres_
Do you mind if …?	**¿Le importa si …?** _leh eemporta see_
I sit here	**me siento aquí** _meh seeyento akee_
I open the window	**abro la ventana** _abro la bentana_

During the trip

How long are we stopping here?	**¿Por cuánto tiempo paramos aquí?** _por kwanto teeyempo paramos akee_
When do we get to …?	**¿Cuándo llegamos a …?** _kwando l-yegamos a_
Have we passed …?	**¿Hemos pasado …?** _emos pasado_
Where is the dining/ sleeping car?	**¿Dónde está el coche restaurante/cama?** _dondeh esta el kocheh restawranteh/kama_
Where is my berth?	**¿Dónde está mi litera?** _dondeh esta mee leetera_
I've lost my ticket.	**He perdido el billete.** _eh perdeedo el beel-yeteh_

YOU MAY SEE

FRENO DE EMERGENCIA	emergency brake
PUERTAS AUTOMÁTICAS	automatic doors

LONG-DISTANCE BUS [COACH]

Long-distance buses are good if you want to visit out-of-the-way places. Most buses only serve towns and villages within a region or province. From larger cities you can book cross-country and international lines – information is available from the local central bus station (**estación de autobuses**).

Where is the bus [coach] station?	**¿Dónde está la estación de autobuses?** *dondeh esta la estatheeyon deh awtobooses*
When's the next bus [coach] to …?	**¿Cuándo sale el próximo autobús a …?** *kwando saleh el prokseemo awtoboos a*
Where does it leave from?	**¿De qué andén sale?** *deh keh anden saleh*
Where are the bus [coach] stops?	**¿Dónde están los andenes?** *dondeh estan los andenes*
Does the bus [coach] stop at …?	**¿Para el autobús en …?** *para el awtoboos en*
How long does the trip [journey] take?	**¿Cuánto dura el viaje?** *kwanto doora el beeyakheh*

YOU MAY SEE

PARADA DE AUTOBUSES	bus stop
PARADA SOLICITADA	request stop
PROHIBIDO FUMAR	no smoking
SALIDA DE EMERGENCIA	(emergency) exit

BUS

In most buses you pay as you enter. For larger cities with fixed fares, a 10-trip pass (**un bonobús**) is cheapest – but remember to use the cancelling machine by the driver for each trip. These tickets are sold at newspaper stands in Madrid; at banks in Barcelona, lottery-ticket shops and metro stations.

Where is the bus station [terminus]?	**¿Dónde está la estación de autobuses?** *dondeh esta la estatheeyon deh awtobooses*
Where can I get a bus to …?	**¿Dónde se coge un autobús a …?** *dondeh se kokheh oon awtoboos a …*

YOU MAY HEAR

Tiene que tomar el autobús número …	You need bus number …
Tiene que cambiar de autobús en …	You must change buses at …

Buying tickets

Where can I buy tickets?	**¿Dónde se puede comprar billetes?** _dondeh seh pwedeh komprar beel-yetes_
A ... ticket to...	**Un billete ... para...** _oon beel-yeteh ... para_
one-way [single]	**de ida** _deh eeda_
round-trip [return]	**de ida y vuelta** _deh eeda ee bwelta_
multiple trip	**bonobús** _bonoboos_
day/weekly/monthly	**para todo el día/la semana/el mes** _para todo el deeya/la semana/el mes_
How much is the fare to ...?	**¿Cuánto cuesta el billete a ...?** _kwanto kwesta el beel-yeteh a_

YOU MAY SEE

PIQUE SU BILLETE	validate your ticket

Traveling

Is this the right bus to ...?	**¿Es éste el autobús a ...?** _es este el awtoboos a_
Could you tell me when to get off?	**¿Podría decirme cuándo me tengo que bajar?** _podreeya detheermeh kwando meh tengo keh bakhar_
Do I have to change buses?	**¿Tengo que hacer transbordo?** _tengo keh ather transbordo_
How many stops are there to ...?	**¿Cuántas paradas hay hasta ...?** _kwantas paradas eye asta_
Next stop please!	**¡Próxima parada, por favor!** _prokseema parada por fabor_

AT A BUS STOP

¿Es éste el autobús al centro? _es este el awtoboos al thentro_ (Is this the bus to downtown?)

Sí, es el número ocho. _see es el noomero ocho_ (Yes, bus number 8.)

Muchas gracias. _moochas gratheeyas_ (Thank you very much.)

De nada. _de nada_ (You're welcome.)

SUBWAY [METRO]

There are extensive subway [metro] systems in Madrid and Barcelona, with a striking new system in Bilbao. Big maps outside each station make the systems easy to use. Cheaper ten-ride tickets (**billete de diez viajes**) are available.

Barcelona offers **un bon-bus T1**, which allows travel on both the metro and the bus networks.

Most metro systems close at 11 p.m. on weekdays and at 1 a.m. on Saturdays.

General inquiries

Where's the nearest subway [metro] station?	**¿Dónde está la próxima estación de metro?** _dondeh esta_ la _prokseema estatheeyon_ deh _metro_
Where do I buy a ticket?	**¿Dónde se compran los billetes?** _dondeh_ seh _kompran_ los _beel-yetes_
Could I have a map of the subway [metro]?	**¿Podría darme un mapa del metro?** _podreeya_ _darmeh_ oon _mapa_ del _metro_

Traveling

Which line should I take for …?	**¿Qué línea tengo que coger para …?** keh _leenaya_ _tengo_ keh _kokher_ _para_
Is this the right train for …?	**¿Es éste el tren para …?** es _esteh_ el tren _para_
Which stop is it for …?	**¿Qué parada es la de …?** keh _parada_ es la _deh_
How many stops is it to …?	**¿Cuántas paradas quedan para …?** _kwantas_ _paradas_ _kedan_ _para_
Is the next stop …?	**¿Es … la próxima parada?** es … la _prokseema_ _parada_
Where are we?	**¿Dónde estamos?** _dondeh_ _estamos_
Where do I change for …?	**¿Dónde tengo que hacer transbordo para …?** _dondeh_ _tengo_ keh _ather transbordo_ _para_

YOU MAY SEE	
A OTRAS LÍNEAS/ CORRESPONDENCIA	to other lines/ transfer

FERRY

Regular ferry services are run to the Balearic Islands (from Valencia) and Canary Islands (by **Compañía Transmediterránea SA**).

Why not spend the day in Africa? A ferry trip to Tangiers (Morocco) and Ceuta (Spanish territory) operates from Algeciras.

When is the car ferry to …?	**¿Cuándo sale el ferry a …?** _kwan_do _sa_leh el _fe_rree a
first/next/last	**primer/próximo/último** _pree_mer/_prok_seemo/_ool_teemo
hovercraft/ship	**el aerodeslizador/el barco** el _aeyrodeslee_thador/el _bar_ko
A round-trip [return] ticket for …	**Un billete de ida y vuelta para …** oon beel-_ye_teh deh _ee_da ee _bwel_ta _pa_ra
one car and one trailer [caravan]	**un coche y una roulotte** oon _ko_cheh ee _oo_na roo_lo_teh
two adults and three children	**dos adultos y tres niños** dos a_dool_tos ee tres _nee_ños
I want to reserve a … cabin.	**Quiero reservar un camarote …** _kee_yero reser_bar_ oon kama_ro_teh
single/double	**individual/doble** eendeebeedoo_wal_/_do_bleh

YOU MAY SEE

BOTE SALVAVIDAS	life boat
PROHIBIDO EL ACCESO	no access
PUNTO DE REUNIÓN	muster station
SALVAVIDAS	life preserver [life belt]

BOAT TRIPS

Is there a …?	**¿Hay …?** eye
boat trip/river cruise	**una excursión en barco/un crucero por el río** _oo_na eks_koorseeynn_ en _bar_ko/ oon kroo_the_ro por el _ree_yo
What time does it leave/return?	**¿A qué hora sale/vuelve?** a keh _o_ra _sa_leh/_bwel_veh
Where can we buy tickets?	**¿Dónde se compran los billetes?** _don_deh seh _kom_pran los beel-_ye_tes

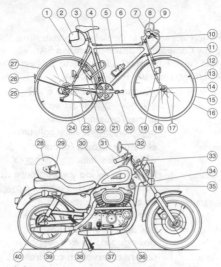

1	brake pad **frenos** mpl	22	generator [dynamo] **dinamo** m
2	bicycle bag **cesta** f	23	chain **cadena** f
3	saddle **sillín** m	24	rear light **luz** f **trasera**
4	pump **bomba** f	25	rim **llanta** f
5	water bottle **botella** f **para el agua**	26	reflectors **reflectores** mpl
6	frame **cuadro** m	27	fender [mudguard] **guardabarros** mpl
7	handlebars **manillar** m	28	helmet **casco** m
8	bell **timbre** m	29	visor **visor** m
9	brake cable **cable** m **de los frenos**	30	fuel tank **depósito** m **del combustible**
10	gear shift [lever] **palanca** f **para cambiar de marcha**	31	clutch **palanca** f **del embrague**
11	gear control cable **cable** m **de las marchas/de control**	32	mirror **espejo** m
12	inner tube **cámara** f	33	ignition switch **interruptor** m **de arranque**
13	front/back wheel **rueda** f **delantera/trasera**	34	turn signal [indicator] **intermitente** m
14	axle **eje** m	35	horn **cláxon** m
15	tire [tyre] **neumático** m	36	engine **motor** m
16	wheel **rueda** f	37	gear shift [lever] **palanca** f **para las marchas**
17	spokes **radio** m	38	kick stand [main stand] **pie** m
18	bulb **luz** f	39	exhaust pipe **tubo** m **de escape**
19	headlamp **luz** f **delantera**	40	chain guard **protector** m **de la cadena**
20	pedal **pedal** m		
21	lock **candado** m		

BICYCLE/MOTORBIKE

I'd like to rent a …	**Quiero alquilar …** _keeyero alkeelar_ **una**
3-/10-speed bicycle	**bicicleta de tres/diez marchas** _oona beetheekleta deh tres/deeyeth marchas_
mountain bike	**una bicicleta de montaña** _oona beetheekleta deh montaña_
moped	**un ciclomotor** _oon theeklomotor_
motorbike	**una moto** _oona moto_
How much does it cost per day/week?	**¿Cuánto cuesta por día/semana?** _kwanto kwesta por deeya/semana_
Do you require a deposit?	**¿Hay que pagar un depósito?** _eye keh pagar oon deposito_
The brakes don't work.	**Los frenos no funcionan.** _los frenos no foontheeyonan_
There are no lights.	**No hay luces.** _no eye loothes_
The front/rear tire [tyre] has a flat [puncture].	**El neumático delantero/trasero está pinchado.** _el neyoomateeko delantero/trasero esta peenchado_

HITCHHIKING

Where are you heading?	**¿Adónde se dirige?** _adondeh seh deereekheh_
I'm heading for …	**Me dirijo a …** _meh deereekho a_
Can you give me/us a lift?	**¿Me/nos puede llevar?** _meh/nos pwedeh l-yebar_
Is that on the way to …?	**¿Está de camino a …?** _esta deh kameeno a_
Could you drop me off …?	**¿Me podría dejar …?** _meh podreeya dekhar_
here	**aquí** _akee_
at the … exit	**a la salida …** _a la saloeda_
downtown	**en el centro** _en el thentro_
Thanks for the lift.	**Gracias por traernos.** _gratheeyas por trayernos_

TAXI/CAB

Taxis are marked **SP** (**servicio público**) and a green sign indicates **libre** when free; in tourist areas they are often unmetered, though fares to most destinations are fixed and displayed at the main taxi stand.

Tipping: 10% for the taxi driver.

Where can I get a taxi?	**¿Dónde puedo coger un taxi?** _dondeh pwedo kokher oon taksee_
Do you have the number for a taxi service?	**¿Tiene el número de alguna empresa de taxi?** _teeyeneh el noomero deh algoona empresa deh taksee_
I'd like a taxi …	**Quiero un taxi …** _keeyero oon taksee_
now	**ahora** _a-ora_
in an hour	**dentro de una hora** _dentro deh oona ora_
for tomorrow at 9:00	**para mañana a las nueve** _para mañana a las nwebeh_
The pick-up address is …	**La dirección es …** _la deerektheeyon es_
I'm going to …	**Me dirijo a …** _meh deereekho a_
Please take me to …	**Por favor, lléveme a …** _por fabor l-yebemeh a_
airport/train station	**el aeropuerto/la estación de trenes** _el ayropwerto/la estatheeyon deh trenes_
this address	**esta dirección** _esta deerektheeyon_
How much will it cost?	**¿Cuánto costará?** _kwanto kostara_
How much is that?	**¿Cuánto es?** _kwanto es_
You said … euros.	**Dijo … euros.** _deekho … eh-ooros_
Keep the change.	**Quédese con el cambio.** _kedeseh kon el kambeeyo_

AT A TAXI STAND

¿Cuánto costará al aeropuerto? _kwanto kostara al ayropwerto_ (How much is it to the airport?)
Quince euros. _keentheh eh-ooros_ (15 euros.)
Gracias. _gratheeyas_ (Thank you.)

CAR/AUTOMOBILE

The minimum driving age is 18. While driving, the following documents must be carried at all times: driver's license, vehicle registration document and insurance documentation. If you don't hold an EU license, an international driving permit is also required. Insurance for minimum third party risks is compulsory in Europe. It is recommended that you take out international motor insurance (Green Card insurance) through your insurer.

The most common crime against tourists in Spain is theft from rental cars. Always look for secure parking areas overnight and never leave valuables in your car at any time.

Essential equipment: warning triangle, national identity (country of origin) sticker, and a set of spare head- and rear-lamp bulbs. Seat belts are compulsory. Children under 10 must travel in the rear.

Traffic on main roads has priority; where 2 roads of equal importance merge, traffic from the right has priority. Tolls are payable on certain roads, they can be high.

Traffic police can give hefty on-the-spot fines. A **boletín de denuncia** is issued, specifying the offense; guidelines in English for an appeal appear on the back.

The use of horns is prohibited in built-up areas except for emergencies.

Alcohol limit in blood: max. 80mg/100ml.

Road network

A (**autopista**) – toll highway [motorway] (blue sign), and (**autovías**) – free highway [motorway] (green sign); **N** (**nacional**) – main road; **C** (**comarcal**) – secondary road (white sign); **V** (**vecinal**) – local road (prefixed by letter denoting province)

Conversion Chart

km	1	10	20	30	40	50	60	70	80	90	100	110	120	130
miles	0.62	6	12	19	25	31	37	44	50	56	62	68	74	81

Speed limits

	Residential	Built-up area	Main road	Highway/motorway
	kmh (mph)	*kmh (mph)*	*kmh (mph)*	*kmh (mph)*
Cars	20 (12)	50 (31)	90-100 (56-62)	120 (74)

Gas [Petrol]	Leaded	Lead-free	Diesel
	Normal (92)	Sin plomo (95)	Gasóleo 'A' (98)

Car rental

Third-party insurance is included in the basic charge, usually with Collision Damage Waiver.

The minimum age varies from 21 if paying by credit card, 23 if paying by cash. In the latter case, a large deposit will be charged.

Where can I rent a car?	**¿Dónde puedo alquilar un coche?** *dondeh pwedo alkeelar oon kocheh*
I'd like to rent …	**Quiero alquilar …** *keeyero alkeelar*
2-/4-door car	**un coche de dos/cuatro puertas** *oon kocheh deh dos/kwatro pwertas*
an automatic	**un coche automático** *oon kocheh aootomateeko*
a car with 4-wheel drive	**un coche con tracción a las cuatro ruedas** *oon kocheh kon traktheeyon a las kwatro roowedas*
a car with air conditioning	**un coche con aire acondicionado** *oon kocheh kon ayreh akondeetheeyonado*
I'd like it for a day/week.	**Lo quiero para un día/una semana.** *lo keeyero para oon deeya/oona semana*
How much does it cost per day/week?	**¿Cuánto cuesta por día/semana?** *kwanto kwesta por deeya/semana*
Is mileage/insurance included?	**¿Va el kilometraje/seguro incluido?** *ba el keelometrakheh/segooro eenklooweedo*
Are there special weekend rates?	**¿Tienen precios especiales de fin de semana?** *teeyenen pretheeyos espetheeyales deh feen deh semana*
Can I return the car at …?	**¿Puedo dejar el coche en …?** *pwedo dekhar el kocheh en*
What kind of fuel does it take?	**¿Qué tipo de combustible gasta?** *keh teepo deh komboosteebleh gasta*
Where is the high [full]/ low [dipped] beam ?	**¿Dónde están las largas/cortas?** *dondeh estan las largas/kortas*
Could I have full insurance?	**¿Podría hacerme un seguro a todo riesgo?** *podreeya athermeh oon segooro a todo rreeyesgo*

Gas [Petrol] station

Where's the next gas [petrol] station, please?	**¿Dónde está la próxima gasolinera, por favor?** _dondeh esta la prokseema gasoleenera por fabor_
Is it self-service?	**¿Es de autoservicio?** _es deh owtoserbeetheeyo_
Fill it up, please.	**Lleno, por favor.** _l-yeno por fabor_
… liters of gasoline, please.	**… litros de gasolina, por favor.** _… leetros deh gasoleena por fabor_
premium [super]/regular	**súper/normal** _sooper/normal_
lead-free/diesel	**sin plomo/diesel** _seen plomo/dee-ehsel_
Where is the air pump/water?	**¿Dónde está el aire/agua?** _dondeh esta el ayreh/agwa_

YOU MAY SEE

PRECIO POR LITRO	price per liter

Parking

Metered parking is common in most towns; some take credit cards as well as coins. In certain zones of Madrid, prepaid slips (**tarjeta de aparcamiento**) are required, available from tobacconists.

It is an offense to park facing against the traffic.

Vehicles that are illegally parked may be towed away (**grúa**); you will find a yellow triangle with your license plate number and address of the car-pound.

Is there a parking lot [car park] nearby?	**¿Hay un aparcamiento cerca?** _eye oon aparkamooyonto therka_
What's the charge per hour/per day?	**¿Cuánto cobran por hora/día?** _kwanto kobran por ora/deeya_
Do you have some change for the parking meter?	**¿Tienen cambio para el parquímetro?** _teeyenen kambeeyo para el parkeemetro_
My car has been booted [clamped]. Who do I call?	**A mi coche le han puesto el cepo.** **¿A quién llamo?** _a mee kocheh leh an pwesto el thepo. a keeyen l-yamo_

15 headlights **los faros**
16 license [number] plate **la matrícula**
17 fog lamp **el faro antiniebla**
18 turn signals [indicators]
   los intermitentes
19 bumper **el parachoques**
20 tires [tyres] **las llantas**
21 wheel cover [hubcap]
   el tapacubos
22 valve **la válvula**
23 wheels **las ruedas**
24 outside [wing] mirror **el espejo
   lateral**
25 automatic locks [central locking]
   el cierre centralizado
26 lock **el seguro [la cerradura]**
27 wheel rim **el rin de la rueda**
28 exhaust pipe **el tubo de escape**
29 odometer [milometer]
   el cuentakilómetros
30 warning light
   la luz de advertencia

1 taillights [back lights] **las luces
   traseras**
2 brakelights **las luces de los frenos**
3 trunk [boot] **el maletero**
4 gas tank door [petrol cap] **la
   tapa del depósito de gasolina**
5 window **la ventana**
6 seat belt **el cinturón de seguridad**
7 sunroof **el techo solar**
8 steering wheel **el volante**
9 ignition **el encendido**
10 ignition key **la llave
   (de encendido)**
11 windshield [windscreen] **el
   parabrisas**
12 windshield [windscreen] wipers
   las escobillas
13 windshield [windscreen] washer
   el limpiaparabrisas
14 hood [bonnet] **el capó**

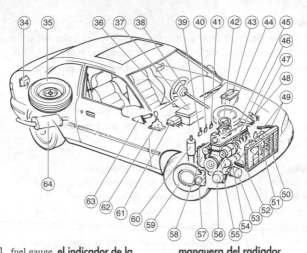

31 fuel gauge **el indicador de la gasolina**
32 speedometer **el velocímetro**
33 oil gauge **el indicador del nivel de aceite**
34 backup [reversing] lights **las luces de marcha atrás**
35 spare tire **la rueda de repuesto**
36 choke **el estárter**
37 heater **la calefacción**
38 steering column **la columna de dirección**
39 accelerator **el acelerador**
40 pedal **el pedal**
41 clutch **el embrague**
42 carburetor **el carburador**
43 battery **la batería**
44 air filter **el filtro de agua**
45 camshaft **el árbol de levas**
46 alternator **el alternador**
47 distributor **el distribuidor**
48 points **las tomas de corriente**
49 radiator hose (top/bottom) **la manguera del radiador (arriba/abajo)**
50 radiator **el radiador**
51 fan **el ventilador**
52 engine **el motor**
53 oil filter **el filtro de aceite**
54 starter motor **el motor de arranque**
55 fan belt **la correa del ventilador**
56 horn **la bocina [el pito]**
57 brake pads **las pastillas de los frenos**
58 transmission [gearbox] **la caja de cambio**
59 brakes **los frenos**
60 shock absorbers **los amortiguadores**
61 fuses **los fusibles**
62 gear shift [lever] **la palanca de cambios**
63 handbrake **el freno de mano**
64 muffler [silencer] **el silenciador**

Breakdown

For help in the event of a breakdown: refer to your breakdown assistance documents; or contact the breakdown service: Spain: ☎ (91) 742 1213.

Where is the nearest garage?	**¿Dónde está el taller más cercano?** _dondeh esta el tal-yer mas therkano_
I've had a breakdown.	**He tenido una avería.** _eh teneedo oona abereeya_
Can you send a mechanic/ tow [breakdown] truck?	**¿Puede mandar a un mecánico/una grúa?** _pwedeh mandar a oon mekaneeko/oona groowa_
I belong to … . rescue service	**Soy del servicio de grúa …** _soy del serbeetheeyo deh groowa_
My license plate [registration] number is …	**Mi número de matrícula es …** _mee noomero deh matreekoola es_
The car is …	**El coche está …** _el kocheh esta_
on the highway [motorway]	**en la autopista** _en la aootopeesta_
2 km from …	**a dos kilómetros de …** _a dos keelometros deh_
How long will you be?	**¿Cuánto tiempo tardará?** _kwanto teeyempo tardara_

What's wrong?

I don't know what's wrong.	**No sé qué le pasa.** _no seh ke leh pasa_
My car won't start.	**Mi coche no arranca.** _mee kocheh no arranka_
The battery is dead.	**La batería no funciona.** _la batereeya no foontheeyona_
I've run out of gas [petrol].	**Se me ha acabado la gasolina.** _seh meh a akabado la gasoleena_
I have a flat [puncture].	**Tengo un pinchazo.** _tengo oon peenchatho_
There is something wrong with …	**Algo va mal en …** _algo ba mal en_
I've locked the keys in the car.	**Me he dejado las llaves en el coche.** _meh eh dekhado las l-yabes en el kocheh_

Repairs

Do you do repairs? **¿Hacen reparaciones?**
athen reparatheeyones

Could you have a look at my car? **¿Podrían echarle un vistazo al coche?**
podreeyan echarleh oon beestatho al kocheh

Can you repair it (temporarily)? **¿Puede hacerle una reparación (provisional)?** _pwedeh atherle oona reparatheeyon (probeeseeyonal)_

Please make only essential repairs. **Por favor, hágale reparaciones básicas solamente.** _por fabor agaleh reparatheeyones baseekas solamenteh_

Can I wait for it? **¿Puedo esperar?** _pwedo esperar_

Can you repair it today? **¿Puede arreglarlo hoy?**
pwedeh arreglarlo oy

When will it be ready? **¿Cuándo estará listo?** _kwando estara leesto_

How much will it cost? **¿Cuánto costará?** _kwanto kostara_

That's outrageous! **¡Eso es un escándalo!**
eso es oon eskandalo

Can I have a receipt for my insurance? **¿Pueden darme un recibo para el seguro?**
pweden darmeh oon retheebo para el segooro

YOU MAY HEAR

El/la … no funciona.	The … isn't working.
No tengo las piezas necesarias.	I don't have the necessary parts.
Tendré que mandar a pedir las piezas.	I will have to order the parts.
Sólo puedo repararlo provisionalmente.	I can only repair it temporarily.
Su coche no tiene arreglo.	Your car is beyond repair.
No se puede arreglar/reparar.	It can't be repaired.
Estará listo …	It will be ready …
hoy mismo	later today
mañana	tomorrow
dentro de … días	in … days

ACCIDENTS

In the event of an accident:

1. put your red warning triangle about 100 meters behind your car;
2. report the accident to the police; don't leave before they arrive;
3. show your driver's license and insurance papers;
4. give your name, address, insurance company to the other party;
5. report the accident to your insurance company;
6. don't make any written statement without advice of a lawyer or automobile club official;
7. note all relevant details of the other party, any independent witnesses, and the accident.

There has been an accident.	**Ha habido un accidente.** *a abeedo oon aktheedenteh*
It's ...	**Ha ocurrido ...** *a okoorreedo*
on the highway	**en la autopista** *en la aootopeesta*
[motorway] near ...	**cerca de ...** *therka deh*
Where's the nearest telephone?	**¿Dónde está el teléfono más cercano?** *dondeh esta el telefono mas therkano*
Call ...	**Llame a ...** *l-yameh a*
the police	**la policía** *la poleetheeya*
an ambulance	**una ambulancia** *oona amboolantheeya*
the fire department [brigade]	**el cuerpo de bomberos** *el kwerpo deh bomberos*
Can you help me, please?	**¿Puede ayudarme, por favor?** *pwedeh ayoodarmeh por fabor*

Injuries

There are people injured.	**Hay gente herida.** *eye khenteh ereeda*
He's seriously injured.	**Está gravemente herido.** *esta grabementeh ereedo*
He's bleeding.	**Está sangrando.** *esta sangrando*
She's unconscious.	**Está inconsciente.** *esta eenkonstheeyenteh*
He can't breathe/move.	**No puede respirar/moverse.** *no pwedeh respeerar/moberseh*

Legal matters

What's your insurance company?	**¿Cuál es su compañía de seguros?** *kwal es soo kompañeeya deh segooros*
What's your name and address?	**¿Cuál es su nombre y su dirección?** *kwal es soo nombreh ee soo deerektheeyon*
The car ran into me.	**Chocó conmigo.** *choko konmeego*
She was driving too fast/ too close.	**Conducía demasiado rápido/cerca.** *kondootheeya demaseeyado rapeedo/therka*
I had the right of way.	**Yo tenía derecho de paso.** *yo teneeya derecho deh paso*
I was (only) driving … kmh.	**(Sólo) conducía a … kilómetros por hora.** *(solo) kondootheeya a … keelometros por ora*
I'd like an interpreter.	**Quiero un intérprete.** *keeyero oon eenterpreteh*
I didn't see the sign.	**No vi la señal.** *no bee la señal*
He/She saw it happen.	**Él/Ella lo vio.** *el/el-ya lo beeyo*
The license plate [registration] number was …	**El número de matrícula era …** *el noomero deh matreekoola era*

YOU MAY HEAR

¿Puedo ver su …, por favor?	Can I see your …, please?
carnet/permiso de conducir	driver's license
certificado del seguro	insurance card [certificate]
documento del registro del coche	vehicle registration
¿A qué hora ocurrió?	What time did it happen?
¿Dónde ocurrió?	Where did it happen?
¿Hubo alguien más involucrado?	Was anyone else involved?
¿Hay testigos?	Are there any witnesses?
Se pasó del límite de velocidad.	You were speeding.
Sus faros no funcionan.	Your lights aren't working.
Tendrá que pagar una multa (en el sitio).	You'll have to pay a fine (on the spot).
Tenemos que tomar su declaración en la comisaría.	You have to make a statement at the station.

ASKING DIRECTIONS

Excuse me, please.	**Disculpe, por favor.** *dees<u>kool</u>peh por fa<u>bor</u>*
How do I get to …?	**¿Cómo se va a …?** <u>ko</u>mo seh ba a
Where is …?	**¿Dónde está …?** <u>don</u>deh es<u>ta</u>
Can you show me where I am on the map?	**¿Puede indicarme dónde estoy en el mapa?** <u>pwe</u>deh eendee<u>kar</u>meh <u>don</u>deh es<u>toy</u> en el <u>mapa</u>
Can you repeat that, please?	**¿Puede repetir eso, por favor?** <u>pwe</u>deh repe<u>teer</u> eso por fa<u>bor</u>
More slowly, please.	**Más despacio, por favor.** mas des<u>pa</u>theeyo por fa<u>bor</u>
Thanks for your help.	**Gracias por su ayuda.** <u>gra</u>theeyas por soo a<u>yoo</u>da

Traveling by car

Is this the right road for …?	**¿Es ésta la carretera para …?** es <u>es</u>ta la karre<u>te</u>ra <u>pa</u>ra
How far is it to … from here?	**¿A qué distancia está … de aquí?** a keh dees<u>tan</u>theeya es<u>ta</u> … deh a<u>kee</u>
Where does this road lead?	**¿Adónde va esta carretera?** a<u>don</u>deh ba <u>es</u>ta karre<u>te</u>ra
How do I get onto the highway [motorway]?	**¿Cómo se va a la autopista?** <u>ko</u>mo seh ba a la aooto<u>pees</u>ta
What's the next town called?	**¿Cómo se llama el próximo pueblo?** <u>ko</u>mo seh l-<u>ya</u>ma el <u>prok</u>seemo <u>pwe</u>blo
How long does it take by car?	**¿Cuánto tiempo se tarda en coche?** <u>kwan</u>to tee<u>yem</u>po seh <u>tar</u>da en <u>ko</u>cheh

ON THE STREET

¿A qué distancia está la estación de trenes? *a keh dees<u>tan</u>theeya es<u>ta</u> la estathee<u>yon</u> deh <u>tre</u>nes* (How far is it to the train station?)

Diez minutos en coche. *dee<u>yeth</u> mee<u>noo</u>tos en <u>ko</u>cheh* (10 minutes by car.)

Gracias. *<u>gra</u>theeyas* (Thank you.)

Location

Está …	It's …
todo recto	straight ahead
a la izquierda	on the left
a la derecha	on the right
al otro lado de la calle	on the other side of the street
en la esquina	on the corner
doblando la esquina	around the corner
yendo hacia …	in the direction of …
frente a …/detrás de …	opposite …/behind …
al lado de …/después de …	next to …/after …
Baje por …	Go down the …
bocacalle/calle principal	side street/main street
Cruce …	Cross the …
plaza/puente	square/bridge
Tome/Coja …	Take the …
el tercer desvío a la derecha	third turn to the right
Tuerza a la izquierda.	Turn left.
después del primer semáforo	after the first traffic light
en el segundo cruce	at the second intersection [crossroad]

By car

Está … de aquí.	It's … of here.
al norte/sur	north/south
al este/oeste	east/west
Tome/coja la carretera para …	Take the road for …
Se ha equivocado de carretera.	You're on the wrong road.
Tendrá que volver a …	You'll have to go back to …
Siga las señales para …	Follow the signs for …

How far?

Está …	It's …
cerca/no está lejos/bastante lejos	close/not far/a long way
a cinco minutos a pie	5 minutes on foot
a diez minutos en coche	10 minutes by car
aproximadamente a cien metros	about 100 meters from
de final de la calle	by the end of the street

ROAD SIGNS

ACCESO SÓLO	access only
CALLE DE SENTIDO ÚNICO	one-way street
CARRETERA CERRADA	road closed
CEDA EL PASO	yield [give way]
DESVÍO	detour [diversion]
ESCUELA/COLEGIO	school
PÓNGASE EN EL CARRIL	stay in lane [get in lane]
PUENTE BAJO	low bridge
RUTA ALTERNATIVA	alternative route
UTILICE LOS FAROS	use headlights

Town plans

aeropuerto	airport
aparcamiento	parking lot [car park]
aseos	restrooms
calle mayor	main [high] street
campo de actividades deportivas	playing field [sports ground]
casco antiguo	old town
cine	movie theater [cinema]
comisaría de policía	police station
correos (oficina de)	post office
edificio público	public building
estación	station
estación de metro	subway [metro] station
estadio	stadium
iglesia	church
oficina de información	information office
parada de autobús	bus stop
parada de taxis	taxi stand [rank]
parque	park
pasaje subterráneo	underpass
paso de peatones	pedestrian crossing
ruta de autobús	bus route
servicios	toilets
teatro	theater
Usted está aquí.	You are here.
zona peatonal	pedestrian zone [precinct]

SIGHTSEEING
TOURIST INFORMATION OFFICE

Tourist information offices are often situated in the town center; look for **Oficina de turismo** and **Información**.

There are numerous local festivals to look for: e.g. **Las Fallas de Valencia** (March), **La Feria de Sevilla** (April), **San Isidro** (Madrid,15 May), **Los Sanfermines de Pamplona** (July), **La Mercè** (Barcelona, 23 September).

Where's the tourist office?	**¿Dónde está la oficina de turismo?** _dondeh esta la ofeetheena deh tooreesmo_
What are the main points of interest?	**¿Cuáles son los sitios de interés?** _kwales son los seeteeyos deh interes_
We're here for …	**Nos quedaremos aquí …** _nos kedaremos akee_
a few hours	**unas horas** _oonas oras_
a day/week	**un día/una semana** _oon deeya/oona semana_
Can you recommend a(n) …?	**¿Puede recomendarme …?** _pwedeh rekomendarmeh_
a sightseeing tour	**un recorrido por los sitios de interés** _oon rekorreedo por los seeteeyos deh eenteres_
an excursion	**una excursión** _oona ekskoorseeyon_
a boat trip	**una excursión en barco** _oona eskoorseeyon en barko_
Are these brochures free?	**¿Son gratis estos folletos?** _son gratees estos fol-yetos_
Do you have any information on …?	**¿Tiene alguna información sobre …?** _teeyeneh algoona eenformatheeyon sobreh_
Are there any trips to …?	**¿Hay excursiones a …?** _eye ekskoorseeyones a_

EXCURSIONS

How much does the tour cost?	**¿Cuánto cuesta la visita?** *kwanto kwesta la beeseeta*
Is lunch included?	**¿Va incluida la comida?** *ba eenklooeeda la komeeda*
Where do we leave from?	**¿De dónde se sale?** *deh dondeh seh saleh*
What time does the tour start?	**¿A qué hora comienza la visita?** *a keh ora komeeyentha la beeseeta*
What time do we get back?	**¿A qué hora volvemos?** *a keh ora bolbemos*
Do we have free time in …?	**¿Tenemos tiempo libre en …?** *tenemos teeyempo leebreh en*
Is there an English-speaking guide?	**¿Hay un guía que hable inglés?** *eye oon geeya keh ableh eengles*

On tour

Are we going to see …?	**¿Vamos a ver …?** *bamos a behr*
We'd like to have a look at …	**Queremos echar un vistazo a …** *keremos echar oon beestatho a*
Can we stop here …?	**¿Podemos parar aquí …?** *podemos parar akee*
to take photographs	**para hacer fotos** *para ather fotos*
to buy souvenirs	**para comprar recuerdos** *para komprar rekwerdos*
for the restrooms [toilets]	**para ir al servicio** *para eer al serbeetheeyo*
Would you take a photo of us, please?	**¿Podría sacarnos una foto, por favor?** *podreeya sakarnos oona foto por fabor*
How long do we have here/in …?	**¿Cuánto tiempo tenemos para estar aquí/en …?** *kwanto teeyempo tenemos para estar akee/en*
Wait! … isn't back yet.	**¡Esperen! … todavía no ha vuelto.** *esperen … todabeeya no a bwelto*
Stop the bus, my child is feeling sick.	**Pare el autobús – mi hijo(-a) se marea.** *pareh el aootoboos mee eekho(-a) se mareya*

98

SIGHTS

Town maps are on display in city centers, train, tram, and many bus stations, and at tourist information offices. Many tourist offices will give you a free folding map of the town with useful tourist information.

Where is the …?	**¿Dónde está …?** _don_deh es_ta_
abbey	**la abadía** _la aba_dee_ya_
battle site	**el lugar de la batalla** _el loo_gar_ deh la ba_tal_-ya_
botanical garden	**el jardín botánico** _el khar_deen_ bo_ta_neeko_
castle	**el castillo** _el kas_teel_-yo_
cathedral	**la catedral** _la kate_dral_
church	**la iglesia** _la eeg_lesee_ya_
downtown area	**el centro** _el_ then_tro_
fountain	**la fuente** _la_ fwen_teh_
library	**la biblioteca** _la beeblee_yo_teka_
market	**el mercado** _el mer_ka_do_
(war) memorial	**el monumento (a los caídos)** _el mono_omen_to (a los ka_ee_dos)_
monastery	**el monasterio** _el monas_tereeyo_
museum	**el museo** _el moo_sey_o_
old town	**el casco antiguo** _el_ kas_ko an_teeg_wo_
opera house	**el teatro de la ópera** _el te_ya_tro deh la_ ope_ra_
palace	**el palacio** _el pa_la_thoeyo_
park	**el parque** _el_ park_heh_
parliament building	**el palacio de las cortes** _el pa_la_thoeyo deh las_ kortes_
ruins	**las ruinas** _la roo_ee_na_
shopping area	**la zona de tiendas** _la_ thona_ deh tee_yendas_
theater	**el teatro** _el te_ya_tro_
tower	**la torre** _la_ torreh_
town hall	**el ayuntamiento** _el ayoontamee_yen_to_
viewpoint	**el mirador** _el meera_dor_
Can you show me on the map?	**¿Puede indicarme en el mapa?** _pwe_deh eendee_kar_meh en el_ mapa_

ADMISSION

Museums are usually closed on Mondays, important holidays, and for the daily siesta (2 p.m. to 4 p.m.). Usual opening hours are 10 a.m.to 1 or 2 p.m. and 4 p.m. to 6 or 7 p.m.

Is the … open to the public?	**¿Está … abierto(-a) al público?** *esta … abeeyerto(-a) al poobleeko*
Can we look around?	**¿Podemos echarle un vistazo a los alredededores?** *podemos echarleh oon beestatho a los alredededores*
What are the hours?	**¿A qué hora abre?** *a keh ora abreh*
When does it close?	**¿A qué hora cierra?** *a keh ora theeyerra*
Is it open on Sundays?	**¿Está abierto los domingos?** *esta abeeyerto los domeengos*
When's the next guided tour?	**¿Cuándo es la próxima visita con guía?** *kwando es la prokseema beeseeta kon geeya*
Do you have a guide book (in English)?	**¿Tiene una guía (en inglés)?** *teeyeneh oona geeya (en eengles)*
Can I take photos?	**¿Puedo hacer fotos?** *pwedo ather fotos*
Is there access for the disabled?	**¿Tiene acceso para minusválidos?** *teyeneh aktheso para meenoosbaleedos*
Is there an audioguide in English?	**¿Tienen auriculares para seguir la visita en inglés?** *teeyenen aooreekoolares para segeer la beeseeta en eengles*

Paying/Tickets

How much is the entrance fee?	**¿Cuánto cuesta la entrada?** *kwanto kwesta la entrada*
Are there any reductions?	**¿Hacen descuento?** *athen deskwento*
children	**los niños** *los neeños*
groups	**los grupos** *los groopos*
senior citizens	**los pensionistas** *los penseeyoneestas*
students	**los estudiantes** *los estoodeeyantes*
the disabled	**los minusválidos** *los meenoosbaleedos*
One adult and two children, please.	**Un adulto y dos niños, por favor.** *oon adoolto ee dos neeños por fabor*

AT THE TICKET COUNTER

Dos adultos, por favor. *dos adooltos por fabor (Two adults, please.)*

Doce euros. *dotheh eh-ooros (12 euros.)*

Aquí tiene. *akee teeyeneh (Here you are.)*

YOU MAY SEE

ABIERTO/CERRADO	open/closed
ENTRADA GRATUITA	free admission
HORARIO DE VISITAS	visiting hours
LA PRÓXIMA VISITA ES A LA/LAS …	next tour at …
PROHIBIDA LA ENTRADA	no entry
PROHIBIDO UTILIZAR EL FLASH	no flash photography
TIENDA DE RECUERDOS	gift shop
ÚLTIMA VISTA A LAS 17H	last entry at 5 p.m.

IMPRESSIONS

It's …	**Es …** *es*
amazing/brilliant	**increíble/maravilloso** *eenkrayeebleh/marabeel-yoso*
beautiful	**bonito** *boneeto*
bizarre/strange	**extraño** *ekstraño*
boring	**aburrido** *aboorreedo*
interesting	**interesante** *eenteresanteh*
magnificent	**magnífico** *magneefeeko*
romantic	**romántico** *romanteeko*
stunning/superb	**precioso/espléndido** *pretheeoso/esplendeedo*
terrible	**terrible** *terreebleh*
ugly	**feo** *feyo*
It's a good value.	**Está muy bien de precio.** *esta mwee beeyen deh pretheeyo*
It's a rip-off.	**Es un timo.** *es oon teemo*
I like/don't like it.	**Me gusta./No me gusta.** *meh goosta/no meh goosta*

TOURIST GLOSSARY

a escala uno:cien scale 1:100

acuarela watercolor

aguja spire

al estilo (de) in the style of

ala wing *(building)*

almena battlement

antigüedades antiques

aposentos apartments *(royal)*

arma weapon

armadura armory

artesanía crafts

baños baths

biblioteca library

boceto sketch

bóveda vault

cementerio churchyard

cenotafio cenotaph

cerámica pottery

conferencia lecture

construido(-a) en … built in …

contrafuerte buttress

corona crown

cripta crypt

cuadro painting

cúpula dome

decorado(-a) por … decorated by …

descubierto(-a) en … discovered in …

destruido(-a) por … destroyed by …

detalle detail

dibujo drawing

diseñado(-a) por … designed by …

diseño design

donado(-a) por … donated by …

dorado(-a) gilded

dorado(-a) gold(en)

edificio building

emperador emperor

emperatriz empress

empezado(-a) en … started in …

entrada doorway

eregido(-a) en … erected in …

escalera staircase

escenario stage

escuela de school of

escultor sculptor

escultura sculpture

exposición exhibit

exposición exhibition

exposición temporal temporary exhibit

fachada facade

foso moat

friso frieze

fundado(-a) en … founded in …

gárgola gargoyle

grabado engraving

grabado etching

jardín de diseño formal formal garden

joyas jewelry

lápida headstone
lienzo canvas
mandado(-a) por ... commissioned by ...
mármol marble
la maqueta model
moneda coin
muebles furniture
muestra display
murió en ... died in ...
muro *(outside)* wall
nacido(-a) en ... born in ...
obra maestra masterpiece
óleos oils
pabellón pavilion
paisaje landscape painting
pared *(inside)* wall
patio courtyard
piedra stone
piedra semipreciosa gemstone
pila bautismal font
pintado(-a) por ... painted by ...
pintor/pintora painter
placa plaque
plata silver/silverware
por ... by ... *(person)*
prestado(-a) a ... on loan to ...

primer piso level 1
puerta gate
reconstruido (-a) en ... rebuilt in ...
reina queen
reino reign
reloj clock
restaurado(-a) en ... restored in ...
retablo tableau
retrato portrait
rey king
salón para grandes recepciones stateroom
siglo century
silla del coro choir (stall)
talla carving
talla de cera waxwork
tapiz tapestry
terminado(-a) en ... completed in ...
torre tower
traje costume
tumba grave
tumba tomb
vestíbulo foyer
vidriera stained-glass window
vivió lived

WHAT?/WHEN?

What's that building?
¿Qué es ese edificio?
keh es eseh edeefeetheeyo

When was it built/painted?
¿Cuándo se construyó/pintó?
kwando seh konstrooyo/peento

What style is that?
¿De qué estilo es eso?
deh keh esteelo es eso

STYLES

realizaciones romanas   200 b.c.–500 a.d.

Ruins of Roman civilization are commonplace in Spain especially the aqueduct at Segovia, the bridge at Córdoba, the triumphal arch in Tarragona, the theatre in Mérida.

arte árabe   ca. 8–end 15

Moorish architecture and art had a huge influence in Spain; especially ornamental brickwork, fretted woodwork, mosaics, calligraphy, carved plaster work. Three great periods can be identified: arte califal (ca. 8–9th, especially the horseshoe-shaped arch of mosque in Córdoba), arte almohade (ca. 10–1250, especially the Giralda tower in Seville), arte granadino (1250–1492, especially the stucco and ceramics in the Alhambra, Granada).

gótico   ca. 13–end 15

Very complex architectural forms, using pointed arches, rib vaults and elaborate stone ornamentation (Isabelline); especially the cathedrals of Burgos, León, Toledo, Seville. This evolved into Plateresque – a lacelike carving of intricate facades; especially the Patio de las Escuelas, Salamanca.

renacimiento   ca. 15–16

The Renaissance left many monuments in Spain; especially El Escorial near Madrid and the palace of Charles V in the Alhambra.

barroco   ca. 17–18

Exuberant architectural style, especially the convent of San Esteban in Salamanca and the Palacio del Marqués de Dos Aguas in Valencia.

siglo de Oro   ca.17

The Golden Century saw a flourishing of the arts; especially the artists El Greco, Velázquez, Zurbarán, and Murillo; and the writers Miguel de Cervantes, Fray Luis de León, and Santa Teresa.

modernismo   ca. late 19–20

A period of crisis in national self-confidence saw world-renowned cultural figures; especially the artists Picasso, Miró, and Dalí; the architect Gaudí; and the writers Unamuno and Lorca.

RULERS

romana   206 b.c.–410 a.d.

The Romans occupied Spain on defeating the Carthaginians in the Second Punic War. 600 years of rule brought a road network, seaports and skills in mining, agriculture and trade. On the collapse of the Roman Empire, Spain was invaded and dominated by the Visigoths.

árabe   711–1492
The first Moorish invasion from North Africa defeated the Visigoths. For almost 800 years Moorish control of Spain fluctuated as the Christian Reconquest expanded. Ferdinand and Isabella completed their expulsion in 1492.

reyes católicos   1474–1516
National unity under Isabel of Castile and Fernando of Aragón saw the Spanish Inquisition (**Inquisición**) set up in 1478 and Columbus claim newly discovered lands for Spain (1492).

la casa de Asturias   1516–1700
The Habsburg House, financed by plundered wealth from the New World, extended its influence: Charles V (**Carlos I**) made claims on Burgundy, the Netherlands, and Italy.

los Borbones   1700–1923
A period of continued military and cultural decline under the Bourbons. The invasion by Napoleon in 1808 forced the abdication of Carlos IV. The 19th century saw the loss of most of Spain's territories in Central and South America.

dictadura del General Franco   1939–75
In the bloody Spanish Civil War (**guerra civil Española**) General Franco's fascist forces overthrow the Republic and declare a dictatorship that lasts until his death.

la democracia   1975–
Juan Carlos I becomes a constitutional monarch. 1992 saw EXPO '92 in Seville, the Olympics in Barcelona, and Madrid nominated the Cultural Capital of Europe.

RELIGION

Predominantly Roman Catholic, Spain is rich in cathedrals and churches. Most large churches are open to the public during the day, services should be respected. Cover bare shoulders before entering.

Catholic/Protestant church	**la Iglesia católica/protestante** *la eegleseeya katoleeku/protestanteh*
mosque/synagogue	**la mezquita/la sinagoga** *la methkeeta/la seenagoga*
mass/the service	**la misa/el servicio** *la meesa/el serveetheeyo*

105

IN THE COUNTRYSIDE

I'd like a map of …	**Quiero un mapa de …** *keeyero oon mapa deh*
this region	**esta región** *esta rekheeyon*
walking routes	**las rutas de senderismo** *las rootas deh sendereesmo*
bicycle routes	**las rutas para bicicletas** *las rootas para beetheekletas*
How far is it to …?	**¿A qué distancia está …?** *a keh deestantheeya esta*
Is there a right of way?	**¿Hay derecho de paso?** *eye derecho deh paso*
Is there a route to …?	**¿Hay una carretera a …?** *eye oona karretera a*
Can you show me on the map?	**¿Puede indicármelo en el mapa?** *pwedeh eendeekarmelo en el mapa*
I'm lost.	**Me he perdido.** *meh eh perdeedo*

Organized walks/hikes

When does the guided walk/hike start?	**¿Cuándo empieza el paseo/la excursión a pie?** *kwando empeeyetha el paseyo/ la ekskoorseeyon a peeyeh*
When will we return?	**¿Cuándo volveremos?** *kwando bolberemos*
What is the walk/hike like?	**¿Cómo es el paseo/la excursión a pie?** *komo es el paseyo/la ekskoorseeyon a peeyeh*
gentle/medium/tough	**fácil/regular/duro** *fatheel/regoolar/dooro*
Where do we meet?	**¿Dónde nos encontramos?** *dondeh nos enkontramos*
I'm exhausted.	**Estoy exhausto(-a).** *estoy eksawsto(-a)*
How high is that mountain?	**¿Qué altura tiene esa montaña?** *keh altoora teeyeneh esa montaña*
What kind of … is that?	**¿Qué clase de … es ése(-a)?** *keh klaseh deh … es ese(-a)*
animal/bird	**animal/pájaro** *aneemal/pakharo*
flower/tree	**flor/árbol** *flor/arbol*

Geographical features

bridge	**el puente**	*el pwenteh*
cave	**la cueva**	*la kweba*
cliff	**el acantilado**	*el akanteelado*
farm	**la granja**	*la grankha*
field	**el campo**	*el kampo*
footpath	**el sendero**	*el sendero*
forest	**el bosque**	*el boskeh*
hill	**la colina**	*la koleena*
lake	**el lago**	*el lago*
mountain	**la montaña**	*la montaña*
mountain pass	**el paso de montaña**	*el paso deh montaña*
mountain range	**la cordillera**	*la kordeel-yera*
nature reserve	**la reserva natural**	*la reserba natooral*
panorama	**el panorama**	*el panorama*
park	**el parque**	*el parkeh*
pass	**el paso**	*el paso*
path	**el camino**	*el kameeno*
peak	**el pico**	*el peeko*
picnic area	**la zona para picnics**	*la thona para peekneeks*
pond	**el estanque**	*el estankeh*
rapids	**los rápidos**	*los rapeedos*
ravine	**el barranco**	*el barranko*
river	**el río**	*el reeyo*
sea	**el mar**	*el mar*
spa (place to stay)	**el balneario**	*el balneareeyo*
stream	**el arroyo**	*el arroyo*
valley	**el valle**	*el bal-yeh*
viewing point	**el mirador**	*el meerador*
village	**el pueblo**	*el pweblo*
vineyard/winery	**el viñedo**	*el beeñedo*
waterfall	**la catarata**	*la katarata*
wood	**el bosque**	*el boskeh*

LEISURE

EVENTS

Local papers and, in large cities, weekly entertainment guides (such as **Guía del Ocio**) will tell you what's on.

Tickets for concerts, theater, and other cultural events are on sale at special ticket agencies. In small towns these may be in kiosks, book or music stores: ask at the local tourist office.

Do you have a program of events?	**¿Tiene un programa de espectáculos?** *teeyeneh oon programa deh espektakoolos*
Can you recommend a …?	**¿Puede recomendarme un(a) …?** *pwedeh rekomendarmeh oon(a)*
Is there a … somewhere?	**¿Hay … en algún sitio?** *eye … en algoon seeteeyo*
ballet/concert	**un ballet/un concierto** *oon bal-yet/oon kontheeyerto*
movie [film]	**una película** *oona peleekoola*
opera	**una ópera** *oona opera*
When does it start?	**¿A qué hora empieza?** *a keh ora empeeyetha*
When does it end?	**¿A qué hora termina?** *a keh ora termeena*

Availability

Where can I get tickets?	**¿Dónde se pueden comprar las entradas?** *dondeh seh pweden komprar las entradas*
Are there any seats for tonight?	**¿Hay entradas para esta noche?** *eye entradas para esta nocheh*
I'm sorry, we're sold out.	**Lo siento, no quedan entradas.** *lo seeyento no kedan entradas*
There are … of us.	**Somos …** *somos*

Tickets

How much are the seats?	**¿Cuánto cuestan estas localidades?** _kwanto kwestan las lokaleedades_
Do you have anything cheaper?	**¿Tiene algo más barato?** _teeyeneh algo mas barato_
I'd like to reserve ...	**Quiero reservar ...** _keeyero reserbar_
three for Sunday evening	**tres para el domingo por la noche** _tres para el domeengo por la nocheh_
one for the Friday matinée	**una para la matiné del viernes** _oona para la mateeneh del beeyernes_
May I have a program, please?	**¿Puede darme un programa, por favor?** _pwedeh darmeh oon programa por fabor_
Where's the coatcheck [cloakroom]?	**¿Dónde está el guardarropa?** _dondeh esta el gwardarropa_
Where's the water fountain?	**¿Dónde está el bebedero?** _dondeh esta el bebehdero_

ESSENTIAL

¿Cuál es ... de su tarjeta de crédito?	What's your credit card ...?
el número	number
la fecha de caducidad	expiration [expiry] date
Por favor, recoja las entradas ...	Please pick up the tickets ...
antes de las ... de la tarde	by ... p.m.
en el mostrador de reservas	at the reservation desk

AT THE BOX OFFICE

¿Tiene un programa de espectáculos? _teeyeneh oon programa de espektakoolos_ (Do you have a program of events?)

Por supuesto. _por soopwesto_ (Of course.)

Gracias. _gratheeyas_ (Thank you.)

MOVIES [CINEMA]

Foreign films are usually dubbed into Spanish, but some movie theaters show films in the original version (**v.o.**).

Spain has a developing film industry of its own, with world-famous directors such as Almodóvar and Buñuel.

Is there a movie theater [multiplex cinema] near here?	**¿Hay un multicine cerca de aquí?** *eye oon moolteetheeneh therka deh akee*
What's playing at the movies [on at the cinema] tonight?	**¿Qué ponen en el cine esta noche?** *keh ponen en el theeneh esta nocheh*
Is the film dubbed/subtitled?	**¿Está doblada/subtitulada la película?** *esta doblada/soobteetoolada la peleekoola*
Is the film in the original English?	**¿Está la película en el inglés original?** *esta la peleekoola en el eengles oreekheenal*
Who's the main actor/actress?	**¿Quién es el actor/la actriz principal?** *keeyen es el aktor/la aktreeth preentheepal*
A …, please.	**…, por favor** *… por fabor*
box [carton] of popcorn	**un cucurucho de palomitas** *oon kookooroocho deh palomeetas*
chocolate ice cream	**un helado de chocolate** *oon elado deh chokolateh*
hot dog	**un perrito caliente** *oon perreeto kaleeyenteh*
soft drink	**un refresco** *oon refresko*
small/regular/large	**pequeño/de tamaño normal/grande** *pekeño/deh tamaño normal/grandeh*

THEATER

What's playing at the …theater?	**¿Qué función ponen en el teatro …?** *keh foontheeyon ponen en el teyatro*
Who's the playwright?	**¿Quién es el autor?** *keeyen es el aootor*
Do you think I'd enjoy it?	**¿Cree que me gustará?** *kreyeh keh meh goostara*
I don't know much Spanish.	**No sé mucho español.** *no seh moocho español*

OPERA/BALLET/DANCE

Who's the composer/soloist?
¿Quién es el/la compositor(a)/solista?
keeyen es el/la komposeetor(a)/soleesta

Is formal dress required?
¿Hay que vestirse de etiqueta?
eye keh besteerseh deh eteeketa

Where's the opera house?
¿Dónde está el teatro de la ópera?
dondeh esta el teyatro deh la opera

Who's dancing?
¿Quién baila? *keeyen bayla*

I'm interested in
contemporary dance.
Me interesa la danza contemporánea.
meh eenteresa la dantha kontemporaneya

MUSIC/CONCERTS

Where's the concert hall?
¿Dónde está la sala de conciertos?
dondeh esta la sala deh kontheeyertos

Which orchestra/band
is playing?
¿Qué orquesta/grupo toca?
keh orkesta/groopo toka

What are they playing?
¿Qué van a tocar? *keh ban a tokar*

Who's the conductor/soloist?
¿Quién es el/la director(a)/solista?
keeyen es el/la deerektor(a)/soleesta

Who's the support band?
¿Quiénes son los teloneros?
keeyenes son los teloneros

I really like …
Me gusta mucho … *meh goosta moocho*

country music
la música country
la mooseeka kaoontree

folk music
la música folk *la mooseeka folk*

jazz
el jazz *el juzz*

music of the sixties
la música de los sesentas
la mooseeku deh los sesentas

pop
la música pop *la mooseeka pop*

rock music
la música rock *la mooseeka rok*

soul music
la música soul *la mooseeka sowl*

Have you ever heard
of her/him?
¿Ha oído hablar de ella/él?
a oyeedo ablar deh el-ya/el

Are they popular?
¿Son famosos? *son famosos*

NIGHTLIFE

What is there to do in the evenings?	**¿Qué se puede hacer por las noches?** *keh seh pwedeh ather por las noches*
Can you recommend a good …?	**¿Puede recomendarme un buen …?** *pwedeh rekomendarmeh oon bwen*
Is there a … in town?	**¿Hay … en esta ciudad?** *eye … en esta theeyoodath*
bar	**un bar** *oon bar*
casino	**un casino** *oon kaseeno*
discotheque	**una discoteca** *oona deeskoteka*
gay club	**un club gay** *oon kloob gay*
nightclub	**un club nocturno** *oon kloob noktoorno*
restaurant	**un restaurante** *oon restawranteh*
Is there a floor show/cabaret?	**¿Hay un espectáculo de cabaret?** *eye oon espektakoolo deh kabaret*
What type of music do they play?	**¿Qué tipo de música tocan?** *keh teepo deh mooseeka tokan*
How do I get there?	**¿Cómo se va allí?** *komo seh ba al-yee*

Admission

What time does the show start?	**¿A qué hora empieza el espectáculo?** *a keh ora empeeyetha el espektakoolo*
Is evening dress required?	**¿Hay que ir con traje de noche?** *eye keh eer kon trakheh deh nocheh*
Is there a cover charge?	**¿Hay un precio de entrada?** *eye oon pretheeyo deh entradah*
Is a reservation necessary?	**¿Hay que hacer una reserva?** *eye keh ather oona reserba*
Do we need to be members?	**¿Hay que ser socios?** *eye keh sehr sotheeyos*
How long will we have to stand in line [queue]?	**¿Cuánto tiempo tendremos que hacer cola?** *kwanto teeyempo tendremos keh ather kola*

YOU MAY SEE

INCLUYE UNA CONSUMICIÓN GRATIS	includes one complimentary drink

112

CHILDREN

Can you recommend something for the children?	**¿Puede recomendarme algo para los niños?** _pwedeh rekomendarmeh algo para los neeños_
Are there changing facilities here for babies?	**¿Tienen instalaciones para cambiar al bebé?** _teeyenen eenstalatheeyones para kambeeyar al bebeh_
Where are the restrooms [toilets]?	**¿Dónde están los servicios?** _dondeh estan los servcetheeyos_
amusement arcade	**el salón recreativo** _el salon rekreateebo_
fairground	**la feria** _la fereeya_
kiddie [paddling] pool	**la piscina infantil** _la peestheena eenfanteel_
playground	**el patio de juegos** _el pateeyo deh khwegos_
play group	**el club infantil** _el kloob eefanteel_
zoo	**el zoológico** _el thoo-o-lokheeko_

Babysitting

Can you recommend a reliable babysitter?	**¿Puede recomendarme una canguro de confianza?** _pwedeh rekomendarmeh oona kangooro deh konfeeyantha_
Is there constant supervision?	**¿Supervisan a los niños constantemente?** _sooperbeesan a los neeños konstantementeh_
Is the staff properly trained?	**¿Están cualificados los empleados?** _estan kwaleefeekados los empleados_
When can I bring them?	**¿Cuándo puedo dejarlos?** _kwando pwedo dekharlos_
I'll pick them up at …	**Los recogeré a las …** _los rekokhereh a las_
We'll be back by …	**Volveremos antes de las …** _bolberemos antes deh las_
She's 3 and he's 18 months.	**La niña tiene tres años y el niño dieciocho meses.** _la neeña teeyeneh tres años ee el neeño deeyetheeocho meses_

SPORTS

Whether you are a fan or a participant, Spain has the weather and facilities to satisfy most sports enthusiasts. Soccer [football] (**fútbol**) is the most popular sport, inspiring fierce devotion – particularly in Madrid and Barcelona. Spain is famous for its golf courses, especially on the Costa del Sol. Tennis, horseback riding, and hill climbing are also popular. And look for **pelota** (**jai alai** in the Basque country and Latin America) – a furiously fast ball game involving curved wicker-basket gloves.

Spectator Sports

Is there a soccer [football] game [match] this Saturday?	**¿Hay un partido de fútbol este sábado?** *eye oon parteedo deh footbol esteh sabado*
Which teams are playing?	**¿Qué equipos juegan?** *keh ekeepos khwegan*
Can you get me a ticket?	**¿Puede conseguirme una entrada?** *pwedeh konsegeermeh oona entrada*
What's the admission charge?	**¿Cuánto cobran por entrar?** *kwanto kobran por entrar*
Where's the racetrack [racecourse]?	**¿Dónde está el hipódromo?** *dondeh esta el eepodromo*
Where can I place a bet?	**¿Dónde puedo hacer una apuesta?** *dondeh pwedo ather oona apwesta*
What are the odds on ...?	**¿A cómo están las apuestas para ...?** *a komo estan las apwestas para*

athletics	**atletismo** *atleteesmo*
basketball	**baloncesto** *balonthesto*
cycling	**ciclismo** *theekleesmo*
golf	**golf** *golf*
horseracing	**carreras de caballos** *karreras deh kabal-yos*
soccer [football]	**fútbol** *footbol*
swimming	**natación** *natatheeyon*
tennis	**tenis** *tenees*
volleyball	**voleybol** *boleebol*

Participating

Where's the nearest …?	**¿Dónde está … más cercano?** _dondeh está … mas therkano_
golf course	**el campo de golf** _el kampo deh golf_
sports club	**el polideportivo** _el poleedeporteebo_
Where are the tennis courts?	**¿Dónde están las pistas de tenis?** _dondeh estan las peestas deh tenees_
What's the charge per …?	**¿Cuánto cuesta por …?** _kwanto kwesta por_
day/hour	**día/hora** _deeya/ora_
game/round	**partido/juego** _parteedo/khwego_
Do I need to be a member?	**¿Hay que ser socio?** _eye keh sehr sotheeyo_
Where can I rent …?	**¿Dónde puedo alquilar …?** _dondeh pwedo alkeelar_
boots	**unas botas** _oonas botas_
clubs	**unos palos de golf** _oonos palos deh golf_
equipment	**el equipo** _el ekeepo_
a racket	**una raqueta** _oona raketa_
Can I get lessons?	**¿Me pueden dar clases?** _meh pweden dar klases_
Is there an aerobics class?	**¿Hay clases de aerobic?** _eye klases deh ayrobeek_
Do you have a fitness room?	**¿Tienen un gimnasio?** _teeyenen oon khimnaseeyo_

YOU MAY SEE

PROHIBIDO PESCAR	no fishing
SÓLO PARA LOS TENEDORES DE LICENCIA	permit holders only
VESTUARIOS	changing rooms

YOU MAY HEAR

Lo siento, no quedan plazas.	I'm sorry, we're booked.
Hay que pagar depósito de …	There's a deposit of …
¿Qué talla tiene?	What size are you?
Necesita una foto tamaño carnet.	You need a passport-size photo.

At the beach

Spain offers hundreds of miles of beaches for every taste. The most developed offer a full range of facilities for water sports; nor is it too difficult to locate near-deserted coves for a quieter time.

Is the beach …?	**¿Es la playa …?** *es la playa*
pebbly/sandy	**de guijarros/de arena** *deh geekharros/deh arena*
Is there a … here?	**¿Hay … aquí?** *eye … akee*
children's pool	**una piscina para niños** *oona peestheena para neeños*
swimming pool	**una piscina** *oona peestheena*
indoor/outdoor	**cubierta/al aire libre** *koobeeyerta/al ayreh leebreh*
Is it safe to swim/dive here?	**¿Es seguro nadar/tirarse de cabeza aquí?** *es segooro nadar/teerarse deh kabetha akee*
Is it safe for children?	**¿Es seguro(-a) para los niños?** *es segooro(-a) para los neeños*
Is there a lifeguard?	**¿Hay socorrista?** *eye sokorreesta*
I want to rent …	**Quiero alquilar …** *keeyero alkeelar*
deck chair	**una tumbona** *oona toombona*
jet ski	**una moto acuática** *oona moto akwateeka*
motorboat	**una motora** *oona motora*
rowboat	**una barca de remos** *oona barka deh remos*
sailboat	**un velero** *oon belero*
diving equipment	**un equipo de buceo** *oon ekeepo deh boothayo*
umbrella [sunshade]	**una sombrilla** *oona sombreel-ya*
surfboard	**una tabla de surf** *oona tabla deh soorf*
water skis	**unos esquís acuáticos** *oonos eskees akwateekos*
windsurfer	**una tabla de windsurf** *oona tabla deh weensoorf*
For … hours.	**Por … horas.** *por … oras*

Skiing

Spain's 27 ski resorts attract an increasing number of devotees. Most are situated in the Pyrenees (e.g. **Baqueira-Beret, La Molina, Pas de la Casa, Cerler**), while the Andalusian **Sierra Nevada** offers Europe's sunniest skiing.

I'd like to rent …	**Quiero alquilar …** _keeyero alkeelar_
poles	**unos bastones** _oonos bastones_
skates	**unos patines** _oonos pateenes_
ski boots/skis	**unas botas de esquiar/unos esquís** _oonas botas deh eskeeyar/oonos eskees_
These are too …	**Estos(-as) son demasiado …** _estos(as) son demaseeyado_
big/small	**grandes/pequeños** _grandes/pekeños_
These are too loose/tight.	**Están demasiado sueltos/apretados.** _estan demaseeyado sweltos/apretados_
A lift pass for a day/ five days, please.	**Un pase de teleférico para un día/cinco días, por favor.** _oon paseh deh telefereeko para oon deeya/theenko deeyas por fabor_
I'd like to join the ski school.	**Quiero tomar clases de esquí.** _keeyero dar klases deh eskee_
I'm a beginner.	**Soy principiante.** _soy preentheepeeyanteh_
I'm experienced.	**Tengo experiencia.** _tengo ekspereeyen theeya_

YOU MAY SEE

ARRASTRE	drag lift
TELEFÉRICO/CABINA	cable car/gondola
TELESILLA	chair lift

Bullfight

The bullfight (**la corrida**) may fascinate or appall you. First the matador goads the bull with a large cape. Then the **picador** weakens the bull by lancing its neck. **Banderilleros** on foot thrust three barbed sticks between its shoulder blades. The matador returns to taunt the bull with a small red cape, leading up to the final climax of the kill. The bullfighting season lasts from March to October.

I'd like to see a bullfight.	**Quiero ver una corrida.** _keeyero behr oona korreeda_

MAKING FRIENDS

INTRODUCTIONS

Greetings vary according to how well you know someone. The following is a guide. It's polite to shake hands, both when you meet and say good-bye; it is considered impolite not to.

Begin any conversation, whether with a friend, shop assistant or policeman, with a "**buenos días**." Speak to them using the formal form of "you" (**usted**) until you are asked to use the familiar form (**tú**).

In Spanish, there are three forms for "you" (taking different verb forms): **tú** (singular) and **vosotros** (plural) are used when talking to relatives, close friends and children (and between young people); **usted** (singular) and **ustedes** (plural) – often abbreviated to **Ud./Uds.** – are used in all other cases. If in doubt, use **usted/ustedes**.

Hello, I don't think we've met.	**Hola, no nos conocemos.** _ola no nos kono<u>the</u>mos_
My name is …	**Me llamo …** _meh l-<u>ya</u>mo_
May I introduce …?	**Quiero presentarle a …** _kee<u>ye</u>ro presen<u>tar</u>leh a_
John, this is …	**John, éste(-a) es …** _jon <u>es</u>teh(-a) es_
Pleased to meet you.	**Encantado(-a) de conocerle(-la).** _enkan<u>ta</u>do(-a) deh kono<u>ther</u>le(-la)_
What's your name?	**¿Cómo se llama?** _<u>ko</u>mo seh l-<u>ya</u>ma_
How are you?	**¿Cómo está?** _<u>ko</u>mo esta_
Fine, thanks. And you?	**Bien, gracias. ¿Y usted?** _bee<u>ye</u>n <u>gra</u>theeyas. ee oos<u>teth</u>_

AT A RECEPTION

Me llamo Sheryl. _meh l-<u>ya</u>mo sheryl (My name is Sheryl.)_
Mucho gusto. Me llamo José. _<u>moo</u>cho <u>goos</u>toh meh l-<u>ya</u>mo ho<u>seh</u> (My pleasure. My name is José.)_
El gusto es mío. _el <u>goos</u>toh es <u>mee</u>oh (The pleasure is mine.)_

Where are you from?

Where are you from?	**¿De dónde es usted?** *deh dondeh es oosteth*
Where were you born?	**¿Dónde nació?** *dondeh natheeyo*
I'm from …	**Soy de …** *soy deh*
Australia	**Australia** *awoostraleeya*
Britain	**Gran Bretaña** *gran bretaña*
Canada	**Canadá** *kanada*
England	**Inglaterra** *eenglaterra*
Ireland	**Irlanda** *eerlanda*
Scotland	**Escocia** *eskotheeya*
the U.S.	**Estados Unidos** *estados ooneedos*
Wales	**Gales** *gales*
Where do you live?	**¿Dónde vive?** *dondeh beebeh*
What part of … are you from?	**¿De qué parte de … es usted?** *deh keh parteh deh … es oosteth*
Spain	**España** *españa*
Argentina	**Argentina** *arkhenteena*
México	**Méjico** *mekheeko*
We come here every year.	**Venimos todos los años.** *beneemos todos los años*
It's my/our first visit.	**Es mi/nuestra primera visita.** *es mee/nwestra preemera beeseeta*
Have you ever been …?	**¿Ha estado alguna vez …?** *a estado algoona beth*
to the U.K./the U.S.	**en Gran Bretaña/Estados Unidos** *en gran bretaña/estados ooneedos*
Do you like it here?	**¿Le gusta esto?** *leh goosta esto*
What do you think of the …?	**¿Qué le parece …?** *keh le paretheh*
food/people	**la cocina/la gente** *la kotheena/la khenteh*
I love the … here.	**Me encanta … de aquí.** *meh enkanta … deh akee*
I don't really like the … here.	**No me gusta demasiado … de aquí.** *no meh goosta demaseeyado … deh akee*

(119)

Who are you with?

Who are you with?	**¿Con quién ha venido?** *kon keeyen a beneedo*
I'm on my own.	**He venido solo(-a).** *eh beneedo solo(-a)*
I'm with a friend.	**He venido con un(a) amigo(-a).** *eh beneedo kon oon(a) ameego(-a)*
I'm with my …	**He venido con …** *eh beneedo kon*
wife	**mi mujer** *mee mookher*
husband	**mi marido** *mee mareedo*
family	**mi familia** *mee fameeleeya*
children	**mis hijos** *mees eekhos*
parents	**mis padres** *mees padres*
boyfriend/girlfriend	**mi novio(-a)** *mee nobeeyo(-a)*
my father/mother	**mi padre/mi madre** *mee padreh/mee madreh*
my son/daughter	**mi hijo/mi hija** *mee eekho/mee eekha*
my brother/sister	**mi hermano/mi hermana** *mee ermano/mee ermana*
my uncle/aunt	**mi tío/mi tía** *mee teeyo/mee teeya*
Are you married?	**¿Está casado(-a)?** *esta kasado(-a)*
I'm …	**Estoy …** *estoy*
married/single	**casado(-a)/soltero(-a)** *kasado(-a)/soltero(-a)*
divorced/separated	**divorciado(-a)/separado(-a)** *deebortheeyado(-a)/separado(-a)*
engaged	**prometido(-a)** *prometeedo*
We live together.	**Vivimos juntos.** *beebeemos khoontos*
Do you have any children?	**¿Tiene hijos?** *teeyeneh eekhos*
We have two boys and a girl.	**Tenemos dos niños y una niña.** *tenemos dos neeños ee oona neeña*
How old are they?	**¿Qué edad tienen?** *keh edath teeyenen*
They're ten and twelve.	**Tienen diez y doce años respectivamente.** *teeyenen deeyeth ee dotheh años respekteebamenteh*

What do you do?

What do you do?	**¿A qué se dedica?** *a keh seh dedeeka*
What are you studying?	**¿Qué estudia?** *keh estoodeeya*
I'm studying …	**Estudio …** *estoodeeyo*
I'm in …	**Me dedico a …** *meh dedeeko a*
business	**asuntos comerciales** *asoontos komertheeyales*
sales	**las ventas** *las bentas*
I'm in engineering.	**Trabajo de ingeniero.** *trabakho deh eenkhenyero*
Who do you work for?	**¿Para quién trabaja?** *para keeyen trabakha*
I work for …	**Trabajo para …** *trabakho para*
I'm a(n) …	**Soy …** *soy*
accountant	**contable** *kontableh*
housewife	**ama de casa** *ama deh kasa*
student	**estudiante** *estoodeeyanteh*
I'm …	**Estoy …** *estoy*
retired	**jubilado(-a)** *khoobeelado(-a)*
between jobs	**entre un trabajo y otro** *entreh oon trabakho ee otro*
I'm self-employed.	**Trabajo por mi cuenta.** *trabakho por mee kwenta*
What are your interests/ hobbies?	**¿Cuáles son sus pasatiempos/hobbies?** *kwales son soos pasateeyempos/hobees*
I like …	**Me gusta(n) …** *me goosta(n)*
music	**la música** *la mooseeka*
reading	**leer** *leh-er*
sports	**los deportes** *los deportes*
I play …	**Juego a …** *khwego a*
Would you like to play …?	**¿Le gustaría jugar a …?** *leh goostareea khoogar a*
cards	**las cartas** *las kartas*
chess	**al ajedrez** *al akhedreth*

What weather!

What a lovely day!	**¡Qué día tan bonito!** _keh deeya tan boneeto_
What terrible weather!	**¡Qué tiempo más feo!** _keh teeyempo mas feyo_
Isn't it cold/hot today!	**¡Vaya frío/calor que hace hoy!** _baya freeyo/kalor keh atheh oy_
Is it usually this warm?	**¿Hace normalmente tanto calor como ahora?** _athe normalmenteh tanto kalor komo a-ora_
Do you think it's going to … tomorrow?	**¿Cree usted que mañana va a …?** _kreyeh oosteth keh mañana ba a_
be a nice day	**hacer buen tiempo** _ather bwen teeyempo_
rain	**llover** _l-yobehr_
snow	**nevar** _nebar_
What's the weather forecast?	**¿Cuál es el pronóstico del tiempo?** _kwal es el pronosteeko del teeyempo_
It's …	**Está …** _esta_
cloudy	**nublado** _nooblado_
rainy	**lluvioso** _l-yoobeeyoso_
stormy	**tronando** _tronando_
It's foggy.	**Hay niebla.** _eye neeyebla_
It's frosty.	**Hay heladas.** _eye eladas_
It's icy.	**Hay hielo.** _eye eeyelo_
It's snowy.	**Hay nieve.** _eye neeyebeh_
It's windy.	**Hace viento.** _atheh beeyento_
Has the weather been like this for long?	**¿Lleva mucho así el tiempo?** _l-yeba moocho asee el teeyempo_
What's the pollen count?	**¿Cuál es el índice de polen?** _kwal es el eendeetheh deh polen_
high/medium/low	**alto/regular/bajo** _alto/regoolar/bakho_

Enjoying your trip?

I'm here on …	**Estoy aquí …** *estoy akee*
business	**en viaje de negocios** *en beeyakheh deh negotheeyos*
vacation [holiday]	**de vacaciones** *deh bakatheeyones*
We came by …	**Vinimos en …** *beeneemos en*
train/bus/plane	**tren/autobús/avión** *tren/aootoboos/abeeyon*
car/ferry	**coche/ferry** *kocheh/ferree*
I have a rental car.	**He alquilado un coche.** *eh alkeelado oon kocheh*
We're staying in/at …	**Nos alojamos en …** *nos alokhamos en*
an apartment	**un apartamento** *oon apartamento*
a hotel/campsite	**un hotel/un cámping** *oon otel/oon kampeen*
with friends	**con unos amigos** *kon oonos ameegos*
Can you suggest …?	**¿Puede sugerirme …?** *pwedeh sookhereermeh*
things to do	**algo que hacer** *algo keh ather*
places to eat/visit	**algunos sitios para comer/ver** *algoonos seeteeyos para komer/behr*
We're having a great/ terrible time.	**Lo estamos pasando muy bien/mal.** *lo estamos pasando mwee beeyen/mal*

YOU MAY HEAR

¿Está de vacaciones?	Are you on vacation?
¿Cómo ha venido aquí?	How did you get here?
¿Qué tal el viaje?	How was the trip?
¿Dónde se aloja?	Where are you staying?
¿Cuánto tiempo lleva aquí?	How long have you been here?
¿Cuánto tiempo va a quedarse?	How long are you staying?
¿Qué ha hecho hasta ahora?	What have you done so far?
¿Qué es lo próximo que va a hacer?	Where are you going next?
¿Está pasando unas buenas vacaciones?	Are you enjoying your vacation?

INVITATIONS

Would you like to have dinner with us on …?	**¿Le gustaría cenar con nosotros el …?** leh goostareea thenar kon nosotros el
Are you free for lunch?	**¿Puedo invitarle(-la) a comer?** pwedo eenbeetarle(-la) a komer
Can you come for a drink this evening?	**¿Puede venir a tomar algo esta noche?** pwede beneer a tomar algo esta nocheh
We are having a party. Can you come?	**Vamos a dar una fiesta. ¿Puede venir?** bamos a dar oona feeyesta. pwede beneer
May we join you?	**¿Podemos ir con ustedes?** podemos eer kon oostedes
Would you like to join us?	**¿Le gustaría venir con nosotros?** leh goostareea beneer kon nosotros

Going out

What are your plans for …?	**¿Qué planes tiene(n) para …?** ke planes teeyeneh(n) para
today/tonight	**hoy/esta noche** oy/esta nocheh
tomorrow	**mañana** mañana
Are you free this evening?	**¿Está libre esta noche?** esta leebreh esta nocheh
Would you like to …?	**¿Le gustaría …?** leh goostareea
go dancing	**ir a bailar** eer a baylar
go for a drink/meal	**ir a tomar una copa/a cenar** eer a tomar oona kopa/a thenar
go for a walk	**dar un paseo** dar oon paseyo
go shopping	**ir de compras** eer deh kompras
Where would you like to go?	**¿Adónde le gustaría ir?** adondeh leh goostareeya eer
I'd like to go to …	**Me gustaría ir a …** meh goostareea eer a
I'd like to see …	**Me gustaría ver …** meh goostareea behr
Do you enjoy …?	**¿Le gusta …?** leh goosta

Accepting/Declining

Great. I'd love to.

Estupendo. Me encantaría.
estoopendo. meh enkantareeya

Thank you, but I'm busy.

Gracias, pero estoy ocupado(-a)
gratheeyas pero estoy okoopado(-a)

May I bring a friend?

¿Puedo llevar a un amigo?
pwedo l-yebar a oon ameego

Where shall we meet?

¿Dónde quedamos? *dondeh kedamos*

I'll meet you ...

Quedamos ... *kedamos*

in the bar

en el bar *en el bar*

in front of your hotel

en frente de su hotel
en frenteh deh soo otel

I'll come by [call for you]
at 8.

Pasaré a recogerle a las ocho.
pasare a rrekokherle a las ocho

Could we make it a bit
earlier/later?

**¿Podríamos quedar un poco antes/
más tarde?** *podreeyamos kedar oon
poko antes/mas tardeh*

How about another day?

¿Qué le parece otro día?
keh leh paretheh otro deeya

That will be fine.

Muy bien. *mwee beeyen*

Dining out/in

If you are invited home for a meal, always take a gift – a bottle of wine,
sparkling wine, chocolates, flowers, for example.

Let me buy you a drink.

Permítame que le/la invite a una copa.
*permeetameh keh leh/la eenbeeteh a
oona kopa*

What are you going to have?

¿Qué va a tomar? *keh ba a tomar*

That was a lovely meal.

Fue una comida estupenda.
fweh oona komeeda estoopenda

IN A BAR

¿Le gustaría ir a bailar? *leh goostareea eer a baylar*
(Would you like to go dancing?)
Me encantaría. *meh enkantareeya (I'd love to.)*

Encounters

Are you waiting for someone?	**¿Espera a alguien?** *espera a algeeyen*
Do you mind if …?	**¿Le importa si …?** *leh eemporta see*
I sit here/smoke	**me siento aquí/fumo** *meh seeyento akee/foomo*
Can I get you a drink?	**¿Puedo invitarle(-la) a una copa?** *pwedo eenbeetarleh(-la) a oona kopa*
I'd love to have some company.	**Me encantaría estar acompañado(-a).** *meh enkantareeya estar akompañado(-a)*
Why are you laughing?	**¿Por qué se ríe?** *por keh seh reeyeh*
Is my Spanish that bad?	**¿Hablo español tan mal?** *ablo español tan mal*
Shall we go somewhere quieter?	**¿Vamos a otro sitio más tranquilo?** *bamos a otro seeteeyo mas trankeelo*
Leave me alone, please!	**¡Déjeme en paz, por favor!** *dekhemeh en path por fabor*
You look great!	**¡Estás guapísimo(-a)!** *estas gwapeeseemo(-a)*
I'm afraid we have to leave now.	**Me temo que tenemos que irnos ahora.** *meh temo keh tenemos keh eernos a-ora*
Thanks for the evening.	**Gracias por la velada.** *gratheeyas por la belada*
Can I see you again tomorrow?	**¿Puedo volver a verle(-la) mañana?** *pwedo bolber a berleh(-la) mañana*
See you soon.	**Hasta luego.** *asta loowego*
Can I have your address?	**¿Puede darme su dirección?** *pwedeh darmeh soo deerektheeyon*

TELEPHONING

Public telephone booths take either coins only (marked with a green T), or coins and phonecards (with a blue T sign). Phonecards (**tarjeta telefónica**) are available from post offices and tobacconists. A few phones accept credit cards.

Most public cafés and bars have public phones – feel free to enter and ask for the telephone.

To phone home from Spain, dial 07 followed by: 61, Australia; 1, Canada; 353, Ireland; 64, New Zealand; 27, South Africa; 44, United Kingdom; 1, United States. Note that you will usually have to omit the initial 0 of the area code.

Can I have your telephone number?	**¿Me da su número de teléfono?** meh da soo _noo_mero deh te_le_fono
Here's my number.	**Aquí tiene mi número.** a_kee_ tee_ye_neh mee _noo_mero
Please call me.	**Llámeme, por favor.** _lya_memeh por fa_bor_
I'll give you a call.	**Le/La llamaré.** leh/la l-yama_reh_
Where's the nearest telephone booth?	**¿Dónde está la cabina más cercana?** _don_deh es_ta_ la ka_bee_na mas ther_ka_na
May I use your phone?	**¿Puedo usar su teléfono?** _pwe_do oo_sar_ soo te_le_fono
It's an emergency.	**Es urgente.** es oor_khen_teh
I'd like to call someone in England.	**Quiero llamar a alguien en Inglaterra.** kee_ye_ro l-ya_mar_ a _al_geeyen en eengla_te_rra
What's the area [dialling] code for …?	**¿Cuál es el prefijo de …?** kwal es el pre_fee_kho deh
I'd like a phone card, please.	**Quiero una tarjeta para llamar por teléfono, por favor.** kee_ye_ro _oo_na tar_khe_ta _pa_ra l-ya_mar_ por te_le_tono por fa_bor_
What's the number for Information [Directory Enquiries]?	**¿Cuál es el número de información?** kwal es el _noo_mero deh eenforma_thee_yon
I'd like the number for …	**Quiero que me consiga el número de teléfono de …** kee_ye_ro keh meh kon_see_ga el _noo_mero deh te_le_fono deh
I'd like to call collect [reverse the charges].	**Quiero llamar a cobro revertido.** kee_ye_ro l-ya_mar_ a _ko_bro reber_tee_do

On the phone

Hello. This is …
Hola. Soy … _ola. soy_

I'd like to speak to …
Quiero hablar con …
keeyero ablar kon

Extension …
Extensión …
ekstenseeyon

Speak louder/more slowly, please.
Hable más alto/despacio, por favor.
ableh mas alto/despatheeyo por fabor

Could you repeat that, please?
¿Puede repetir eso, por favor?
pwedeh repeteer eso por fabor

I'm afraid he's/she's not in.
Me temo que no está.
meh temo keh no esta

You have the wrong number.
Se ha equivocado de número.
seh a ekeebokado deh noomero

Just a moment.
Un momento. _oon momento_

Hold on, please.
Espere, por favor.
espereh por fabor

When will he/she be back?
¿Cuándo volverá?
kwando bolbera

Will you tell him/her that I called?
¿Puede decirle que he llamado?
pwedeh detheerleh keh eh l-yamado

My name is …
Me llamo …
meh l-yamo

Would you ask him/ her to phone me?
¿Puede decirle que me llame?
pwedeh detheerleh keh meh l-yameh

Would you take a message, please?
¿Puede darle un recado, por favor?
pwedeh darleh oon rekado por fabor

I must go now.
Tengo que irme. _tengo keh eermeh_

Nice to speak to you.
Me encantó hablar con usted.
meh enkanto ablar kon oosteth

I'll be in touch.
Nos mantendremos en contacto.
nos mantendremos en kontakto

Bye.
Adiós. _adeeyos_

STORES & SERVICES

For a view of what Spaniards are buying, take a look in the big department stores El Corte Inglés and Galerías Preciados, which have branches in most size-able towns. Although chain stores are becoming popular, most shops are still individually owned and each is individual in character. Many smaller stores are still to be found outside of the main town centers.

STORES AND SERVICES

Where is …?

Where's the nearest …?	**¿Dónde está … más cercano(-a)?** _dondeh esta_ … _mas therkano(-a)_
Where's there a good …?	**¿Dónde hay un(a) buen(a) …?** _dondeh eye oon(a) bwen(a)_
Where's the main shopping mall [centre]?	**¿Dónde está el centro comercial principal?** _dondeh esta el thentro komertheeyal preentheepal_
Is it far from here?	**¿Está lejos de aquí?** _esta lekhos deh akee_
How do I get there?	**¿Cómo se llega hasta allí?** _komo seh l-yega asta al-yee_

Stores

antiques store	**la tienda de antigüedades** _la teeyenda deh anteegwedades_
bakery	**la panadería** _la panadereeya_
bank	**el banco** _el banko_
bookstore	**la librería** _la leebrereeya_
butcher	**la carnicería** _la karneethereeya_
camera store	**la tienda de fotografía** _la teeyenda deh fotografeeya_
clothing store [clothes shop]	**la tienda de ropa** _la teeyenda deh rropa_
delicatessen	**la charcutería** _la charkootereeya_
department store	**los grandes almacenes** _loss grandes almathenes_
drugstore	**la farmacia** _la farmatheeya_

fish store [fishmonger]	**la pescadería** *la peskade**ree**ya*
florist	**la floristería** *la floreeste**ree**ya*
gift shop	**la tienda de regalos/bazar** *la tee**yen**da deh rre**ga**los/ba**thar***
greengrocer	**la verdulería** *la berdoole**ree**ya*
health food store	**la tienda de alimentos naturales** *la tee**yen**da deh alee**men**tos natoo**ra**les*
jeweler	**la joyería** *la khoye**ree**ya*
liquor store [off-licence]	**la tienda de bebidas alcohólicas** *la tee**yen**da deh be**bee**das alko-o**lee**kas*
market	**el mercado** *el mer**ka**do*
music store	**la tienda de discos** *la tee**yen**du deh **dees**kos*
pastry shop	**la pastelería** *la pastele**ree**ya*
pharmacy [chemist]	**la farmacia** *la far**ma**theeya*
produce store	**la tienda de alimentación** *la tee**yen**da deh aleementa**thee**yon*
shoe store	**la zapatería** *la thapate**ree**ya*
shopping mall [centre]	**el centro comercial** *el **then**tro komer**thee**yal*
souvenir store	**la tienda de recuerdos** *la tee**yen**da deh re**kwer**dos*
sporting goods store	**la tienda de deportes** *la tee**yen**da deh de**por**tes*
supermarket	**el supermercado** *el soopermer**ka**do*
tobacconist	**el estanco** *el es**tan**ko*
toy store	**la juguetería** *la khoogete**ree**ya*

YOU MAY HEAR

¿Necesita ayuda?	Can I help you?
¿Le atienden?	Are you being served?
¿Qué desea?	What would you like?
Ahora mismo voy a comprobarlo.	I'll just check that for you.
¿Eso es todo?	Is that everything?
¿Algo más?	Anything else?

Services

clinic	**el ambulatorio** *el amboolatoreeo*
dentist	**el dentista** *el denteesta*
doctor	**el médico/doctor** *el medeeko/doktor*
dry cleaner	**la tintorería** *la teentorereeya*
hairdresser/barber	**la peluquería de señoras/caballeros** *la pelookereeya deh señoras/kabalyeros*
hospital	**el hospital** *el ospeetal*
laundomat	**la lavandería** *la labandereeya*
library	**la biblioteca** *la beebleeoteka*
optician	**el óptico** *el opteeko*
police station	**la comisaría de policía** *la komeesareeya deh poleetheeya*
post office	**correos** *korreos*
travel agency	**la agencia de viajes** *la akhentheeya deh beeyakhes*

Hours

In tourist resorts, stores are generally open on Sunday and holidays and stay open until late. In larger towns, local markets are open daily in the mornings, and in the afternoons on Fridays only. In smaller towns, they operate one morning a week.

When does the … open/close?	**¿A qué hora abre/cierra …?** *a keh ora abreh/theeyerra*
Are you open in the evening?	**¿Abren por la noche?** *abren por la nocheh*
Do you close for lunch?	**¿Cierran a la hora de comer?** *theeyerran a la ora deh komer*
Where is the …?	**¿Dónde está …?** *dondeh esta*
escalator	**la escalera mecánica** *la eskalera mekaneeka*

YOU MAY SEE	
AUTOSERVICIO	self-service
CAJA CENTRAL	customer service
OFERTA ESPECIAL	special offer

elevator [lift]	**el ascensor** *el asthen<u>sor</u>*
cashier	**caja** <u>*kaha*</u>
store directory [guide]	**el directorio de la tienda** *el deerek<u>tor</u>eeyo deh la tee<u>yen</u>da*
It's in the basement.	**Está en el sótano.** *es<u>ta</u> en el <u>so</u>tano*
It's on the … floor.	**Está en la planta …** *es<u>ta</u> en la <u>plan</u>ta*
first [ground *(U.K.)*] floor	**baja** <u>*ba*</u>*kha*
second [first *(U.K.)*] floor	**primer piso** *pree<u>mer</u> <u>pee</u>so*

Service

Can you help me?	**¿Puede ayudarme?** <u>*pwe*</u>*deh ayoo<u>dar</u>meh*
I'm looking for …	**Estoy buscando …** *estoy boos<u>kan</u>do*
I'm just browsing.	**Sólo estoy mirando.** <u>*so*</u>*lo es<u>toy</u> mee<u>ran</u>do*
Do you have any …?	**¿Tienen …?** *tee<u>yen</u>en*
I'd like to buy …	**Quiero comprar …** *kee<u>yer</u>o kom<u>prar</u>*
Could you show me …?	**¿Podría enseñarme …?** *pod<u>ree</u>ya ense<u>ñar</u>meh*
How much is this/that?	**¿Cuánto cuesta esto/eso?** <u>*kwan*</u>*to <u>kwes</u>ta <u>es</u>to/<u>es</u>o*
That's all, thanks.	**Eso es todo, gracias.** <u>*es*</u>*o es <u>to</u>do <u>gra</u>theeyas*

IN A STORE

¿Necesita ayuda? *neseh<u>see</u>tah ay<u>oo</u>dar (Can I help you?)*
Gracias. Sólo estoy mirando. <u>*gra*</u>*theeyas <u>so</u>lo es<u>toy</u> mee<u>ran</u>do (Thanks. I'm just browsing.)*

YOU MAY SEE

ABIERTO TODO EL DÍA	open all day
CERRADO A LA HORA DE LA COMIDA	closed for lunch
ENTRADA	entrance
ESCALERAS	stairs
HORAS DE TRABAJO	business hours
SALIDA	exit
SALIDA DE EMERGENCIA	emergency exit
SALIDA DE INCENDIOS	fire exit

Preferences

I want something …	**Quiero algo …**	_keeyero algo_
It must be …	**Debe ser …**	_debeh sehr_
big/small	**grande/pequeño(-a)** _grandeh/pekeño(-a)_	
cheap/expensive	**barato(-a)/caro(-a)** _barato(-a)/karo_	
dark/light (color)	**oscuro(-a)/claro(-a)** _oskooro(-a)/klaro(-a)_	
light/heavy	**ligero(-a)/pesado(-a)** _leekhero(-a)/pesado(-a)_	
oval/round/square	**ovalado(-a)/redondo(-a)/cuadrado(-a)** _obalado(-a)/redondo(-a)/kwadrado(-a)_	
genuine/imitation	**auténtico(-a)/de imitación** _aootenteeko(-a)/deh eemeetatheeyon_	
I don't want anything too expensive.	**No quiero nada demasiado caro.** _no keeyero nada demaseeyado karo_	
Around … euros.	**Alrededor de las … euros.** _alrrededor deh las … eh-ooros_	
Do you have anything …?	**¿Tiene(n) algo …?** _teeyeneh(n) algo_	
larger/smaller	**más grande/pequeño** _mas grandeh/pekeño_	
better quality	**de mejor calidad** _deh mekhor kaleedath_	
cheaper	**más barato** _mas barato_	
Can you show me …?	**¿Puede enseñarme …?** _pwedeh enseñarmeh_	
this/that one	**éste/ése-aquél** _esteh/eseh-akel_	
these/those	**estos/esos-aquéllos** _esos-akel-yos/ostos_	

YOU MAY HEAR

¿Qué … quiere?	What … would you like?
color/forma	color/shape
calidad/cantidad	quality/quantity
¿De qué clase quiere?	What kind would you like?
¿Qué precio está dispuesto a pagar aproximadamente?	What price range are you thinking of?

Conditions of purchase

Is there a guarantee?	**¿Tiene garantía?** *teeyeneh garanteeya*
Are there any instructions with it?	**¿Lleva instrucciones?** *l-yeba eenstrooktheeyones*

Out of stock

Can you order it for me?	**¿Me lo puede mandar a pedir?** *meh lo pwedeh mandar a pedeer*
How long will it take?	**¿Cuánto tiempo tardará?** *kwanto teeyempo tardara*
Is there another store that sells ...?	**¿En qué otro sitio puedo conseguir ...?** *en keh otro seeteeyo pwedo konsegeer*

Decisions

That's not quite what I want.	**Eso no es realmente lo que quiero.** *eso no es reyalmenteh lo keh keeyero*
No, I don't like it.	**No, no me gusta.** *no no meh goosta*
That's too expensive.	**Es demasiado caro.** *es demaseeyado karo*
I'd like to think about it.	**Quiero pensármelo.** *keeyero pensarmelo*
I'll take it.	**Me lo quedo.** *meh lo kedo*

IN A STORE

¿Quiere comprarlo? *keeyere komprarloh*
(Would you like to buy this?)
Quiero pensármelo. Gracias. *keeyero pensarlmeoh gratheeyas (I'd like to think about it. Thanks.)*

Paying

Small businesses may not accept credit cards; however, large stores, restaurants, and hotels accept major credit cards or traveler's checks. Non-EU citizens can reclaim the sales tax on larger purchases.

Where do I pay?	**¿Dónde pago?** _dondeh pago_
How much is that?	**¿Cuánto cuesta eso?** _kwanto kwesta eso_
Could you write it down?	**¿Podría escribirlo?** _podreeya eskreebeerlo_
Do you accept traveler's checks [cheques]?	**¿Aceptan cheques de viaje?** _atheptan chekehs deh beeyakheh_
I'll pay …	**Pago …** _pago_
by cash	**en metálico** _en metaleeko_
by credit card	**con tarjeta de crédito** _kon tarkheta deh kredeeto_
I don't have any small change.	**No tengo monedas más pequeñas.** _no tengo monedas mas pekeñas_
Sorry, I don't have enough money.	**Lo siento, no tengo suficiente dinero.** _lo seeyento no tengo soofeetheeyenteh deenero_
Could I have a receipt please?	**¿Podría darme un recibo?** _podreeya darmeh oon rretheebo_
I think you've given me the wrong change.	**Creo que me ha dado el cambio equivocado.** _kreyo keh meh a dado el kambeeyo ekeebokado_

YOU MAY HEAR

¿Cómo va a pagar?	How are you paying?
Esta transacción no ha sido autorizada.	This transaction has not been approved/accepted.
Esta tarjeta no es válida.	This card is not valid.
¿Me puede enseñar otra prueba de identificación?	May I have additional identification?
¿No tiene billetes más pequeños?	Do you have any small change?

YOU MAY SEE

POR PAVOR PAGUE AQUÍ	please pay here
SE DETENDRÁ A LOS CLEPTÓMANOS	shoplifters will be prosecuted

Complaints

This doesn't work.	**Esto no funciona.** *esto no foontheeyona*
Where can I make a complaint?	**¿Dónde puedo hacer una reclamación?** *dondeh pwehdo ather oona rreklamatheeyon*
Can you exchange this, please?	**¿Puede cambiarme esto, por favor?** *pwedeh kambeeyarmeh esto por fabor*
I'd like a refund.	**Quiero que me devuelvan el dinero.** *keeyero keh meh debwelban el deenero*
Here's the receipt.	**Aquí tiene el recibo.** *akee teeyeneh el rretheebo*
I don't have the receipt.	**No tengo el recibo.** *no tengo el rretheebo*
I'd like to see the manager.	**Quiero ver al encargado.** *keeyero behr al enkargado*

Repairs/Cleaning

This is broken. Can you repair it?	**Esto está roto. ¿Me lo puede arreglar?** *esto esta rroto. meh lo pwedeh arreglar*
Do you have ... for this?	**¿Tiene(n) ... para esto?** *teeyeneh(n) para esto*
a battery	**una pila** *oona peela*
replacement parts	**piezas de recambio** *peeyethas deh rrekambeeyo*
There's something wrong with ...	**Hay algo que no funciona en ...** *eye algo keh no foontheeyona en*
Can you ... this?	**¿Puede ... esto?** *pwedeh esto*
clean	**limpiar** *leempeeyar*
press	**planchar** *planchar*
patch	**remendar** *rremendar*
alter	**hacerle un arreglo a** *atherleh oon arrehglo a*
When will it (they) be ready?	**¿Cuándo estará(n) listo(s)?** *kwando estara(n) leesto(s)*
This isn't mine.	**Esto no es mío.** *esto no es meeyo*
There's ... missing.	**Falta ...** *falta*

BANK/CURRENCY EXCHANGE

At some banks, cash can be obtained from ATMs (cash machines) with Visa, Eurocard, American Express and many other international cards. Instructions are often given in English. You can also change money at travel agencies and hotels, but the rate will not be as good.

Remember your passport when you want to change money.

Where's the nearest …?	**¿Dónde está … más cercano?** _dondeh esta … mas therkano_
bank	**el banco** _el banko_
currency exchange office [bureau de change]	**el despacho de cambio** _el despacho deh kambeeyo_

Changing money

Can I exchange foreign currency here?	**¿Puedo cambiar divisas extranjeras aquí?** _pwedo kambeeyar deebeesas ekstrankheras akee_
I'd like to change some dollars/pounds into euros.	**Quiero cambiar dólares/libras a euros.** _keeyero kambeeyar dolares/leebras a eh-ooros_
I want to cash some traveler's checks/cheques/ Eurocheques.	**Quiero cobrar cheques de viaje/ eurocheques.** _keeyero kobrar chekes deh beeyakheh/eurochekes_
What's the exchange rate?	**¿A cuánto está el cambio?** _a kwanto esta el kambeeyo_
How much commission do you charge?	**¿Cuánto se llevan de comisión?** _kwanto seh l-yeban deh komeeseeyon_
I've lost my traveler's checks. These are the numbers.	**He perdido los cheques de viaje. Aquí tiene los números.** _eh perdeedo los chekes deh beeyakheh. akee teeyeneh los noomeros_

In 2002 the currency in most EU countries, including Spain, changed to the euro (€), divided into 100 cents (**céntimos**).

Coins: 1, 2, 5, 10, 20, 50 cts.; €1, 2
Notes: €5, 10, 20, 50, 100, 200, 500

YOU MAY HEAR

¿Podría ver ...	Could I see …?
su pasaporte	your passport
alguna forma de identificación	some identification
su tarjeta bancaria	your bank card
¿Cuál es su dirección?	What's your address?
¿Cuál es su nacionalidad?	What's your nationality?
¿Dónde se aloja(n)?	Where are you staying?
Rellene este impreso,	Fill out this form,
por favor.	please.
Firme aquí, por favor.	Please sign here.

Cash machines/ATMs

Can I withdraw money on my credit card here?	**¿Puedo sacar dinero aquí con mi tarjeta de crédito?** _pwedo sakar deenero akee kon mee tarkheta deh kredeeto_
Where are the ATMs/cash machines?	**¿Dónde están los cajeros (automáticos)?** _dondeh estan los kakheros (aootomateekos)_
Can I use my … card in the ATM?	**¿Puedo usar mi tarjeta … en el cajero (automático)?** _pwedo oosar mee tarkheta … en el kakhero (aootomateeko)_
The ATM has eaten my card.	**El cajero (automático) se ha tragado la tarjeta.** _el kakhero (aootomateeko) seh a tragado la tarkheta_

YOU MAY SEE

CAJEROS	ATMs/cash machines
EMPUJAR	push
TIRAR	pull
APRETAR	press
COMISIÓN DEL BANCO	bank charges
DIVISA EXTRANJERA	foreign currency
TODAS LAS OPERACIONES	all transactions

PHARMACY

Pharmacies are easily recognized by their sign: a green or red cross, usually lit up.

If you are looking for a pharmacy at night, on Sundays or holidays, you'll find the address of duty pharmacies (**famacia de guardia**) listed in the newspaper, and displayed in all pharmacy windows.

Where's the nearest (all-night) pharmacy?	**¿Dónde está la farmacia (de guardia) más próxima?** _dondeh esta la farmatheeya (deh gwardeeya) mas prokseema_
What time does the pharmacy open/close?	**¿A qué hora abre/cierra la farmacia?** _a keh ora abreh/theeyerra la farmatheeya_
Can you make up this prescription for me?	**¿Puede darme el medicamento de esta receta?** _pwedeh darmeh el medeekamento deh esta rretheta_
Shall I wait?	**¿Me espero?** _meh espero_
I'll come back for it.	**Volveré a recogerlo.** _bolbereh a rrekokherlo_

Dosage instructions

How much should I take?	**¿Cuánto tengo que tomar?** _kwanto tengo keh tomar_
How often should I take it?	**¿Cada cuánto tiempo lo tomo?** _kada kwanto teeyempo lo tomo_
Is it suitable for children?	**¿Lo pueden tomar los niños?** _lo pweden tomar los neeños_

YOU MAY HEAR

Tómese ...	Take ...
... comprimidos/... cucharaditas	... tablets/... teaspoons
antes/después de cada comida	before/after meals
con agua	with water
enteros(-as)	whole
por la mañana/noche	in the morning/at night
durante ... días	for ... days

NO DEBE APLICARSE	not to be taken
INTERNAMENTE	internally
PARA/DE USO TÓPICO	for external use only
VENENO	poison

Asking advice

What would you recommend for …?	**¿Qué recomienda usted para …?** *keh rrekomeeyenda oosteth para*
a cold	**el resfriado** *el rresfreeyado*
a cough	**la tos** *la tos*
diarrhea	**la diarrea** *la deeyarreya*
a hangover	**la resaca** *la rresaka*
hay fever	**la fiebre del heno** *la feeyebreh del eno*
insect bites	**las picaduras de insectos** *las peekadooras deh eensektos*
a sore throat	**el dolor de garganta** *el dolor deh garganta*
sunburn	**las quemaduras producidas por el sol** *las kemadooras prodootheedas por el sol*
motion [travel] sickness	**el mareo** *el mareyo*
an upset stomach	**el dolor de estómago** *el dolor deh estomago*
Can I get it without a prescription?	**¿Puedo comprarlo sin receta?** *pwedo komprarlo seen rretheta*
Can I have …?	**¿Puede darme …?** *pwedeh darmeh*
antiseptic cream	**una crema antiséptica** *oona krema anteesepteeka*
(soluble) aspirin	**aspirinas (solubles)** *aspeereenas (soloobles)*
bandage	**vendas** *bendas*
condoms	**condones** *kondones*
cotton [cotton wool]	**algodón** *algodon*
insect repellent/spray	**repelente/espray para insectos** *repelenteh/espray para eensektos*
pain killers	**analgésicos** *analkheseekos*
vitamins	**vitaminas** *beetameenas*

Toiletries

I'd like …	**Quiero …** *keeyero*
aftershave	**aftershave** *"aftershabe"*
after-sun lotion	**aftersun** *aftersoon*
deodorant	**desodorante** *desodoranteh*
razor blades	**cuchillas de afeitar** *koocheel-yas deh afeyeetar*
sanitary napkins [towels]	**compresas** *kompresas*
soap	**jabón** *khabon*
sunscreen	**crema bronceadora** *krema brontheyadora*
tampons	**tampones** *tampones*
tissues	**pañuelos de papel** *pañwelos deh papel*
toilet paper	**papel higiénico** *papel eekheeyeneeko*
toothpaste	**pasta de dientes** *pasta deh deeyentes*

Haircare

comb	**peine** *peyneh*
conditioner	**suavizante** *swabeethanteh*
hairbrush	**cepillo** *thepeel-yo*
hair mousse	**espuma para el pelo** *espooma para el pelo*
hair spray	**espray fijador** *espray feekhador*
shampoo	**champú** *champoo*

For the baby

baby food	**comida para bebés** *komeeda para bebes*
baby wipes	**toallitas** *toal-yeetas*
diapers [nappies]	**pañales** *pañales*
sterilizing solution	**solución esterilizante** *solootheeyon estereeleethanteh*

CLOTHING

You'll find that airport boutiques offering tax-free shopping may have cheaper prices but less selection.

General

I'd like …	**Quiero …** *keeyero*
Do you have any …?	**¿Tiene(n) …?** *teeyeneh(n)*

Color

I'm looking for something in …	**Estoy buscando algo …** *estoy booskando algo*
beige	**beige** *beich*
black	**negro** *negro*
blue	**azul** *athool*
brown	**marrón** *marron*
green	**verde** *berdeh*
gray	**gris** *grees*
orange	**naranja** *narankha*
pink	**rosa** *rrosa*
purple	**morado** *morado*
red	**rojo** *rrokho*
white	**blanco** *blanko*
yellow	**amarillo** *amareel-yo*
light …	**… claro** *klaro*
dark …	**… oscuro** *oskooro*
I want a darker/lighter shade.	**Quiero un tono más oscuro/claro.** *keeyero oon tono mas oskooro/klaro*
Do you have the same in …?	**¿Lo tiene igual en …?** *lo teeyeneh eegwal en*

Clothes and accessories

belt	**cinturón**	*theentooron*
bikini	**bikini**	*beekeenee*
blouse	**blusa**	*bloosa*
bra	**sujetador/sostén**	*sookhetador/sosten*
briefs	**calzoncillos**	*kalthontheel-yos*
coat	**abrigo**	*abreego*
dress	**vestido**	*besteedo*
handbag	**bolso**	*bolso*
hat	**sombrero**	*sombrero*
jacket	**chaqueta**	*chaketa*
jeans	**vaqueros**	*bakeros*
leggings	**mallas**	*mal-yas*
pants (U.S.)	**pantalones**	*pantalones*
pantyhose [tights]	**medias**	*medeeyas*
raincoat	**impermeable**	*eempermeableh*
scarf	**bufanda**	*boofanda*
shirt	**camisa**	*kameesa*
shorts	**pantalones cortos**	*pantalones kortos*
skirt	**falda**	*falda*
socks	**calcetines**	*kaltheteenehs*
stockings (a pair of …)	**unas medias**	*medeeya*
suit	**traje de chaqueta**	*trakheh deh chaketa*
sunglasses	**gafas de sol**	*gafas deh sol*
sweater	**jersey**	*khersay*
sweatshirt	**sudadera**	*soodadera*
swimming trunks/ swimsuit	**bañador (de hombre/de mujer)**	*bañador (deh ombreh/deh mookher)*
T-shirt	**camiseta**	*kameeseta*
tie	**corbata**	*korbata*
trousers	**pantalones**	*pantalones*
underpants	**calzoncillos**	*kalthontheel-yos*
with long/short sleeves	**de manga larga/corta**	*deh manga larga/korta*

| with a V-/round neck | **de cuello en pico/redondo** |
| | *kon kwel-yo deh peeko/redondo* |

a pair of …	**un par de …** *oon par deh*
boots	**botas** *botas*
flip-flops	**chancletas** *chankletas*
sandals	**sandalias** *sandaleeyas*
shoes	**zapatos** *thapatos*
slippers	**zapatillas** *thapateel-yas*

knapsack	**mochila** *mocheela*
walking boots	**botas de montaña** *botas deh montaña*
waterproof jacket [anorak]	**chaquetón impermeable**
	chaketon eempermehable
windbreaker [cagoule]	**chubasquero** *choobaskero*

I want something in …	**Quiero algo de …** *keeyero algo deh*
cotton	**algodón** *algodon*
denim	**tela vaquera** *tela bakera*
lace	**encaje** *enkakheh*
leather	**cuero** *kwero*
linen	**lino** *leeno*
wool	**lana** *lana*
Is this …?	**¿Es esto …?** *es esto*
pure cotton	**puro algodón** *pooro algodon*
synthetic	**sintético** *seenteteeko*
Is it hand/machine washable?	**¿Se puede lavar a mano/a máquina?**
	seh pwedeh labar a mano/a makeena

YOU MAY SEE

SÓLO LAVAR A MANO	handwash only
SÓLO LIMPIAR EN SECO	dry clean only
NO DESTIÑE	colorfast

Does it fit?

Can I try this on?	**¿Puedo probarme esto?**
	pwedo probarmeh esto
Where's the fitting room?	**¿Dónde está el probador?**
	dondeh esta el probador
I'll take it.	**Me lo quedo.** _meh lo kedo_
It doesn't fit.	**No me está bien.**
	no meh esta beeyen
It's too…	**Es demasiado …**
	es demaseeyado
short/long	**corto(-a)/largo(-a)**
	korto(-a)/largo(-a)
tight/loose	**estrecho(-a)/ancho(-a)**
	estrecho(-a)/ancho(-a)
Do you have this in size …?	**¿Tienen esto en la talla …?**
	teeyenen esto en la tal-ya
Could you measure me?	**¿Podría tomarme las medidas?**
	podreeya tomarmeh las medeedas

Size

	Dresses/Suits						Women's shoes			
American }	8	10	12	14	16	18	6	7	8	9
British }	10	12	14	16	18	20	4½	5½	6½	7½
Continental	38	40	42	44	46	48	37	38	39	40

	Shirts				Men's shoes							
American }	15	16	17	18	6	7	8	8½	9	9½	10	11
British }												
Continental	38	41	43	45	38	39	41	42	43	43	44	44

YOU MAY SEE	
XL	extra large (XL)
GRANDE	large (L)
MEDIANA	medium (M)
PEQUEÑA	small (S)

HEALTH AND BEAUTY

I'd like a …	**Quiero que me …** *keeyero keh meh*
facial	**haga una limpieza de cutis/cara** *aga oona leempeeyetha deh kootees/kara*
manicure	**haga la manicura** *aga la maneekoora*
massage	**dé un masaje** *deh oon masakheh*
waxing	**haga la cera** *aga la thera*

Hairdresser

Tipping: 5-10% is normal.

I'd like to make an appointment for …	**Quiero pedir hora para …** *keeyero pedeer ora para*
Can you make it a bit earlier/later?	**¿Puede venir un poco más tarde/ temprano?** *pwedeh beneer oon poko mas tardeh/ttemprano*
I'd like a …	**Quiero …** *keeyero*
cut and blow-dry	**que me corte el pelo y me lo seque** *keh meh korteh el pelo ee meh lo sekeh*
shampoo and set	**un lavado y marcado** *oon labado ee markado*
trim	**que me corte las puntas** *keh meh korteh las poontas*
I'd like my hair …	**Quiero que me …** *keeyero keh meh*
colored/tinted	**tiña el pelo** *teeña el pelo*
highlighted	**haga mechas** *aga mechas*
permed	**haga la permanente** *aga la permanenteh*
Don't cut it too short.	**No me lo corte demasiado.** *no meh lo korteh demaseeyado*
A little more off the …	**Un poquito más por …** *oon pokeeto mas por*
back/front	**detrás/delante** *detras/delanteh*
neck/sides	**el cuello/por los lados** *el kwel-yo/por los lados*
top	**arriba** *arreeba*

HOUSEHOLD ARTICLES

I'd like a(n)/some …	**Quiero …** *keeyero*
adapter	**un adaptador** *oon adaptador*
alumin[i]um foil	**papel de aluminio** *papel deh aloomeeneeyo*
bottle opener	**un abrebotellas** *oon abrebotel-yas*
can [tin] opener	**un abrelatas** *oon abrelatas*
candles	**velas** *belas*
clothespins [pegs]	**pinzas de la ropa** *peenthas deh la rropa*
corkscrew	**un sacacorchos** *oon sakakorchos*
lightbulb	**una bombilla** *oona bombeel-ya*
matches	**cerillas** *thereel-yas*
paper napkins	**servilletas de papel** *serbeel-yetas deh papel*
plastic wrap [cling film]	**film transparente** *feelm transparente*
plug *(electrical)*	**un enchufe** *oon enchoofeh*
scissors	**tijeras** *teekheras*
screwdriver	**un destornillador** *oon destorneel-yador*

Cleaning items

bleach	**lejía** *lekheeya*
detergent [washing powder]	**detergente de lavadora** *deterkhenteh deh labadora*
dishcloth	**balleta** *bal-yeta*
dishwashing liquid	**lavavajillas** *lababakheel-yas*
garbage [refuse] bags	**bolsa de basura** *bolsa deh basoora*

Dishes/Utensils [Crockery/Cutlery]

cups	**tazas** *tathas*
forks	**tenedores** *tenedores*
glasses	**vasos/copas** *basos/kopas*
knives	**cuchillos** *koocheel-yos*
mugs	**tazas** *tathas*
plates	**platos** *platos*
spoons/teaspoons	**cucharas/cucharillas** *koocharas/koochareel-yas*

Could I see …?	**¿Podría ver …?** *podreeya behr*
this/that	**esto/eso** *esto/eso*
It's in the window/display case.	**Está en el escaparate/en la vitrina.** *esta en el eskaparateh/en la beetreena*
I'd like a(n)/some …	**Quiero …** *keeyero*
battery	**una pila** *oona peela*
bracelet	**una pulsera** *oona poolsera*
brooch	**un broche** *oon brocheh*
chain	**una cadena** *oona kadena*
clock	**un reloj de pared** *oon relokh deh pareth*
earrings	**unos pendientes** *oonos pendeeyentes*
necklace	**un collar** *oon kol-yar*
ring	**un anillo** *oon aneel-yo*
watch	**un reloj de pulsera** *oon relokh deh poolsera*

Materials

Is this real silver/gold?	**¿Es esto plata/oro de ley?** *es esto plata/oro deh ley*
Is there a certificate for it?	**¿Tiene el sello?** *teeyeneh el sel-yo*
Do you have anything in …?	**¿Tiene(n) algo …?** *teeyeneh(n) algo*
copper	**de cobre** *deh kobreh*
crystal (quartz)	**de vidrio** *deh beedreeyo*
cut glass	**de vidrio tallado** *deh beedreeyo tal-yado*
diamond	**de diamantes** *deh deeyamantes*
enamel	**esmaltado** *esmaltado*
goldplate	**chapado en oro** *chapado en oro*
pearl	**de perlas** *deh perlas*
pewter	**de peltre** *deh peltreh*
platinum	**de platino** *deh plateeno*
silverplate	**chapado en plata** *chapado en plata*
stainless steel	**de acero inoxidable** *deh athero eenokseedableh*

Foreign newspapers can usually be found at train stations, airports, and in major cities at newsstands. Cigarettes are widely available. Spanish cigarettes are strong (**negro**) or light (**rubio**). Cigars from the Canary Islands and Cuba are widely available in Spain.

Do you sell English-language books/newspapers?	**¿Venden libros/periódicos en inglés?** _benden leebros/pereeyodeekos en eengles_
I'd like a(n)/some …	**Quiero …** _keeyero_
book	**un libro** _oon leebro_
candy [sweets]	**caramelos** _karamelos_
chewing gum	**chicles** _cheekles_
chocolate bar	**una barra de chocolate** _oona barra deh chokolateh_
cigarettes (pack of)	**un paquete de tabaco** _oon paketeh deh tabako_
cigars	**unos puros** _oonos pooros_
(English-Spanish) dictionary	**un diccionario (de inglés-español)** _oon docktheeyonareeyo (deh eengles español)_
guidebook of …	**una guía de …** _oona geeya deh_
lighter	**un encendedor** _oon enthendedor_
magazine	**una revista** _oona rebeesta_
map of the town	**un plano de la ciudad** _oon plano deh la theeyoodath_
matches	**unas cerillas** _oonos thereel-yas_
newspaper	**un periódico** _oon pereeyodeeko_
paper	**papel** _papel_
pen	**un bolígrafo** _oon boleegrafo_
postcard	**una postal** _oona postal_
road map of …	**un mapa de carreteras de …** _oon mapa deh karreteras deh_
stamps	**unos sellos** _oonos sel-yos_
tobacco	**tabaco** _tabako_
writing pad	**un cuaderno** _oon kwaderno_

Photography

I'm looking for a(n) … camera.	**Busco una cámara …** boosko oona kamara
automatic	**automática** aootomateeka
compact	**compacta** kompakta
disposable	**de usar y tirar** deh oosar ee teerar
SLR (single lens reflex)	**cámara reflex** kamara refleks
I'd like a(n) …	**Quiero …** keeyero
battery	**una pila** oona peela
camera case	**una funda para la cámara** oona foonda para la kamara
electronic flash	**un flash electrónico** oon flash (elektroneeko)
filter	**un filtro** oon feeltro
lens	**una lente** oona lenteh
lens cap	**una tapa para la lente** oona tapa para la lenteh

Film/Processing

I'd like a …	**Quiero un carrete …** keeyero oon karreteh
black and white	**en blanco y negro** en blanko ee negro
color	**de color** deh kolor
I'd like this film developed.	**Quiero que me revelen este carrete.** keeyero keh meh rebelen esteh karreteh
Would you enlarge this?	**¿Podrían ampliarme esto?** podreeyan ampleeyarmeh esto
How much do … exposures cost?	**¿Cuánto cuesta revelar … fotos?** kwanto kwesta rebelar … fotos
When will the photos be ready?	**¿Cuándo estarán listas las fotos?** kwando estaran leestas las fotos
I'd like to pick up my photos. Here's the receipt.	**Vengo a recoger mis fotos. Aquí tiene el recibo.** bengo a rekokher mees fotos. akee teeyeneh el retheebo

POLICE

There are 3 police forces in Spain. In rural areas and smaller towns, any crime or road accident has to be reported to the **Cuartel de la Guardia Civil**. In larger towns, responsibilities are divided between the local police (**Policía Municipal**) for traffic control, lost property, commerce, etc., and the national police (**Cuerpo Nacional de Policía**) for all aspects of personal protection, crime, injury, and immigration.

Beware of pickpockets, particularly in crowded places. Report all thefts to the local police within 24 hours for insurance purposes. In an emergency: ☎ 091 for the police; ☎ 092 for medical assistance.

Where's the nearest police station?	**¿Dónde está la comisaría (de policía) más cercana?** _dondeh esta la komeesareeya (deh poleetheeya) mas therkana_
Does anyone here speak English?	**¿Hay alguien aquí que hable inglés?** _eye algeeyen akee keh ableh eengles_
I want to report an ...	**Quiero denunciar ...** _keeyero denoontheeyar_
accident/attack	**un accidente/asalto** _oon aktheedenteh/asalto_
My child is missing.	**Mi hijo(-a) ha desaparecido.** _mee ockho(-a) u desaparetheedo_
Here's a photo of him/her.	**Aquí tiene una foto de él/ella.** _akee teeyeneh oona foto deh el/el-ya_
I need to make a phone call.	**Tengo que hacer una llamada.** _tengo keh ather oona l-yamada_
I need to contact the ... (American/British) Consulate.	**Tengo que ponerme en contacto con el consulado ... (americano/británico)** _tengo keh ponermeh en kontakto kon el konsoolado ... (amereekano/breetaneeko)_

YOU MAY HEAR

¿Puede describirle/la?	Can you describe him/her?
hombre/mujer	male/female
con el pelo largo/corto	long/short hair
altura aproximada ...	approximate height ...
edad (aproximada) ...	aged (approximately) ...
Llevaba puesto ...	He/She was wearing ...

I want to report a theft/break-in.	**Quiero denunciar un robo.** *keeyero denoontheeyar oon rrobo*
I've been robbed/mugged.	**Me han robado/atracado.** *meh an rrobado/atrakado*
I've lost my …	**He perdido mi …** *eh perdeedo mee*
My … has been stolen.	**Me han robado …** *meh an rrobado*
bicycle	**la bicicleta** *la beetheekleta*
camera	**la cámara** *la kamara*
(rental) car	**el coche (alquilado)** *el kocheh (alkeelado)*
credit cards	**las tarjetas de crédito** *las tarkhetas deh kredeeto*
handbag	**el bolso** *el bolso*
money	**el dinero** *el deenero*
passport	**el pasaporte** *el pasaporteh*
purse/wallet	**el monedero/la billetera** *el monedero/la beel-yetera*
watch	**el reloj (de pulsera)** *el relokh (deh poolsera)*
What shall I do?	**¿Qué debo hacer?** *keh debo hacer*
I need a police report for my insurance claim.	**Necesito un certificado de la policía para el seguro.** *netheseeto oon therteefeekado deh la poleetheeya para el segooro*

YOU MAY HEAR

¿Qué falta?	What's missing?
¿Cuándo ocurrió?	When did it happen?
¿Dónde se hospeda?	Where are you staying?
¿De dónde lo cogieron?	Where was it taken from?
¿Dónde estaba usted entonces?	Where were you at the time?
Le vamos a conseguir un intérprete.	We're getting an interpreter for you.
Por favor, rellene este impreso/formulario.	Please fill out this form.

POST OFFICE

Spanish post offices are recognized by a red hunting-horn symbol on a bright yellow background. Mailboxes are yellow and red. Stamps can be bought from tobacconists, as well as from post offices.

General inquiries

Where is the main/nearest post office?	**¿Dónde está la oficina de correos principal/más cercana?** _dondeh esta la ofeetheena de korreyos preentheepal/mas therkana_
What time does the post office open/close?	**¿A qué hora abre/cierra la oficina de correos?** _a keh ora abreh/theeyera la ofeetheena deh korreyos_
Does it close for lunch?	**¿Se cierra para comer?** _seh theeyerra para komer_
Where's the mailbox [postbox]?	**¿Dónde está el buzón?** _dondeh esta el boothon_

Buying stamps

A stamp for this postcard/letter, please.	**Un sello para esta postal/carta, por favor.** _oon selyo para esta postal/karta por fabor_
A … cent stamp, please.	**Un sello de … céntimos, por favor.** _oon sel-yo deh … sentimos por fabor_
What's the postage for a postcard/letter to …?	**¿Cuántos sellos se necesitan para una postal/carta a …?** _kwantos sel yos seh netheseetan para oona postal/karta a_
Is there a stamp machine here?	**¿Hay una máquina expendedora de sellos aquí?** _eye oona makeena expendedora deh sol yos ukee_

IN A POST OFFICE

Quiero mandar estas postales. _keeyero mandar estas postales_ (I'd like to send these postcards.)
Son tres euros, cincuenta. _son tres eh-ooros theenkwenta_ (That's 3 euros, 50.)
Aquí tiene. _akee teeyeneh_ (Here you are.)

153

Sending packages

I want to send this package [parcel] by …	**Quiero mandar este paquete por …** *keeyero mandar esteh paketeh por*
airmail	**correo aéreo** *korreyo ayreyo*
special delivery [express]	**correo urgente** *korreyo oorkhenteh*
registered mail	**correo certificado** *korreyo therteefeekado*
It contains …	**Contiene …** *konteeyeneh*

Telecommunications

I'd like a phonecard.	**Quiero una tarjeta para llamar por teléfono.** *keeyero oona tarkheta para l-yamar por telefono*
10/20/50 units	**de diez/veinte/cincuenta unidades** *deh deeyeth/beynteh/theenkwenta ooneedades*
Do you have a photocopier?	**¿Tienen una fotocopiadora?** *teeyenen oona fotokopeeyadora*
I'd like to send a message by fax/e-mail.	**Quiero mandar un mensaje por fax/correo electrónico.** *keeyero mandar oon faks/mensakheh por korreyo elektroneeko*
What's your e-mail address?	**¿Cuál es tu dirección de correo electrónico?** *kwal es too deerektheeyon deh korreyo elektroneeko*
Can I access the Internet here?	**¿Puedo acceder a Internet desde aquí?** *pwedo aktheder ah eenternet desdeh akee*
What are the charges per hour?	**¿Cuánto cuesta por hora?** *kwanto kwesta por ora*
How do I log on?	**¿Cómo entro?** *komo entro*

SOUVENIRS

You'll find no shortage of gift ideas from the Spanish souvenir industry.

Bullfight poster (**el cartel de toros**), bullfighter's cap (**la montera**), bullfighter dolls (**los muñecos de torero**), bullfighter sword (**la espada de torero**), cape (**la capa**), castanets (**las castañuelas**), fan (**el abanico**), guitar (**la guitarra**), mantilla (**la mantilla**), pitcher (**el botijo**), poncho (**el poncho**), reproduction painting (**la reproducción de un cuadro**), tambourine (**la pandereta**).

You will also find a wide selection of fine hand-crafted articles, particularly in special outlets called **artesanía** or the government-sponsored **Artespaña**: carpets (**las alfombras**), ceramics (**objetos de cerámica**), copperware (**objetos de cobre**), earthenware (**la loza de barro**), embossed leather (**el cuero repujado**), embroidery (**el bordado**), fashion (**la moda**), jewelry [jewellery] (**las joyas**), lace (**los encajes**), leather goods (**artículos de piel**), Valencian porcelain (**la cerámica de Valencia**), wood carving (**la talla en madera**).

Gifts

bottle of wine	**una botella de vino**
	oona botel-ya deh beeno
box of chocolates	**una caja de bombones**
	oona kakha deh bombones
calendar	**un calendario** _oon kalendareeyo_
key ring	**un llavero** _oon l-yabero_
postcard	**una postal** _oona postal_
souvenir guide	**un catálogo de recuerdos**
	oon katalago deh rekwerdos
dish towel	**un paño de cocina** _oon paño de kotheena_
T-shirt	**una camiseta** _oona kameeseta_

Music

I'd like a …	**Quiero …** _keeyero_
cassette	**una cinta/cassette** _oona theenta/kasetch_
compact disc	**un compact disc** _oon "compact disc"_
record	**un disco** _oon deesko_
videocassette	**una cinta de vídeo** _oona theenta deh beedeyo_
Who are the popular native singers/bands?	**¿Quiénes son los cantantes/grupos populares de aquí?** _keeyenes son los kantantes/groopos popoolares deh akee_

Toys and games

I'd like a toy/game …	**Quiero un juguete/juego …** *keeyero oon khoogeteh/khwego*
for a boy	**para un niño** *para oon neeño*
for a 5-year-old	**para un(a) niño(a) de cinco años** *para oon(a) neeño(a) deh theenko años*
chess set	**un juego de ajedrez** *oon khwego deh akhedreth*
board game	**un juego de mesa** *oon khwego deh mesa*
doll	**una muñeca** *oona mooñeka*
electronic game	**un juego electrónico** *oon khwego elektroneeko*
pail and shovel [bucket and spade]	**un cubo y una pala** *oon koobo ee oona pala*
teddy bear	**un osito** *oon oseeto*
small/big	**pequeño/grande** *pekenio/grandeh*

Antiques

How old is this?	**¿Qué antigüedad tiene esto?** *keh anteegwedath teeyeneh esto*
Do you have anything from the … period?	**¿Tiene algo del periodo …?** *teeyeneh algo del pereeyodo*
Can you send it to me?	**¿Puede mandármelo?** *pwedeh mandarmelo*
Will I have problems with customs?	**¿Tendré problemas en la aduana?** *tendreh problemas en la adwana*
Do I have to fill out any forms?	**¿Tengo que llenar alguna forma?** *tengo keh l-yenar algoona forma*
Is there a certificate of authenticity?	**¿Tiene certificado de autenticidad?** *teeyeneh therteefeekado deh aootenteetheedath*

SUPERMARKET/MINIMART

Supermarkets such as **Dia** and **Spar** can be found in town centers; **Alcampo**, **Caprabo**, **Jumbo** and **Pryca** are hypermarket chains situated around larger cities. You will also encounter minimarts (**galería comercial**) and modern substitutes for the tradtional market (**galería de alimentación**).

Opening times for these stores are generally 9:30 a.m. to 1:30 p.m., 4 p.m. to 8 p.m., and Saturdays from 9:30 to 1.30 p.m., with a few open in the afternoon.

At the supermarket

Excuse me. Where can I find (a) …?	**Disculpe. ¿Dónde puedo encontrar …?** dees<u>kool</u>peh <u>don</u>deh <u>pwe</u>do enkon<u>trar</u>
Do I pay for this here or at the checkout?	**¿Pago esto aquí o en la caja?** <u>pa</u>go <u>es</u>to a<u>kee</u> o en la <u>ka</u>kha
Where are the carts [trolleys]/baskets?	**¿Dónde están los carritos/las cestas?** <u>don</u>deh es<u>tan</u> los ka<u>rree</u>tos/las <u>thes</u>tas
Is there a … here?	**¿Hay … aquí?** eye … a<u>kee</u>
delicatessen	**una charcutería** <u>oo</u>na charkoote<u>ree</u>ya
pharmacy	**una farmacia** <u>oo</u>na farma<u>thee</u>ya

YOU MAY SEE

ARTÍCULOS PARA EL HOGAR	household goods
CARNE DE AVE	poultry
CARNE FRESCA	fresh meat
CONGELADOS	frozen foods
FRUTA/VERDURA EN CONSERVA	canned fruit/vegetables
PAN Y PASTELES	bread and cakes
PESCADO FRESCO	fresh fish
PRODUCTOS DE LIMPIEZA	cleaning products
FRUTAS Y VERDURAS	fresh produce
PRODUCTOS LÁCTEOS	dairy products
VINOS Y LICORES	wines and spirits

Food hygiene

At the minimart

I'd like some of that/those.	**Quiero un poco de eso/unos cuantos de esos.** _keeyero oon poko deh eso/oonos kwantos deh esos_
this one/these	**éste/estos** _este/estos_
over there/here	**ahí/allí** _aee/al-yee_
I'd like …	**Quiero …** _keeyero_
kilo/half-kilo of apples	**un kilo/medio kilo de manzanas** _oon keelo/medeeyo keelo deh manthanas_
100 grams of cheese	**cien gramos de queso** _theeyen gramos deh keso_
liter of milk	**un litro de leche** _oon leetro deh lecheh_
half-dozen eggs	**media docena de huevos** _medeeya dothena deh webos_
… slices of ham	**… rodajas de jamón** _rrodakhas deh khamon_
piece of cake	**un trozo de pastel/tarta** _oon trotho deh pastel/tarta_
bottle of wine	**una botella de vino** _oona botel-ya deh beeno_
carton of milk	**un cartón de leche** _oon karton deh lecheh_
jar of jam	**un bote de mermelada** _oon boteh deh mermelada_
package of potato chips [crisps]	**una bolsa de patatas fritas** _oona bolsa deh patatas freetas_

IN A SUPERMARKET

¿Dónde puedo encontrar azúcar? _dondeh pwedo enkontrar ahzoogahr_ (Where can I find sugar?)

Ahí, a la derecha. _aee ala dehrecha_ (Over there, to the right.)

PROVISIONS/PICNIC

beer	**cerveza** _therbetha_
butter	**mantequilla** _mantehkeelya_
cheese	**queso** _kehso_
cookies [biscuits]	**galletas** _galyehtas_
French fries [chips]	**patatas fritas** _patatas freetas_
cold meats	**fiambres** _feeyambrehs_
potato chips [crisps] (a bag of)	**patatas fritas (de bolsa)** _patatas freetas (deh bolsa)_
eggs	**huevos** _wehbos_
grapes	**uvas** _oobas_
ice cream	**helado** _ehlado_
instant coffee	**café soluble** _kafeh solooble_
bread	**pan** _pan_
margarine	**margarina** _margareena_
milk	**leche** _lecheh_
rolls	**panecillos** _panetheel-yos_
sausages	**salchichas** _salcheechas_
soft drink/soda	**refresco** _rehfrehsko_
wine	**vino** _beeno_

Una barra de pan _oona barra deh pan_
Similar to a French breadstick; other types of bread include **colines** (breadsticks), **rosquillas** (ring-shaped), **pan integral** (wholemeal bread).

Empanadillas _empanadeel-yas_
Pasties, usually with a meat or tuna filling.

Una tarta/un pastel _oona tarta/oon pastel_
A cake/small cakes; other types include **roscón** (ring-shaped cake, often flavored), **bizcocho** (sponge cake), **magdalenas** (small sponge cakes).

CONVERSION CHARTS

The following conversion charts contain the most commonly used measures.

1 Gramo (g)	= 1000 milligrams	= 0.35 oz.
1 Libra (lb)	= 500 grams	= 1.1 lb
1 Kilogramo (kg)	= 1000 grams	= 2.2 lb
1 Litro (l)	= 1000 milliliters	= 1.06 U.S / 0.88 Brit. quarts
		= 2.11 /1.8 US /Brit. pints
		= 34 /35 US /Brit. fluid oz.
		= 0.26 /0.22 US /Brit. gallons
1 Centímetro (cm)	= 100 millimeter	= 0.4 inch
1 Metro (m)	= 100 centimeters	= 39.37 inches/3.28 ft.
1 Kilómetro (km)	= 1000 meters	= 0.62 mile
1 Metro cuadrado (m²)	= 10.8 square feet	
1 Hectárea (qm)	= 2.5 acres	
1 Km cuadrado (km²)	= 247 acres	

Not sure whether to put on a bathing suit or a winter coat? Here is a comparison of Fahrenheit and and Celsius/Centigrade degrees..

-40°C	–	-40°F	5°C	–	41°F	Oven Temperatures	
-30°C	–	-22°F	10°C	–	50°F	100°C	212°F
-20°C	–	-4°F	15°C	–	59°F	121°C	250°F
-10°C	–	14°F	20°C	–	68°F	154°C	300°F
-5°C	–	23°F	25°C	–	77°F	177°C	350°F
-1°C	–	30°F	30°C	–	86°F	204°C	400°F
0°C	–	32°F	35°C	–	95°F	260°C	500°F

When you know	Multiply by	To find
ounces	28.3	grams
pounds	0.45	kilograms
inches	2.54	centimeters
feet	0.3	meters
miles	1.61	kilometers
square inches	6.45	sq. centimeters
square feet	0.09	sq. meters
square miles	2.59	sq. kilometers
pints (US/Brit)	0.47 / 0.56	liters
gallons (US/Brit)	3.8 / 4.5	liters
Fahrenheit	5/9, after subtracting 32	Centigrade
Centigrade	9/5, then add 32	Fahrenheit

HEALTH

Before you leave, make sure your health insurance policy covers illness and accident while you are abroad. If not, ask your insurance representative, automobile association or travel agent for details of special health insurance. A special Spanish health and accident insurance is available from tourist boards (**ASTES**), covering doctors' fees and clinical care. In Spain, EU citizens with Form E111 are eligible for free medical treatment. However, this only applies to clinics that belong, or are connected, to the **Seguridad Social** (national health service). Dental care in this program is limited to extractions.

A list of English-speaking doctors is available at local tourist offices. There are hospitals in all principal towns and a first-aid station (**casa de socorro**) in smaller places. For emergerncies, ☎ 092

DOCTOR (GENERAL)

Where can I find a doctor/dentist?	**¿Dónde puedo encontrar un médico/ dentista?** _dondeh pwedo enkontrar oon medeeko/denteesta_
Where's there a doctor who speaks English?	**¿Dónde hay un médico que hable inglés?** _dondeh eye oon medeeko keh ableh eengles_
What are the office [surgery] hours?	**¿Cuáles son las horas de consulta?** _kwales son las oras deh konsoolta_
Could the doctor come to see me here?	**¿Podría el médico venir a verme aquí?** _podreeya el medeeko beneer a bermeh akee_
Can I make an appointment for …?	**¿Puede darme una cita para …?** _pwedeh darmeh oona theeta para_
today/tomorrow	**hoy/mañana** _oy/mañana_
as soon as possible	**lo antes posible** _lo antes poseebleh_
It's urgent.	**Es urgente.** _es oorkhenteh_
I've got an appointment with Doctor …	**Tengo una cita con el /la doctor(a) …** _tengo oona theeta kon el/la doktor(a)_

(161)

Accident and injury

My … is hurt/injured.	**Mi … está herido(-a).**	*mee … esta ereedo(-a)*
husband/wife	**marido/mujer**	*mareedo/mookher*
son/daughter	**hijo/hija**	*eekho/eekha*
friend	**amigo(-a)**	*ameego(-a)*
He/She is …	**El/Ella está …**	*el/el-ya esta*
unconscious	**inconsciente**	*eenkonstheeyenteh*
bleeding (heavily)	**sangrando (mucho)**	*sangrando (moocho)*
I've got a(n) …	**Tengo …**	*tengo*
boil/bruise	**un forúnculo/cardenal**	*oon foroonkoolo/kardenal*
cut/graze	**un corte/rasguño**	*oon korteh/rasgooño*
rash/sting	**un sarpullido/ardor**	*oon sarpool-yeedo/ardor*
sprained muscle	**un esguince**	*oon esgeentheh*
swelling	**una hinchazón**	*oon eenchathon*

Symptoms

I've been feeling ill for … days.	**Llevo … días sintiéndome enfermo.**	*l-yebo … deeyas seenteeyendomeh enfermo*
I feel faint.	**Estoy mareado(-a).**	*estoy mareado(-a)*
I'm feverish.	**Tengo fiebre.**	*tengo feeyebreh*
I've been vomiting.	**He estado vomitando.**	*eh estado bomeetando*
I've got diarrhea.	**Tengo diarrea.**	*tengo deeyarreya*
It hurts here.	**Me duele aquí.**	*meh dweleh akee*
I have a(n) …	**Tengo …**	*tengo*
backache	**dolor de espalda**	*dolor deh espalda*
cold	**un resfriado**	*oon resfreeyado*
cramps	**retortijones**	*rretorteekhones*
earache	**dolor de oídos**	*dolor deh oyeedos*
headache	**dolor de cabeza**	*dolor deh kabetha*
stomachache	**dolor de estómago**	*dolor deh estomago*
sunstroke	**insolación**	*eensolatheeyon*

Health conditions

I am …	**Soy …** *soy*
asthmatic	**asmático(-a)** *asmateeko(-a)*
diabetic	**diabético(-a)** *deeyabeteeko(-a)*
epileptic	**epiléptico(-a)** *epeelepteeko(-a)*
handicapped	**minusválido(-a)** *meenoosbaleedo(-a)*
I have arthritis.	**Tengo artritis.** *tengo artreetees*
I'm (… months) pregnant.	**Estoy embarazada (de … meses).** *estoy embarathada (deh … meses)*
I have a heart condition/ high blood pressure.	**Padezco del corazón/de tensión alta.** *padethko del korathon/deh tenseeyon alta*
I had a heart attack … years ago.	**Me dio un infarto hace … años.** *meh deeyo oon eenfarto atheh … años*

Parts of the body

appendix	**el apéndice** *el apendeetheh*	kidney	**el riñón** *el reeñon*
		knee	**la rodilla** *la rrodeel-ya*
arm	**el brazo** *el bratho*	leg	**la pierna** *la peeyerna*
back	**la espalda** *la espalda*	lip	**el labio** *el labeeyo*
bladder	**la vejiga** *la bekheega*	liver	**el hígado** *el eegado*
bone	**el hueso** *el weso*	mouth	**la boca** *la boka*
breast	**el pecho** *el pecho*	muscle	**el músculo** *el mooskoolo*
chest	**el pecho** *el pecho*		
ear	**el oído** *el oyeedo*	neck	**el cuello** *el kwel-yo*
eye	**el ojo** *el okho*	nose	**la nariz** *la nareeth*
face	**la cara** *la kara*	rib	**la costilla** *la kosteel-ya*
finger	**el dedo** *el dedo*	shoulder	**el hombro** *el ombro*
foot/toe	**el pie/el dedo del pie** *el peeyeh/dedo del peeyeh*	skin	**la piel** *la peeyel*
		spine	**la columna vertebral** *la koloomna bertebral*
hand	**la mano** *la mano*		
head	**la cabeza** *la kabetha*	stomach	**el estómago** *el estomago*
heart	**el corazón** *el korathon*		
jaw	**la mandíbula** *la mandeeboola*	thigh	**la cadera** *la kadera*
		throat	**la garganta** *la garganta*
joint	**la articulación** *la arteekoolatheeyon*	tongue	**la lengua** *la lengwa*

Doctor's Inquiries

¿Cuánto tiempo lleva sintiéndose así?	How long have you been feeling like this?
¿Es ésta la primera vez que le pasa?	Is this the first time you've had this?
¿Está tomando otros medicamentos?	Are you taking any other medication?
¿Es alérgico(a) a algo?	Are you allergic to anything?
¿Lo/la han vacunado contra el tétano?	Have you been vaccinated against tetanus?
¿Ha perdido el apetito?	Have you lost your appetite?

Examination

Le tomaré la temperatura/ tensión.	I'll take your temperature/ blood pressure.
Súbase la manga, por favor.	Roll up your sleeve, please.
Desvístase de cintura para arriba, por favor.	Please undress to the waist.
Túmbese, por favor.	Please lie down.
Abra la boca.	Open your mouth.
Respire profundamente.	Breathe deeply.
Tosa, por favor.	Cough please.
¿Dónde le duele?	Where does it hurt?
¿Le duele aquí?	Does it hurt here?

Diagnosis

Quiero que le hagan una radiografía.	I want you to have an X-ray.
Necesito una muestra de sangre/heces/orina.	I want a specimen of your blood/stool/urine.
Quiero que vea a un especialista.	I want you to see a specialist.
Quiero mandarlo al hospital.	I want you to go to the hospital.
Está roto(-a)/tiene un esguince.	It's broken/sprained.
Está dislocado(a)/desgarrado(a).	It's dislocated/torn.

Tiene ...	You have a(n) ...
apendicitis	appendicitis
cistitis	cystitis
gripe	flu
intoxicación	food poisoning
una fractura	fracture
gastritis	gastritis
una hernia	hernia
una inflamación de ...	inflammation of ...
la varicela	measles
neumonía	pneumonia
ciática	sciatica
amigdalitis	tonsilitis
un tumor	tumor
una enfermedad venérea	venereal disease
Está infectado(-a).	It's infected.
Es contagioso(a).	It's contagious.

Treatment

Le daré ...	I'll give you ...
un antiséptico	an antiseptic
un analgésico	a pain killer
Voy a recetarle ...	I'm going to prescribe ...
un tratamiento de antibióticos	a course of antibiotics
unos supositorios	some suppositories
¿Es usted alérgico(a) a algún medicamento?	Are you allergic to any medication?
Tome una pastilla ...	Take one pill ...
cada ... horas	every ... hours
... veces al día	... times a day
antes de las comidas	before meals
Consulte a un médico cuando vuelva a casa.	Consult a doctor when you get home.

GYNECOLOGIST

I have …	**Tengo …** _tengo_
abdominal pains	**dolores abdominales** _dolores abdomeenales_
period pains	**molestias del periodo** _molesteeyas del pereeyodo_
a vaginal infection	**una infección vaginal** _oona eenfektheeyon bakheenal_
I haven't had my period for … months.	**No me ha venido el periodo desde hace … meses.** _no meh a beneedo el pereeyodo desdeh atheh … meses_
I'm on the Pill.	**Estoy tomando la píldora.** _estoy tomando la peeldora_

HOSPITAL

Please notify my family.	**Por favor, avise a mi familia.** _por fabor abeeseh a mee fameeleeya_
What are the visiting hours?	**¿Qué horas de visita tienen?** _keh oras deh beeseeta teeyenen_
I'm in pain.	**Tengo dolores.** _tengo dolores_
I can't eat/sleep.	**No puedo comer/dormir.** _no pwedo komer/dormeer_
When will the doctor come?	**¿Cuándo viene el médico?** _kwando beeyeneh el medeeko_
Which section [ward] is … in?	**¿En qué sala está …?** _en keh sala esta_
I'm visiting …	**Vengo a hacer una visita a …** _bengo a ather oona beeseeta a_

Optician

I'm near- [short-] sighted/far- [long-] sighted.	**Soy miope/hipermétrope.** _soy meeyopeh/eepermetropeh_
I've lost …	**He perdido …** _eh perdeedo_
one of my contact lenses	**una lentilla** _oona lenteel-ya_
my glasses	**mis gafas** _mees gafas_
a lens	**una lente** _oona lenteh_

DENTIST

I have a toothache.	**Tengo dolor de muelas.** *tengo dolor deh mwelas*
This tooth hurts.	**Este diente me duele.** *esteh deeyenteh meh dweleh*
I don't want it extracted.	**No quiero que me lo saque.** *no keeyero keh me lo sakeh*
I've lost a filling/tooth.	**Se me ha caído un empaste/un diente.** *seh meh a kaeedo oon empasteh/* *oon deeyenteh*
Can you repair this denture?	**¿Puede arreglar esta dentadura postiza?** *pwedeh arreglar esta dentadoora posteetha*

YOU MAY HEAR

Voy a ponerle una inyección/ anestesia local.	I'm going to give you an injection/ a local anesthetic/anesthetic.
Le hace falta un empaste/ una funda/una corona.	You need a filling/cap (crown).
Tendré que sacárselo.	I'll have to take it out.
Sólo puedo arreglárselo provisionalmente.	I can only fix it temporarily.
Vuelva dentro de … días.	Come back in … days.
No coma nada durante … horas.	Don't eat anything for … hours

PAYMENT AND INSURANCE

How much do I owe you?	**¿Cuánto le debo?** *kwanto leh debo*
I have insurance.	**Tengo un seguro.** *tengo oon segooro*
Can I have a receipt for my health insurance?	**¿Puede darme un recibo para mi seguro médico?** *pwede darmeh oon rretheebo para mee segooro medeeko*
Would you fill out this health insurance form?	**¿Me rellena este formulario para el seguro médico?** *meh rrel-yena esteh formoolareeyo para el segooro medeeko*
Do you have Form E111/ health insurance?	**¿Tiene el impreso E111/seguro médico?** *teeyeneh el eempreso ehtheeyento onthe/ segooro medeeko*

DICTIONARY
ENGLISH-SPANISH

A

a few unos(-as) pocos(-as)
a little un poco
a lot mucho
a.m. de la mañana
able, to be (also ➤ can, could)
poder/ser capaz de
about (approximately) aproximadamente
above (place) encima de/
por encima de
abroad el extranjero m
abscess abceso m
accept, to aceptar;
do you accept ...? ¿aceptan ...?
access (noun) acceso m
accessories accesorios mpl
accident accidente m
accidentally sin querer
accommodations alojamiento m
accompany to acompañar
accountant contable m/f
ace (cards) as m
acne acné m
across cruzando; al otro lado de
acrylic acrílico(-a)
action film película f de acción
actor/actress actor m/actriz f
adaptor adaptador m
address dirección f
adjoining room
habitación f conjunta
admission charge precio f
de la entrada
adult adulto m
advance, in (booking) con antelación;
(paying) por adelantado
aerial (car/TV) antena f
after (time) después de; (place)
después de
aftershave loción f para después del
afeitado; aftershave m

after-sun lotion aftersun m
afternoon, in the por la tarde
age: what age? ¿qué edad?
ago hace
agree: I agree estoy de acuerdo
air conditioning aire m acondicionado
airline compañía f aérea
air mattress colchón m inflable
airplane avión m
air pump bomba f de aire
airmail correo m aéreo
airport aeropuerto m
air steward azafato(-a) m/f
alcoholic (drink) alcohólico(-a)
all todo
all-night pharmacy farmacia f de
guardia
allergic, to be ser alérgico(-a)
allergy alergia f
allowance permitido m
allowed: is it allowed?
¿está permitido?
almost casi
alone solo(-a)
already ya; todavía
also también
alter, to hacer un arreglo
alternative route ruta f alternativa
always siempre
am: I am soy, estoy
ambassador embajador(a) m/f
ambulance ambulancia f
American (noun/adj.) americano(-a)
American football fútbol americano m
amount cantidad f
amusement arcade salón m
recreativo
anchor, to echar el ancla
and y
anesthetic anestesia f
angling ángulo m
animal animal m
anorak anorak m
another otro(-a)
antibiotics antibióticos mpl
antifreeze anticongelante m
antique antigüedad f
antiques shop tienda f de antigüedades

antiseptic cream crema f antiséptica
any alguno(-a)
anyone alguien
anyone else alguien más
anything cheaper algo más barato
anything else? ¿algo más?
apartment apartamento m
apologize: I apologize pido perdón; me disculpo
apple manzana f
appointment cita f
approximately aproximadamente
April abril m
archery tiro m con arco
architect arquitecto m
area code prefijo m
are you…? ¿está/es usted…?
Argentina Argentina
Argentine (noun/adj.) argentino(-a)
arm brazo m
armbands (swimming) manguitos mpl
around (time) a eso de ; (place) alrededor de
arrange: can you arrange it? ¿puede organizarlo?
arrest, to be under estar detenido(-a)
arrive, to llegar
art; ~ gallery arte m; galería f de arte
artery arteria f
arthritis, to have tener artritis
articulated truck camión m articulado
artificial sweetener edulcorante m artificial
artist artista m/f
as soon as possible lo más pronto; lo antes posible
ashtray cenicero m
ask, to pedir; **asked for …** pedí …
asleep, to be estar dormido(a)
aspirin aspirina f
asthmatic, to be ser asmático(a)
at (place) en; (time) a
at least por lo menos
attack asalto m; (medical) ataque m
attendant asistente m/f
attractive atractivo(-a)
August agosto m
aunt tía f

Australia Australia
Australian (person) australiano(-a) m/f
authenticity autenticidad f
automatic (car, camera) automático(-a)
automobile coche m -
autumn otoño m
avalanche avalancha f
away lejos
awful horrible

B

baby bebé m; **~ food** comida f para bebés; **~ seat** asiento m para bebés; **~sitter** canguro f; **~ wipes** toallitas fpl
baby's bottle biberón m
back (body) espalda f
backache dolor m de espalda
backpacking ir de mochilero
baggage equipaje f; **~ allowance** peso m máximo; **~ check** facturación f de equipajes
baggage claim recogida f de equipajes
bakery panadería f
balcony balcón m
ball pelota f
ballet ballet m
banana plátano m
band (musical group) grupo m
bandage vendas fpl
bank banco m; **~ account** cuenta de banco f; **~ card** tarjeta f de banco; **~ loan** préstamo m
bar bar m
barbecue barbacoa f; parrilla f
barber shop barbería f
basement sótano m
basin palangana f
basket cesta f
bath: to take a darse un baño
bath towel toalla f de baño
bathing hut (cabana) caseta f
bathroom cuarto m de baño
battery pila f; (car) batería f
be, to (also ➤ **am**, **are**) ser/estar; **I am** soy/estoy; **we are** somos/estamos
beach playa f

beard barba f

beautiful bonito(-a)

because porque : ~ **of** por

bed cama f; **I'm going to ~** me voy a la cama

bed and breakfast desayuno y habitación

bedroom dormitorio m

beer cerveza f

before (time) antes de

begin, to (also ➤ **start**) empezar/comenzar

beginner principiante m/f

beginning principio m; comienzo m

beige beige m

belt cinturón m

beneath debajo de

berth litera f

best el/la mejor; los/las mejores

better mejor

between entre

bib babero m

bicycle bicicleta f; **~ rental** alquiler m de bicicletas

bidet bidet m

big grande

bikini bikini m

bill cuenta f; factura f; **put it on the bill** póngalo en la cuenta

binoculars prismáticos mpl

bird pájaro m

birthday cumpleaños m

bishop (chess) alfil m

bite (insect) picadura f

bitten: I've been bitten by a dog me ha mordido un perro

bitter amargo(-a)

black negro m; **~ and white film** (camera) carrete m en blanco y negro

blanket manta f

bleeding, to be estar sangrando(-a)

blind (window) persiana f

blister ampolla f

blocked, to be estar atascado(-a); **the road is blocked** la carretera está cortada

blood sangre f; **~ group** grupo m sanguíneo; **~ pressure** tensión f

blouse blusa f

blow-dry secado m de pelo

blue azul m

blush (rouge) colorete m

boarding embarque m; **~ pass** tarjeta f de embarque

boat bote m

boat trip excursión f en barco

body: parts of the body partes fpl del cuerpo

boil (ailment) forúnculo m

boiler calentador m

bone hueso m

book libro m

book, to reservar; hacer una reserva

booking reserva f; **~ office** oficina f de reservas

booklet of tickets taco m de papeletas

bookstore librería f

boots botas fpl

border (country) frontera f

boring aburrido(-a)

born: I was born in nací en

borrow: may I borrow your…? ¿puedo coger prestado(-a) su…?

botanical garden jardín m botánico

bottle botella f

bow (ship) proa f

bowel intestino m

box of chocolates caja f de bombones

box office taquilla f

boxing boxeo m

boy niño m

boyfriend novio m

bra sujetador m

bread pan m

break, to romper; partir

break-in robo m (con intrusión)

breakage avería f

breakdown (mechanical) avería f; **to have a ~** tener una avería; **~ truck** camión m de reparto

breakfast desayuno m

breast pecho m

breathe, to respirar

breathtaking impresionante

bridge puente m

briefcase maleta f

briefs calzoncillos mpl
brilliant maravilloso(-a)
bring, to traer; llevar
Britain Gran Bretaña
British *(noun/adj.)* británico(-a)
brochure folleto m
broken, to be estar roto(-a); *(bone)*
bronchitis bronquitis f
bronze *(adj)* de bronce
brother hermano m
brown marrón m
browse, to mirar
bruise cardenal m
brush cepillo m
bucket *(pail)* cubo m
buffet car coche m restaurante
build, to construir
building edificio m
built construido(-a)
bureau de change despacho m de cambio; oficina f de cambio; ventanilla f de cambio
burger hamburguesa f; **~ stand** hamburguesería f
burglary *(also > theft)* robo m
burn quemadura f
burnt, to be *(food)* está quemado(-a)
bus autobús m; **~ route** ruta f de autobús; **~ station** estación f de autobuses; **~ stop** parada f de autobús
business: on ~ en viaje de negocios; **~ class** clase f preferente; **~ trip** viaje m de negocios; **~man** hombre m de negocios; **~woman** mujer m de negocios
busy, to be estar ocupado(-a)
but pero
butane gas gas butano m
butcher carnicería f
butter mantequilla f
button botón m
buy, to comprar
by *(time)* para/antes de; **~ car** en coche, **~ credit card** con tarjeta de crédito
bye! ¡adiós!

C

cabana caseta f

cabaret cabaret m
cabin camarote m
cable car teleférico m
café cafetería f
cake *(small)* dulce m; *(big)* pastel m; tarta f; **~ shop** pastelería f
calendar calendario m
call, to *(phone)* llamar (por teléfono); **~ for someone** llamar a alguien; **~ the police!** ¡llame a la policía!; **I'll call back** volveré a llamar
call collect, to llamar a cobro revertido
camcorder cámara f de video
camel hair pelo m de camello
camera cámara f; **~ case** funda de/para la cámara f; **~ store** tienda f de fotografía
camp, to acampar
campbed cama f de cámping f
camping acampada f; **~ equipment** equipo m de cámping
campsite cámping m
can *(noun)* lata f
can I? ¿puedo?; **~ I have?** ¿puedo tomar?
can you help me? ¿puede ayudarme?
can you recommend…? ¿puede recomendar(me/nos)…?
can opener abrelatas m
Canada Canadá
Canadian *(noun/adj.)* canadiense m/f
canal canal m
cancel, to cancelar
candy caramelos mpl
canoe canoa f
canoeing piragüismo m
canyon cañón m
cap *(clothing)* gorra f; *(dental)* funda f
capital city capital f
car coche m; **by ~** en coche; **~ alarm** alarma f (del coche); **~ ferry** transportador m de coches; **~ rental** alquiler de coches; **~ park** *(parking lot)* aparcamiento m; **~ parts** —; **~ pound** depósito m de coches; **~ repairs** reparaciones fpl de coches; **~ wash** lavado m de coches

carafe garrafa f

caravan *(trailer)* roulotte f; **~ site**
(trailer park) cámping m para roulottes

cardphone teléfono m a tarjeta

cards cartas fpl

careful: be careful! ¡tenga(n) cuidado!

carpet *(rug)* alfombra f; *(fitted)*
moqueta f

carrier bag bolsa f

carton cartón m

cash, to cobrar

cash dinero m en metálico; **~ card** tarjeta m del cajero automático; **~ desk**
caja f; **~ machine** *(ATM)* cajero m
automático

casino casino m

cassette cinta f; cassette f

castle castillo m

casualty deptartment *(hospital)*
(servicio m de) urgencias

cat gato(-a) m/f

catch, to *(bus)* coger

cathedral catedral f

cause, to causar

cave cueva f

CD CD m; **~-player** aparato m de
compact (disc)

cent céntimo m

central heating calefacción central f

center of town centro m de la ciudad

ceramics cerámica f

certificate certificado m

chair silla f

chair-lift telesilla m

change *(coins)* cambio m; suelto m;
keep the ~ quédese con el cambio/la
vuelta

change, to *(money, reservation)*
cambiar; *(bus, train)* cambiar de/
hacer trasbordo; *(clothes)* cambiarse

**change: where can I change the
baby?** ¿dónde puedo cambiar al bebé?

change clothes, to cambiarse de ropa

change lanes, to cambiar de carril

changing facilities instalaciones para
cambiar al bebé fpl

changing rooms vestuarios mpl

channel *(sea)* canal m

charcoal carbón m

charge precio m

charter flight vuelo chárter m

cheap barato(-a)

cheaper más barato(-a)

check *(bill)* cuenta f [factura f]

checkbook [cheque book] talonario m
de cheques

check: please check the ... por favor,
compruebe ...

check guarantee card tarjeta f de
crédito/débito

check in, to facturar

check-in desk mostrador de facturación m

checked *(patterned)* de cuadros

checkers damas fpl

check out, to *(hotel)* salir

checkout caja f

cheers! ¡salud!

cheese queso m

chess ajedrez m; **~ set** juego de ajedrez
m

chest *(body)* pecho m

chewing gum chicle m

chickenpox sarampión m

child niño(-a) m/f; hijo(-a)

child's seat silla f para niños; *(in car)*
asiento m para niños

children niños mpl; hijos mpl

children's meals comidas fpl para niños

Chinese *(cuisine)* chino(-a)

chips *(UK)* patatas fritas fpl

chips *(U.S.)* patatas fritas fpl de bolsa

chocolate chocolate m; *(flavour)* (de)
chocolate; **~ bar** barra f de chocolate;
box of ~ caja f de bombones

chocolate ice cream helado de
chocolate

chop *(meat)* chuleta f

Christmas Navidad f

church iglesia f

cigarettes, pack of
paquete de tabaco m

cigars puros mpl

cinema *(movie theater)* cine m

circle *(balcony)* anfiteatro m

city wall muralla f de la ciudad

clean *(adj)* limpio(-a)
clean, to limpiar
cleaned: I'd like my shoes cleaned quiero que me limpien los zapatos
cleaner limpiador(a) m/f;
cleaning limpieza f; **~ utensils** artículos de limpieza mpl; **~ lotion** loción limpiadora f; **~ solution (for lenses)** solución limpiadora f
close *(near)* cerca
close, to cerrar
clothes ropa f; **~ line** tendedero m
clothing store tienda de ropa f
cloudy, to be estar nublado
clown payaso m
clubs *(golf)* palos mpl
coach autobús m; *(train compartment)* compartimento m; **~ bay** andén m; **~ station** estación f de autobuses
coast costa f
coat abrigo m
coathanger percha f
cockroach cucaracha f
code *(area/dialling)* prefijo m
coffee café m
coin moneda f
cold *(adj)* frío(-a); *(flu)* resfriado m
cold meats fiambres mpl
collapse: he's collapsed se ha desmayado
collect, to recoger
college universidad f
color color m; **~ film** carrete m de color
comb peine m
come back to volver
comedy comedia f
commission comisión f
communion comunión f
compact camera cámara f compacta
compact disc compact disc m
company *(companionship)* compañía f; *(business)* empresa f
compartment *(train)* compartimento m
compass brújula f
complaint queja fpl; **to make a ~** hacer una reclamación
computer ordenador m

concert concierto m; **~ hall** sala f de conciertos
concession *(reduction)* descuento m
concussion, to have a sufrir una conmoción cerebral
conditioner suavizante/acondicionador m
condoms condones mpl
conductor director(a) m/f
confirm, to confirmar
confirmation confirmación f
congratulations! ¡felicidades!
connection *(transport)* enlace m
conscious, to be estar consciente
constipation estreñimiento m
consulate consulado m
consult, to consultar
consultant *(medical)* asesor(a) m/f médico(-a)
contact, to ponerse en contacto con
contact lenses lentillas fpl
contact-lens fluid líquido m para las lentillas
contagious, to be ser contagioso(-a)
contain, to llevar/tener; contener
contemporary dance danza f contemporánea
contraceptive anticonceptivo m
convenient conveniente
cook cocinero(-a) m/f
cook, to cocinar
cooker cocina f
cookie galleta f
cooking *(cuisine)* cocina f
copper cobre m
copy copia f
corked *(wine)* con sabor a corcho
corner esquina f
correct correcto(-a)
cosmetics cosméticos mpl
cot cuna f
cottage casita f
cotton algodón m; **~ wool** *(absorbent cotton)* algodón m
cough tos f; **~ syrup** jarabe m para la tos
cough, to toser
could I have...? ¿puedo tomar...?
counter mostrador m

country *(nation)* país m
country music música f country
countryside campo m
couple *(pair)* pareja f
courier *(guide)* guía m/f
course *(meal)* plato m
cousin primo(-a) m/f
cover *(lid)* tapa f
cover charge *(nightclub)* consumición f mínima; *(restaurant)* cubierto m
craft shop tienda f de artesanía
cramps retortijones mpl
crash: I've had a crash he tenido un accidente
creaks: the bed creaks la cama cruje
crèche guardería f
credit card tarjeta f de crédito; ~ **number** número m de tarjeta de crédito
credit status estado m de cuentas
credit, in saldo m positivo
crockery vajilla f
cross *(crucifix)* cruz f
cross, to *(road)* cruzar
cross-country skiing track pista f de esquí de montaña
crossing *(boat)* travesía f
crossroad cruce m
crowded abarrotado
crown *(dental)* corona f
cruise crucero m
crutches muletas fpl
crystal vidrio m
cuisine cocina f
cup taza f
cupboard armario m
curlers rulos mpl
currency moneda/divisa f
currency exchange office oficina f de cambio
curtains cortinas fpl
cushion cojín m
customs *(control)* aduana f; ~ **declaration** declaración f para la aduana
cut corte m
cut and blow-dry cortar y secar
cut and style cortar y peinar
cut glass vidrio tallado m

cutlery cubiertos mpl
cycle helmet casco m para bicicletas
cycle path carril m para bicicletas
cycle route ruta f para bicicletas
cycling ciclismo m
cyclist ciclista m/f
cystitis cistitis f

D

daily diariamente
damaged, to be estar estropeado(-a)
damp *(noun)* humedad; *(adj.)* húmedo (-a), mojado(-a)
dance *(performance)* baile m
dancing, to go ir a bailar
dangerous peligroso(-a)
dark oscuro(-a)
daughter hija f
dawn amanecer m
day día m; ~ **ticket** tarjeta f para un día; ~ **trip** excursión f
dead muerto(-a); *(battery)* descargado(-a)
deaf, to be ser sordo(-a)
dear *(greeting)* querido(-a)
December diciembre m
decide: we haven't decided yet no nos hemos decidido todavía
deck *(ship)* cubierta f
deck chair tumbona f
declare, to declarar
deduct, to *(money)* deducir
deep hondo(-a), profundo(-a)
deep-freeze congelar
defrost, to descongelar
degrees *(temperature)* grados mpl
delay retraso m
delicate delicado(-a)
delicatessen charcutería f
delicious *(food)* delicioso(-a)
deliver, to repartir
denim tela vaquera f
dental floss hilo m dental
dentist dentista m/f
dentures dentadura postiza f
deodorant desodorante m
depart, to *(train, bus)* salir

department *(store)* sección f; **~ store** grandes almacenes mpl

departure *(train)* salida f; **~ lounge** sala de embarque f

depend: it depends on depende de

deposit señal f; fianza f

describe, to describir

design *(dress)* diseño m

designer diseñador(a) m/f

destination destino m

detergent detergente m

develop, to *(photos)* revelar

diabetes diabetes f

diabetic diabético(-a); **to be ~** ser diabético(a)

diagnosis diagnosis f

dialing (area) code prefijo m

diamond diamante m

diamonds *(cards)* diamantes mpl

diapers pañales mpl

diarrhea diarrea f; **to have ~** tener diarrea

dice dado m

dictionary diccionario m

diesel diesel

diet, I'm on a estoy a régimen

different, something algo diferente

dine, to cenar

dinghy lancha hinchable f

dining car coche restaurante m

dining room comedor m

dinner jacket chaqueta f de esmóking

dinner, to have cenar

direct directo(-a)

direct, to indicar

direct-dial telephone teléfono m de llamada directa

direction dirección f; **in the ~ of** de camino a

director *(film, company)* director(a) m/f

directory *(telephone)* guía f telefónica

Directory Enquiries Información f

dirty sucio(-a)

disabled *(n)* minusválido(-a)

disco discoteca f

discount descuento m; **can you offer me a ~** ¿puede hacerme un descuento?; **is there a ~ for children?** ¿hacen descuento a los niños?

disgusting asqueroso(-a)

dish *(meal)* plato m

dish cloth balleta f

dishes *(crockery)* vajilla f

dishwashing detergent lavavajillas m

disk film disquete m

dislocated, to be estar dislocado(a)

display cabinet/case vitrina f

disposable camera cámara de usar y tirar f

distilled water agua destilada f

district distrito m

disturb: don't disturb no molestar; no moleste

dive, to tirarse de cabeza

diving equipment equipo m de buceo

diversion desvío m

divorced, to be estar divorciado(-a)

dizzy, to feel estar mareado

do you accept …? ¿acceptan …?

do you have…? ¿tiene…?

do: things to do cosas que hacer

dock muelle m

doctor médico(-a)/doctor(a) m/f

does anyone here speak English? ¿Hay alguien que hable inglés?

dog perro m

doll muñeca f

door puerta f

dosage dosificación f

double doble

double bed cama f de matrimonio

double room habitación f doble

down abajo

downstairs abajo; en el piso de abajo

downtown area centro m

dozen docena f

draft *(wind)* corriente f

drama drama m

draughts damas fpl

dress vestido m

drink copa f; bebida f

drinking water agua potable f
drip: the faucet [tap] drips el grifo gotea
drive, to conducir
driver conductor(a) m/f
driver's licence [driving license] carnet/permiso de conducir m
drop off, to (*someone*) dejar
drowning: someone is drowning alguien se está ahogando
drugstore droguería f
drunk borracho(-a)
dry cleaner tintorería f
dry clothes, to secar la ropa
dry clean, to limpiar en seco
dubbed, to be estar doblado(-a)
dummy (*baby's*) chupete m
during durante
dusty polvoriento(-a)
duty-free goods artículos mpl libres de impuestos
duty-free shopping compra f de artículos libres de impuestos
duvet edredón m nórdico

E

each: how much each? ¿a cuánto cada uno(-a)?
ear (*internal*) oído m; (*external*) oreja f
ear drops gotas para el oído fpl
earache dolor m de oídos
earlier antes
early temprano
east este m
Easter Pascua f
eat, to comer; **places to ~** sitios para comer
economical económico(-a)
economy class clase f turista
eggs huevos mpl
eight ocho
eighteen dieciocho
eighty ochenta
either … or … o … o …
elastic (*adj*) elástico(-a)
electric shaver máquina f de afeitar eléctrica

electrician electricista m
electricity electricidad f
electric meter contador m de la luz
elevator ascensor m
eleven once
else, something ~ algo más
embark, to (*boat*) embarcar
embarkation point punto m de embarque
embassy embajada f
emerald esmeralda f
emergency emergencia f; **it's an ~** es una emergencia; **~ exit** salida f de emergencia
emergency room servicio m de urgencias
enamel esmalte m
end, to terminar
end: at the ~ al final
engaged, to be estar prometido(-a)
engine motor m
engineer ingeniero m/f
England Inglaterra
English (*noun/adj.*) inglés(a) m/f
English-speaking que hable inglés
enjoy, to gustar; disfrutar; pasarlo bien
enlarge, to (*photos*) ampliar
enough bastante
enquiry desk ventanilla f de información
ensuite bathroom cuarto de baño dentro de la habitación m
entertainment: what ~ is there? ¿qué espectáculos hay?
entirely completamente
entrance fee precio m de entrada
entry visa visado m de entrada
envelope sobre m
epileptic epiléptico(-a)
equally igualmente
equipment (*sports*) equipo m
error error m
escalator escalera f mecánica
essential fundamental, básico(-a)
estate agent agente m/f inmobiliario(-a)
EU UE f
euro (€) euro m
evening dress traje m de noche

evening, in the por la noche
events espectáculos mpl
every day todos los días
every week todas las semanas
examination *(medical)* reconocimiento m
example, for por ejemplo
except excepto
excess baggage exceso m de equipaje
exchange rate tasa f de cambio
exchange, to cambiar
excursion excursión
excuse me disculpe
exhausted, to be estar exhausto(-a)
exhibition exposición f
exit salida f
expected, to be suponerse
expensive caro(-a)
expiration [expiry] date fecha de caducidad f
expire: when does it ~? ¿cuándo caduca?
exposure *(photos)* fotos fpl
express *(special delivery)* exprés, urgente
extension extensión f
extension cord alargador m
extra *(additional)* más
extremely sumamente
eye ojo m
eyeliner delineador m de ojos
eyeshadow sombra f de ojos

F

fabric *(material)* tela f
face cara f
facial limpieza f de cutis/cara
facilities instalaciones fpl
factor factor m
factory outlet almacén m
faint, to feel sentirse desfallecer
fairground feria f
fall *(season)* otoño m
fall: he's had a fall se ha caído
family familia f
famous famoso(-a)
fan *(air)* ventilador m

fan: I'm a fan of soy un fan/admirador(a)
far lejos; **how ~ is it?** ¿a qué distancia está?
fare tarifa f
farm granja f
far-sighted hipermétrope
fashionable, to be estar de moda
fast rápido(-a)
fast food comida f rápida; **~ restaurant** restaurante m de comida rápida
fast, to be *(clock)* estar adelantado
fast: you were driving too fast conducías demasiado deprisa
fat *(substance)* grasa f
father padre m
faucet grifo m
fault: it's my/your fault es culpa mía/vuestra
faulty defectuoso(-a)
favorite favorito(-a)
fax *(facilities, machine)* fax m
fax bureau papelería f con servicio de fax
February febrero m
feed, to dar de comer
feeding bottle biberón m
feel ill, to sentise enfermo(a)
feel sick, to marearse
female mujer, hembra
fence valla f
ferry ferry, transbordador m
festival festival m
fetch help! ¡vaya a buscar ayuda!
feverish, to feel tener fiebre
few pocos(as)
fiancé(e) prometido(-a) m/f
field campo m
fifteen quince
fifth quinto(a)
fifty cincuenta
fight *(brawl)* pelea f
fill out, to rellenar
filling *(dental)* empaste m; *(sandwich)* relleno m
film *(movie)* película f; *(camera)* carrete m; **~ speed** velocidad f del carrete

filter filtro m; **~ paper** *(for coffee)* papel m de filtro

fine *(penalty)* multa f; *(well)* bien

finger dedo m

fire: there's a fire! ¡hay un incendio!; **~ alarm** alarma f contra incendios; **~ brigade** bomberos mpl; **~ escape** salida f de incendios; **~ extinguisher** extintor m; **~ lighters** pastillas para encender fuegos fpl; **~place** chimenea f; **~wood** leña f

first *(adj.)* primer(a)

first class (de) primera clase

first floor *(U.K.)* primera f planta

first floor *(U.S.)* planta f baja

first-aid kit botiquín m

fishing rod caña f de pescar

fishing, to go ir de pesca/a pescar

fishmonger pescadería f

fit, to *(clothes)* estar/quedar bien

fitting room probador m

five cinco

fix: can you fix it? ¿puede arreglarlo?

flag bandera f

flannel *(washing)* manopla f; *(material)* franela f

flash *(camera)* flash m

flashlight linterna f

flat *(tire [tyre])* pinchazo m

flavor: what flavors do you have? ¿qué sabores tiene?

flea pulga f; **~ market** mercadillo m

flight vuelo m; **~ number** número m de vuelo; **~ attendant** azafato(-a) m/f

flip-flops chancletas fpl

flood inundación f

floor *(story [storey])* piso m; planta f

floor mop fregona f

floor show espectáculo m de cabaret

florist floristería f

flour harina f

flower flor f

flu gripe f

fluent: to speak fluent Spanish hablar español fluido

fly *(insect)* mosca f

fly, to volar

foggy, to be haber niebla

folk art arte m popular

folk music música f folk

follow, to seguir

food comida f; **~ poisoning** intoxicación f

foot pie m

football *(soccer)* fútbol m

footpath sendero

for a day por un día

for a week por una semana

forecast pronóstico m

foreign extranjero(-a); **~ currency** divisa/moneda f extranjera

forest bosque m

forget, to olvidar

fork tenedor m; *(in road)* bifurcación f

form impreso m, formulario m

formal dress vestido m de etiqueta

fortnight dos semanas, medio mes

fortunately afortunadamente

forty cuarenta

foundation *(makeup)* base f

fountain fuente f

four cuatro

four-door car coche m de cuatro puertas

four-wheel drive tracción f a las cuatro ruedas

fourteen catorce

fourth cuarto(-a)

foyer *(hotel/theater)* vestíbulo m

frame *(glasses)* montura f

France Francia

free *(available)* libre; *(of charge)* gratis, sin pagar

freezer congelador m

frequent: how frequent? ¿con qué frecuencia?

frequently con frecuencia

fresh fresco(-a)

Friday viernes m

fried frito(-a)

friend amigo(a) m/f

friendly amistoso(-a)

fries patatas fpl fritas

frightened, to be estar aterrorizado(-a)

fringe flequillo m

from de; **~ ... to ...** *(time)* de ... a ...

front door puerta f principal; **~ key** llave f de la puerta principal

frosty, to be haber helado
frozen congelado(-a)
fruit juice zumo m de fruta
frying pan sartén f
fuel *(gasoline)* combustible m
full board *(A.P.)* pensión f completa
full insurance seguro m a todo riesgo
fun, to have divertirse
funny *(amusing)* divertido(-a); *(odd)* raro(-a)
furniture muebles mpl
further: how much further to ¿cuánto falta para llegar a…?
fuse fusible m; ~ **box** caja f de fusibles; ~ **wire** cable m de fusible

---

G

game *(toy)* juego m
garage garaje m
garbage bags bolsas fpl de basura
garden jardín m
gardening jardinería f
gas: I smell gas! ¡huelo a gas!; ~ **bottle** bombona f de butano
gas permeable lenses lentes fpl permeables
gas station gasolinera f
gasoline gasolina f ~ **can (gas can)** lata de gasolina f
gastritis gastritis f
gate *(airport)* puerta f
gay club club m gay
general delivery *(poste restante)* reparto general m
genuine auténtico(-a)
geology geología f
get, to: ~ **by** pasar; ~ **off** *(transport)* bajarse (de); ~ **out** *(of vehicle)* salir; ~ **to** llegar a; **how do I get to…?** ¿cómo se llega a…?; ¿cómo se va a…?
gift regalo m; ~ **shop** tienda f de regalos, bazar f
girl niña f
girlfriend novia f
give, to dar
give way, to *(on road)* dejar/ceder paso
glass *(wine)* vaso m, copa f

glasses *(optical)* gafas fpl
gliding vuelo m sin motor
glossy finish *(photos)* acabado m con brillo
go, to ir; **let's go!** ¡vamos!; **go away!** ¡váyase!; ~ **back** *(turn around)* volver; ~ **for a walk** ir de paseo; ~ **out** *(in evening)* salir; ~ **shopping** ir de compras; **where does this bus ~?** ¿a dónde va este autobús?
goggles gafas fpl de bucear
gold oro m; ~**-plate** baño m de oro
golf golf m; ~ **course** campo m de golf
good *(adj)* bueno(-a); ~ **afternoon** buenas tardes; ~ **evening** buenas tardes; ~ **morning** buenas días; ~ **night** buenas noches
good value, to be estar muy bien de precio
good-bye adiós
gorge garganta f
got: have you got any …? tiene(n)…?
grade *(fuel)* grado m
gram gramo m
grammar gramática f
grandparents abuelos mpl
grapes uvas fpl
grass hierba f
gratuity *(tip)* propina f
gray [grey] gris m
greasy *(hair)* graso(-a)
green verde m
greengrocer verdulería f
greetings saludos mpl
grilled a la parrilla
grocery store tienda f de alimentación
ground *(camping)* suelo m
groundcloth [groundsheet] aislante m para el suelo
ground floor planta f baja
group grupo m
guarantee garantía f
guarantee: is it guaranteed? ¿tiene garantía?
guide *(person)* guía m/f turístico(-a)
guidebook guía f

guided tour visita f con guía
guitar guitarra f
gum *(mouth)* encía f
gynecologist ginecólogo(a) m/f

hair pelo/cabello m; **~ brush** cepillo m (para el pelo); **~ dryer** secador m; **~ gel** fijador m; **~ mousse** espuma (para el pelo) f; **~ spray** espray (para el pelo) m
haircut corte m de pelo
hairdresser *(person)* peluquero(-a) m/f; *(salon)* **(ladies/men)** peluquería f de señoras/caballeros
half, a la mitad
half board *(M.A.P.)* media pensión f
half fare tarifa reducida f
half past *(time)* y media
hammer martillo m
hand mano f; **~ cream** crema f para las manos; **~ luggage** equipaje m de mano; **~ towel** toalla f de las manos; **~ washable** se puede lavar a mano
handbag bolso m
handicap *(golf)* hándicap m
handicapped, to be ser minusválido(-a)
handicrafts trabajos mpl de artesanía
handkerchief pañuelo m
handle *(cup)* asa f; *(drawer/door)* tirador m
hang-gliding vuelo m con ala delta
hanger percha f
hangover *(n)* resaca f
happen: what happened? ¿qué ocurrió?
happy: I'm not happy with the service no estoy contento(-a) con el servicio
harbor bahía f
hard shoulder *(road)* arcén m
hat sombrero m
hatchback coche m con tres/cinco puertas
have, to tener
have to, to *(must)* tener que

hayfever fiebre f del heno; alergia f primaveral
head cabeza f
head, to ~ for *(go to)* dirigirse
head waiter metre m
headache dolor m de cabeza
headband cinta f del pelo
health food store tienda f de alimentos naturales
health insurance seguro m médico
hear, to oír
hearing aid aparato para el oído m
heart corazón m; **~ attack** infarto m
hearts *(cards)* corazones mpl
heater calentador m
heating calefacción f
heavy pesado(-a)
height altura f
helicopter helicóptero m
hello hola
help, to ayudar; **can you help me?** ¿puede ayudarme?
hemorrhoids hemorroides fpl
her *(adj.)* su; *(pron.)* ella
here aquí
hernia hernia f
hers suyo(-a); **it's ~** es suyo(-a), es de ella
high alto(-a)
high street *(main)* calle f mayor
high tide marea f alta
highlight, to *(hair)* hacer mechas
highway autopista f
hike *(walk)* paseo m
hiking senderismo m
hill colina f
him él
his suyo(-a); su
history historia f
hitchhike, to hacer autostop
hitchhiking autostop m
HIV-positive seropositivo(-a)
hobby *(pastime)* pasatiempo m
hockey hockey m
hold, to *(contain)* contener
hold on, to esperar
hole *(in clothes)* agujero m
home, to go ir a casa

homosexual *(adj.)* homosexual
honeymoon, to be on estar de luna de miel
horse caballo m
horseracing carreras fpl de caballos
horseback trip excursión f a caballo
hospital hospital m
hot caliente; **~ spring** fuente f termal; **~ water** agua f caliente; **~ water bottle** bolsa f de agua caliente
hot dog perrito m caliente
hotel hotel m; **~ reservation** reservas de hotel
hour hora f; **in an ~** dentro de una hora
hours horas fpl; *(open)* **hours** horas fpl (de apertura)
house casa f
housewife ama f de casa
hovercraft aerodeslizador m
how? ¿cómo?
how are you? ¿cómo está?
how far? ¿a qué distancia?
how long? ¿cuánto tiempo?
how many? ¿cuántos(-as)?
how much? ¿cuánto?
how often? ¿cada cuánto tiempo?
how old? ¿qué edad?
however sin embargo
hundred cien
hungry, to be tener hambre
hurry, to be in a tener prisa
hurt, to be estar herido(-a); **it hurts** duele
husband marido m

I

I'd like ... quiero ...
I'll have ... tomaré ...
I've lost ... he perdido ...
ice hielo m; **~ dispenser** máquina f de hielo m; **~ pack** bolsa de hielo f; **~ rink** pista f de hielo
ice cream helado m; **~ café/parlor** heladería f; **~ cone** cucurucho m de helado
icy, to be haber hielo
identification identificación f
ill, to be estar enfermo(-a)
illegal, to be ser ilegal
illness enfermedad f
imitation de imitación
immediately inmediatamente
impressive impresionante
in *(place)* en; *(time)* dentro de
in-law: mother-in-law suegra f; **father-in-law** suegro m
included: is ... included? ¿va ... incluido(-a)?
Indian *(cuisine)* indio(-a)
indicate, to indicar
indigestion indigestión f
indoor cubierto(-a); **~ pool** piscina f cubierta
inexpensive no muy caro(-a)
infected, to be estar infectado(-a)
infection infección f
inflammation inflamación f
informal *(dress)* informal
information información f; **~ desk** ventanilla f de información; **~ office** oficina f de información
injection inyección f
injured, to be estar herido(-a); *(athletes)* estar lesionado(-a)
insect insecto m; **~ bite** picadura f; **~ repellent/spray** repelente para insectos/espray m
inside dentro
insist: I insist insisto
insomnia insomnio m
instant coffee café instantáneo m
instead of en lugar de
instructions instrucciones fpl
instructor instructor(a) m/f
insulin insulina f
insurance seguro m; **~ certificate** certificado del seguro m; **~ claim** reclamación del seguro f; **~ company** compañía de seguros f
interest *(hobby)* pasatiempo m
interesting interesante
international internacional
International Student Card Carnet m Internacional de Estudiante
interpreter intérprete m/f

intersection cruce m
interval intervalo m
into dentro, en
introduce oneself, to presentarse
invitation invitación f
invite, to invitar
involved, to be estar involucrado(-a)
Ireland Irlanda
Irish *(noun/adj.)* irlandés(a) m/f
iron *(electrical)* plancha f
iron, to planchar
is there…? ¿hay…?
island isla f
it is… es…
Italian *(adj.)* italiano(-a)
itch: it itches pica
itemized bill cuenta f detallada

jack *(cards)* sota f
jacket chaqueta f
jam mermelada f
jammed, to be estar atascado(-a)
January enero m
jaw mandíbula f
jeans vaqueros mpl
jellyfish medusa f
jet lag, I have estoy sufriendo el cambio de horario
jet ski moto acuática f
jeweler *(store)* joyería f
Jewish *(adj.)* judío(-a)
job: what's your job? ¿en qué trabaja?
jogging, to go ir a hacer footing
join: may we join you ¿podemos ir con ustedes?
joint *(body)* articulación f; *(meat)* pierna f
joint passport pasaporte m conjunto
joke chiste m
journey viaje m
jug *(water)* jarra f
July julio m
jumper jersey m
junction *(exit)* salida f; *(intersection)* cruce m
June junio m

kaolin caolín m
keep: keep the change quédese con el cambio/la vuelta
kerosene queroseno m
kerosene stove hornillo m de queroseno
ketchup ketchup m
kettle hervidor m
key llave f; ~ **ring** llavero m
kiddie pool piscina f infantil
kidney riñón m
kilo(gram) kilo m
kilometer kilómetro m
kind *(pleasant)* amable
kind: what kind of… ¿qué tipo/clase de…?
king *(cards, chess)* rey m
kiosk quiosco m
kiss, to besar
kitchen cocina f
kitchen paper rollo m de cocina
knapsack mochila f
knee rodilla f
knickers bragas fpl
knife cuchillo m
knight *(chess)* caballo m
know: I don't know no sé
kosher kosher

label etiqueta f
lace encaje m
ladies *(toilet)* servicio/aseo m de señoras
lake lago m
lamp lámpara f
landing *(house)* descansillo m
landlord/landlady casero(-a) m/f
language course curso m de idiomas
large grande
last último(-a)
last, to *(time)* durar
late tarde; *(delayed)* con retraso
later más tarde
laugh, to reír
laundromat lavandería f

laundry service servicio m de lavandería
laundry soap detergente m en polvo
lavatory baño m
lawyer abogado(-a) m/f
laxative laxante m/f
lead, to (road) dirigirse; ir
lead-free (gas) sin plomo
leader (of group) líder m/f
leaflet folleto m
leak, to (roof/pipe) gotear
learn, to (language) aprender
leather cuero m
leave, to (depart) salir; (drop off) dejar; **leave me alone!** ¡déjeme en paz!; **I've left my bag in…** me he dejado el bolso en…; **are there any left?** ¿quedan algunos/algunas?
lecturer (at conference) conferenciante m/f; (occupation) profesor(a) m/f
left, on the a la izquierda
left-hand side en el lado izquierdo
left-handed zurdo(-a)
leg pierna f
legal, to be ser legal
leggings mallas fpl
lemon limón m
lemonade (soda) gaseosa f; (real lemons) limonada f
lend, to: could you lend me …? ¿podría prestarme …?
length longitud f
lens (camera) objetivo m; (glasses) lente m/f; (contact) lentilla f; **~ cap** (camera) tapa f del objetivo
lesbian club bar m de lesbianas; discoteca f de lesbianas
less menos
lesson clase f
let, to: please let me know por favor, hágamelo saber
letter carta f, **by ~** por carta
level (flat) nivel m
library biblioteca f
license plate number número m de matrícula
lie down, to echarse/tumbarse
lifeboat bote m salvavidas

lifeguard socorrista m/f
life jacket chaleco m salvavidas
life preserver [belt] flotador m
light (color) claro(-a); (cigarette) fuego m; (electric) luz f; (weight) ligero(-a); **~bulb** bombilla f
lighter (cigarette) encendedor m, mechero m
lighthouse faro m
like: I like it me gusta; **I don't like it** no me gusta; **I'd like …** quiero …
like this (similar) así
limousine limusina f
line (subway/metro) línea f; (profession) campo m
linen lino m
lip labio m
lipsalve protector m de labios
lipstick barra f de labios
liqueur licor m
liter litro m
little (small) pequeño(-a); **a ~** un poco
live, to vivir; **~ together** vivir juntos
liver hígado m
living room salón m/sala f de estar
lobby (theater/hotel) vestíbulo m; hall m
local (area) local
local anesthetic anestesia m local
local road carretera f comarcal
lock (door) pestillo m; (canal) exclusa f
locked, to be estar cerrado(-a) (con llave)
locker taquilla f
lollipop chupachup m
long (clothing) largo(-a); (time) mucho (tiempo), **how long?** ¿cuánto tiempo?; **how much longer?** ¿cuánto tiempo más?
long-distance bus autobús m de largo recorrido
long-distance call conferencia f
long-sighted hipermétrope
look, to mirar; **~ for** buscar; **I'm looking forward to it** me hace mucha ilusión; **I'm just looking** (browsing) sólo estoy mirando
look after: please look after my case for a minute por favor, cuídeme la maleta un momento

look, to have a (*check*) echarle un vistazo

loose ancho(-a), suelto(-a)

lose, to perder; **I've lost...** he perdido...

lost pérdida f

lost-and-found [lost property office] oficina de objetos perdidos f

lotion loción f

lots muchos(-as)

loud: it's too ~ (*noise*) es demasiado alto(-a)

louder más alto

love: I love you te quiero/amo

low-fat de bajo contenido graso

lower berth litera f de abajo

luck: good luck buena suerte

luggage (*baggage*) equipaje m; **~ allowance** límite m de equipaje permitido; **~ locker** taquilla f; **~ tag** etiqueta f de equipaje; **~ carts [trolleys]** carritos mpl para el equipaje

lumpy (*mattress*) con bultos

lunch almuerzo m, comida f

lung pulmón m

luxury lujo m

M

machine washable se puede lavar a máquina

madam señora f

made of, what is it ¿de qué está hecho?

magazine revista f

maid chica f de servicio

maiden name nombre m de soltera

mail correo m

mail, to mandar por correo

mailbox buzón m

main principal; **~ course** segundo m plato; **~ train station** estación f de tren central; **~ street** calle principal f

mains (*services*) red f

make (*brand*) marca f

make-up (*cosmetics*) maquillaje m

make: to make tea/coffee hacer té/café

male hombre m, varón m

mallet mazo m

man hombre m

manager encargado/administrador m

manicure manicura f

manual (*car*) coche m con cambio de marchas manual

many muchos(-as)

map mapa m

March marzo m

margarine margarina f

market mercado m; **~ day** día m de mercado

married, to be estar casado(-a)

mascara rímel m

mask (*diving*) gafas fpl de bucear

mass misa f

massage masaje m

match (*game*) partido m

matches cerillas fpl

material material m; (*fabric*) tela f

matinée matiné f

matte finish (*photos*) acabado m mate

matter: it doesn't matter no importa; **what's the matter?** ¿qué pasa?

mattress (air) colchón m (inflable)

May mayo m

may I ...? ¿puedo ...?

maybe quizás

me mí

meal comida f

mean, to significar

measles varicela f

measure, to medir

measurement medida f

meat carne f

medical certificate certificado m médico

medicaton [medicine] medicina f; medicamento m

medium (*regular*) mediano(-a); (*steak*) medio hecho(-a)

meet, to quedar; encontrarse; **pleased to meet you** encantado(-a) de conocerle/a

meeting place [point] lugar m de encuentro

member (*of club*) socio(-a) m/f

men (toilets) servicio/aseo m de caballeros
mend, to arreglar
menu menú m
message recado m
metal metal m
meter (taxi) taxímetro m
metro (subway) metro m; **~ station** estación f de metro
Mexican (person) mejicano(-a)
Mexico Méjico
microwave (oven) microondas m
midday medio día m
midnight doce fpl de la noche
might: I might not puede que no
migraine jaqueca f; migraña f
mileage kilometraje m
milk leche f; **with ~** con leche; **~ of magnesia** leche de magnesio f
million un millón
mind: do you mind? ¿le importa?;
I've changed my mind he cambiado de opinión
mine mío(-a), míos(as); **it's ~** es mío(-a)
mineral water agua f mineral
minibar minibar m
minibus microbús m
minimart autoservicio m
minimum (n) mínimo m
minister pastor m
minor road carretera f secundaria
minute minuto m
mirror espejo m
miss, to (train/bus) perder; (stop) pasarse de
missing, to be faltar; (person) desaparecer
mistake error m
mittens mitones mpl
modern moderno(-a); **~ art** arte m moderno
moisturizing cream crema f hidratante
monastery monasterio m
Monday lunes m
money dinero m
money order giro m postal
money-belt cinturón-monedero m
month mes m

monthly ticket tarjeta f para un mes
monument monumento m
moor, to atracar
moped ciclomotor m
more más; **I'd like some more** quiero un poco más (de)
morning, in the por la mañana
Morocco Marruecos
moslem (adj.) musulmán(a)
mosquito mosquito m;
~ bite picadura f de mosquito
mother madre f
motion sickness mareo m
motorbike moto f
motorboat motora f
motorway autopista f
mountain montaña f; **~ bike** bicicleta f de montaña; **~ pass** paso m de montaña; **~ range** cordillera f
mountaineering montañismo m
moustache bigote m
mouth boca f; **~ ulcer** llaga f
move, to (change) mudarse de; **don't move him!** ¡no le muevan!
movie theater cine m
Mr. sr. (señor)
Mrs. sra. (señora)
much mucho
mugging atraco m
multiple trip (ticket) bonobús m
multiplex cinema multicine m
mumps paperas fpl
muscle músculo m
museum museo m
music música f; **~ box** caja f de música, **~ store** tienda f de discos
musical (n) musical m
musician músico(-a) m/f
Muslim (person) musulmán(a) m/f
must: I must debo
mustard mostaza f
my mi, mis
myself: I'll do it myself lo haré yo mismo

nail polish esmalte m de uñas

nail scissors tijeras fpl para las uñas
name nombre m; **my ~ is ...** me llamo
...; **what's your ~?** ¿cómo se llama?
napkin *(serviette)* servilleta f
nappies pañales mpl
narrow estrecho(-a)
national nacional
national health seguridad f social
nationality nacionalidad f
nature reserve reserva f natural
nausea náuseas fpl
navy blue azul m marino
near cerca de
nearby cerca, por aquí
nearest el/la más cercano(-a); el/la
próximo(-a)
near-sighted miope
necessary necesario(-a)
neck cuello m
need: I need to ... necesito ...
needle aguja f
negative *(photo)* negativo m
neighbor vecino(-a) m/f
nephew sobrino m
nerve nervio m
nervous system sistema m nervioso
never nunca
never mind no tiene importancia
New Year año m nuevo
New Zealand Nueva Zelanda
newspaper periódico m
newsstand [newsagent] kiosko m de
prensa; puesto m de periódicos
next próximo(-a); **~ stop!** ¡próxima
parada!
next to al lado de
nice agradable, bonito(-a)
niece sobrina f
night noche f; **at ~** por la noche,; **per ~**
por noche; **~ porter** portero m de noche
nightclub club nocturno m
nightgown camisón m de noche
nine nueve
nineteen diecinueve
ninety noventa
no no
no one nadie
noisy ruidoso(-a)

non-alcoholic sin alcohol
non-smoking *(adj)* para no fumador;
~ area zona de no-fumadores f
none ninguno(-a)
noon mediodía m; doce del mediodía
normal normal
north norte m
Northern Ireland Irlanda del Norte
nose nariz f
not that one ese(-a) no
note billete m
notebook cuaderno m
nothing: nothing else nada más;
nothing to declare nada que declarar
notice board tablón m de anuncios
notify, to notificar
not yet todavía no
November noviembre m
now ahora
nudist beach playa f nudista
number número m; *(telephone)*
número (de teléfono); **sorry, wrong ~**
lo siento, se ha equivocado de número
nurse enfermero(-a) m/f
nut *(for bolt)* tuerca f

O

o'clock, it's ... son las ... en punto
occasionally de vez en cuando
occupied ocupado(-a)
October octubre m
of de
of course por supuesto
off-peak fuera de temporada
off-road (multipurpose) vehicle vehículo m todoterreno
office oficina f
often a menudo
oil aceite m; **~ lamp** lámpara f de aceite
oily *(hair)* graso(-a)
okay de acuerdo
old viejo(-a); **~ fashioned** antiguo(-a);
~ town casco m antiguo
olive oil aceite de oliva m
omelet tortilla f francesa
on *(day, date)* el, en; *(place)*
en/encima de

on: ~ **board** *(ship, plane)* a bordo;
~ **foot** a pie; ~ **the left** a la izquierda;
~ **the other side** al otro lado; ~ **the
right** a la derecha
on/off switch interruptor m
on: this round's on me esta ronda la
pago yo
once una vez; ~ **a week** una vez a la
semana
one uno; ~ **like that** uno(-a) como
ése(-a)
open abierto(-a); ~ **to the public** abier-
to(-a) al público; ~ **to traffic** abierto(-a)
al tráfico
open, to abrir
opening hours horas fpl de apertura
opera ópera f; ~ **house** teatro m de la
ópera
operation operación f
opposite enfrente de/frente a
optician óptico(-a) m/f; oculista m/f
or o
orange *(color/fruit)* naranja f
orchestra orquesta f
order, to pedir; encargar
organized walk/hike paseo organiza-
do m
others otros(-as)
our nuestro(-a); **ours** nuestro(-a),
nuestros(as)
out: he's out ha salido
outdoor al aire libre
outdoor pool piscina f al aire libre
outside a la salida de, afuera;
fuera
outside lane carril m de
adelantamiento
oval ovalado(-a)
oven horno m
over there allí
overcharged, I've been me han co-
brado de más
overdone *(adj.)* demasiado
hecho(-a)
overdraft descubierto m
overheat sobrecalentamiento m
overnight service revelado m
en un día

owe: how much do I owe you?
¿cuánto le debo?
own: on my own solo(-a)
owner propietario(-a) m/f

pacifier chupete m
pack of cards baraja f de cartas
pack, to hacer las maletas
package paquete m
packed lunch bocadillo m
pack[et] paquete m; ~ **of cigarettes**
paquete m de tabaco
paddling pool piscina f infantil
padlock candado m
pain, to be in tener dolores
pain killer analgésico m
paint, to pintar
painted pintado(-a)
painter pintor(a) m/f
painting cuadro m
pair (of) par m (de)
pajamas pijama m
palace palacio m
palpitations taquicardia f
panorama panorama m
pants *(U.S.)* pantalones mpl
pantyhose medias fpl
paper papel m
paralysis parálisis f
parcel paquete m
pardon? ¿cómo?
parents padres mpl
park parque m
park, to aparcar
parking aparcamiento m; ~ **disk**
ficha f para el aparcamiento; ~ **lot**
aparcamiento m; ~ **meter** parquímetro m
parliament building palacio m de las
cortes
parting raya f
partner *(boyfriend/girlfriend)* pareja m/f
parts *(components)* piezas fpl
party *(social)* fiesta f
pass *(mountain)* paso m
pass, to pasar; ~ **through** estar de paso
passenger pasajero(-a) m/f

passport pasaporte m; ~ **control** m de pasaportes
pastry shop pastelería f
patch, to remendar
path camino m
patient paciente m/f
pavement, on the en la acera
pay, to pagar; ~ **a fine** pagar una multa; ~ **by credit card** pagar con tarjeta de crédito
pay phone teléfono público m
payment pago m
pearl perla f
pebbly *(beach)* de guijarros
pedestrian: ~ **crossing** paso m de peatones; ~ **zone [precinct]** zona f peatonal f
pedicure pedicura f
pen pluma estilográfica f; *(ballpen)* bolígrafo
pencil lápiz m
penicillin penicilina f
penknife navaja f
penpal [penfriend] amigo(-a) m/f por correspondencia
pensioner pensionistas mpl
people gente f
pepper *(spice)* pimienta f ; *(vegetable)* pimiento m
per: ~ **day** por día; ~ **hour** por hora; ~ **night** por noche; ~ **week** por semana
performance función f
perhaps quizá
period época f; *(menstrual)* periodo m; ~ **pains** molestias fpl del periodo
permanent *(hair)* permanente f
perm, to hacer la permanente
permit permiso m
personal stereo equipo m de música personal
pet animal m de compañía
petrol gasolina f; ~ **station** gasolinera f
pharmacy farmacia f
phone teléfono m; ~ **call** llamada f telefónica; ~ **card** tarjeta para llamar por teléfono f
phone, to llamar por teléfono
photo, to take a hacer una foto

photocopier fotocopiadora f
photographer fotógrafo(-a) m/f
photography fotografía f
phrase frase; ~ **book** libro m de frases
piano piano m
pick up, to recoger
pickup truck camión de reparto m
picnic picnic m; ~ **area** zona f para picnics
piece *(slice)* trozo m; porción f
Pill *(contraceptive)* píldora f
pillow almohada f; ~ **case** funda f de almohada
pilot light piloto m
pink rosa m
pint pinta f
pipe *(smoking)* pipa f; *(tube)* cañería f
pipe cleaners limpiapipas m
pipe tobacco tabaco m de pipa
pitch *(camping)* parcela m; ~ **charge** tarifa f de acampada
pity: it's a pity es una lástima
pizzeria pizzería f
place *(space)* sitio m
place a bet, to hacer una apuesta
plain *(not patterned)* sencillo(-a)
plane avión m
plans *(intentions)* planes mpl
plant planta f
plastic bags bolsas fpl de plástico
plate plato m
platform andén m
platinum platino m
play, to *(sport)* jugar; *(instrument)* tocar; *(drama)* representar
playground patio m de juegos
play group sala f de juegos
playing cards cartas fpl
playing field campo m de actividades deportivas
playwright escritor(a) m/f
pleasant agradable
please por favor
pliers alicates mpl
plug *(electrical)* enchufe m
plumber fontanero m
p.m. de la tarde/noche
pneumonia neumonía f

point of interest punto m de interés
point to, to señalar a
poison veneno m
poisonous venenoso(-a)
poker *(cards)* póker m
police policía f; **~ report** certificado m de la policía; **~ station** comisaría f de policía
pollen count índice m de polen
polyclinic policlínico m
polyester poliéster m
pond estanque m
pony ride vuelta f en pony
pop music música f pop
popcorn palomitas fpl
popular popular
port *(harbor)* puerto m
porter mozo m
portion porción f
Portugal Portugal
possible: as soon as possible lo antes/más pronto posible
possibly posiblemente
post, to *(mail)* mandar por correo
post *(mail)* correo m; **~ office** oficina f de correos, correos m
postcard postal f
poster póster m
postman cartero m
potatoes patatas fpl
pottery cerámica f
pound *(sterling)* libra (esterlina) f
power failure corte m de luz
power point toma f de corriente
pregnant, to be estar embarazada
premium *(gas [petrol])* súper
prescribe, to recetar
prescription receta f
present *(gift)* regalo m
press, to planchar
pretty bonito(-a)
priest sacerdote m
prison cárcel f
private bathroom cuarto de baño dentro de la habitación m
probably probablemente
program programa m; **~ of events** programa de espectáculos m

prohibited: is it prohibited? ¿está prohibido?
pronounce, to pronunciar
properly correctamente
pub bar m
public holiday fiesta f nacional
pump bomba f; *(gas/petrol)* surtidor m
puppet show teatro m de marionetas
purple morado m
purpose propósito m
purse monedero m
put, to poner; **where can I put…?** ¿dónde puedo poner…?; **~ aside** *(in shop)* guardar; **can you put me up for the night?** ¿puede alojarnos en su casa esta noche?
putting course pista f de putting golf

quality calidad f
quantity cantidad f
quarantine cuarentena f
quarter cuarto m; **~ past** *(after)* y cuarto; **~ to** *(before)* menos cuarto
quay muelle m
queen *(cards, chess)* reina f
question pregunta f
quick rápido(-a)
quickest: what's the quickest way to … ¿cuál es la forma más rápida de llegar a …?
quickly rápidamente
quiet silencioso(-a)
quieter más tranquilo(-a)

rabbi rabino m
race *(cars, horses)* carrera f; **~track [~course]** pista f de carreras
racket *(tennis, squash)* raqueta f
radio radio m
rail station estación f de trenes/ferrocarriles f
railroad ferrocarril m
rain, to llover

raincoat impermeable m, chubasquero m
rape violación f
rapids rápidos m
rare *(steak)* poco hecho(-a); *(unusual)* raro(-a)
rarely rara vez
rash *(ailment)* sarpullido m
ravine barranco m
razor maquinilla f de afeitar; **~ blades** cuchillas fpl de afeitar
re-enter, to volver a entrar
reading *(interest)* lectura f; **~ glasses** gafas de leer fpl
ready, to be estar listo (a)
real *(genuine)* auténtico(-a)
real estate agent agente m/f inmobiliario(-a)
receipt recibo m
reception *(desk)* recepción f
receptionist recepcionista m/f
reclaim tag etiqueta f de reclamación
reclaim, to reclamar
recommend, to recomendar; **can you recommend ...** ¿puede recomendar(me/nos) ...?; **what do you recommend?** ¿qué me/nos recomienda?
record *(LP)* disco m; **~ store** tienda f de discos
recovery service asistencia f en carretera
red rojo m; **~ wine** vino m tinto
reduction descuento m
refreshments bebidas fpl
refrigerator frigorífico m
refund devolución f del dinero
refuse dump basurero m
regards to ... saludos a ...
region región f
registered mail correo m certificado
registration form formulario m de registro
registration number número m de matrícula
regular *(gas [petrol])* normal; *(size)* de tamaño normal

regulations: I didn't know the regulations no conocía las normas
religion religión f
remember: I don't remember no me acuerdo
rent, to alquilar; **for ~** de alquiler; *(in notices)* se alquila
rental car coche m alquilado
repair, to arreglar
repairs reparaciones fpl
repeat, to repetir; **please repeat that** por favor, repítalo
replacement part pieza f de recambio
report, to denunciar
representative representante m/f
required, to be requerirse
rescue service asistencia f en carretera
reservation reserva f
reservation desk despacho m de reservas
reserve, to reservar
rest, to descansar
restaurant restaurante m
retired, to be estar jubilado(-a)
return, to *(come back)* volver
return ticket billete m de ida y vuelta
reverse the charges, to llamar a cobro revertido
rheumatism reumatismo/reuma m
rib costilla f
right *(correct)* correcto(-a)
right of way derecho m de paso
right, on the a la derecha
right-handed diestro(-a)
rip-off *(n)* timo m
river río m **~ cruise** crucero m por el río
road carretera f; *(street)* calle f;
~ accident accidente m de carretera;
~ assistance asistencia f en carretera;
~ map mapa m de carreteras;
~ sign señal f de tráfico
roast(ed) asado(-a); **~ chicken** pollo m asado
robbery robo m
rock climbing escalada f en roca
rock concert concierto m de rock

rocks rocas fpl
roller blades patines de ruedas mpl
rolls *(bread)* bollos mpl
romance *(film)* película f romántica
romantic romántico(-a)
roof *(house/car)* techo m
roof-rack baca f
rook *(chess)* torre f
room habitación f; **~ service** servicio m de habitaciones
rope cuerda f
round redondo(-a); *(of golf)* juego m
round-trip ticket billete m de ida y vuelta
roundabout rotonda f
route camino m; ruta f
rowboat barca f de remos
rubbish *(trash)* basura f
rucksack mochila f
rude, to be ser grosero(-a)
rugby rugby m
ruins ruinas fpl
run into, to *(crash)* chocar con
running shoes zapatillas fpl de deporte
run out, to *(fuel)* quedarse sin
rush hour horas fpl punta

S

safe *(lock box)* caja fuerte f; *(not dangerous)* seguro(-a);
to feel ~ sentirse seguro(-a)
safety
safety pins imperdibles mpl
sag: the bed sags la cama se hunde
sailboard tabla f de windsurf
sailboarding windsurfing m
sailboat velero m
salad ensalada f
sales representative representante m/f
sales tax IVA m; **~ receipt** recibo m con el IVA
salt sal f
same mismo(-a);
the ~ again lo mismo otra vez
sand arena f
sandals sandalias fpl

sandwich bocadillo m
sandy *(beach)* de arena
sanitary napkins [towels] compresas fpl
satellite TV televisión f por satélite; antena f parabólica
satin raso/satén m
satisfied: I'm not satisfied with this no estoy satisfecho(-a) con esto
Saturday sábado m
sauce salsa f
saucepan cazo m
sauna sauna f
sausage salchicha f,
say, to decir; **how do you say …?** ¿cómo se dice …?; **what did he say?** ¿qué dijo …?
scarf *(wool)* bufanda f; *(silk)* pañuelo m
scenic route carretera f panorámica
scheduled flight vuelo m regular
school colegio m; escuela f
sciatica ciática f
scientist científico(-a) m/f
scooter vespa®/vespino f/m
Scotland Escocia f
Scottish *(noun/adj.)* escocés(a) m/f
scouring pad estropajo m
screw tornillo m
sea mar m
seafront paseo m marítimo
seasick, I feel me mareo
season ticket abono m de temporada
seasoning aderezo m
seat *(movies)* asiento m; *(plane/train)* plaza f
second segundo(-a); **~ class** de segunda clase; **~ [first (U.K.)] floor** *(U.S.)* primera planta f
secondhand de segunda mano; **~ shop** tienda f de artículos de segunda mano
secretary secretario(-a) m/f
security guard guardia m/f de seguridad
sedative sedante m
see, to ver; **~ someone again** volver a ver a alguien

self-employed, to be trabajar por cuenta propia
self-service autoservicio m
sell, to vender
send, to *(help)* mandar
senior citizen pensionista m/f
separated, to be estar separado(-a)
separately por separado
September septiembre m
serious grave
served, to be *(meal)* servirse
service servicio m; *(religious)* servicio m; ~ **charge** servicio m
service station *(gas station)* estación f de servicio
services servicios mpl
set menu menú del día m
seven siete
seventeen diecisiete
seventy setenta
sex *(act)* acto m sexual
shade tono m
shallow poco hondo(-a)
shampoo champú m; ~ **for dry/oily hair** champú para cabello seco/graso m
shape forma f
share, to *(room)* compartir
sharp *(object)* afilado(-a)
shatter, to *(glass)* romperse
shaver máquina f de afeitar; ~ **socket** enchufe m para la máquina de afeitar
shaving brush brocha f de afeitar
shaving cream espuma f de afeitar
she ella
sheet *(bedding)* sábana f
shelf estante m
ship barco m
shirt camisa f
shock *(electric)* calambre m
shoe: shoes zapatos mpl; ~ **laces** cordones mpl de zapatos; ~**maker** zapatero m; ~ **polish** betún m; ~ **repair** zapatero m; ~ **store** zapatería f; *(in signs)* calzados f
shop tienda f; ~ **assistant** dependiente(a) m/f
shopping area zona f de tiendas

shopping basket cesta f de la compra
shopping cart [trolley] carrito m de la compra
shopping mall [centre] centro m comercial
shopping list lista f de la compra
shopping, to go ir de compras/a comprar
shore *(sea/lake)* orilla f
short corto(-a); ~-**sighted** miope
shorts pantalones fpl cortos
shoulder hombro m
show, to enseñar; **can you ~ me?** ¿puede indicarme?
shower ducha f; ~ **gel** gel m de la ducha
shut cerrado(-a); **when do you shut?** ¿a qué hora cierran?
shutter persiana f
shy tímido(-a)
sick, to feel sentirse mal
sick: I'm going to be sick voy a devolver/vomitar
sickbay *(ship)* enfermería f
side *(road)* lado m
side order guarnición f
side street bocacalle f
sidewalk acera f
sights lugares mpl de interés
sightseeing, to go ir a visitar lugares de interés
sightseeing tour recorrido por los lugares de interés m
sign/signpost señal f
silk seda f
silver plata f; ~ **plate** baño m de plata
similar, to be parecerse
since *(time)* desde
singer cantante m/f
single individual; ~ **room** habitación f individual; **to be ~** estar soltero(-a)
single ticket billete m de ida
sink *(basin)* lavabo m; *(kichen)* fregadero m
sister hermana f
sit, to sentarse; **sit down, please** siéntese, por favor
six seis
sixteen dieciséis

sixty sesenta
size talla f
skates patines mpl
skating rink pista f de patinaje
ski: skis esquí m; **~ boots** botas fpl de esquí; **~ instructor** instructor(a) m/f de esquí; **~ lift** teleférico m; **~ poles** bastones mpl de esquí; **~ school** academia de esquí; **~ suit** traje m de esquí; **~ trousers** pantalones mpl de esquí; **~ wax** cera f para los esquíes
ski, to esquiar
skid: we skidded resbalamos/patinamos
skin piel f
skirt falda f
sleep, to dormir
sleeping bag saco m de dormir
sleeping car coche-cama m
sleeping pill somnífero m; pastilla f para dormir f
sleeve manga f
slice rodaja f
slide film diapositiva f; filmina f
slope *(ski)* cuesta f
slot machine máquina f tragaperras
slow lento(-a)
slow down! ¡vaya más despacio!
slow, to be *(clock)* estar atrasado
slowly despacio
SLR SRL m
small pequeño(-a)
small change calderilla f; suelto m
smell: there's a bad smell huele mal
smoke, to fumar; **I don't smoke** no fumo
smoking *(adj.)* para fumador; **~ area** zona f de fumadores
smoky: it's too smoky hay demasiado humo
snack bar bar m
snacks aperitivos mpl
sneakers zapatillas fpl de deporte
snooker snooker m
snorkel esnórkel m
snow nieve f
snow, to nevar

soaking solution *(contact lenses)* solución f para lentillas/lentes de contacto
soap jabón m
soap powder detergente m en polvo
socket caja de enchufe m
socks calcetines mpl
sofa sofá m
sofa-bed sofá-cama m
soft drink refresco m
sole *(shoes)* suela f
soluble aspirin aspirinas fpl solubles
some algunos(-as); algo de
someone alguien
something algo
sometimes a veces
son hijo m
soon pronto; **as ~ as possible** tan pronto como sea posible
sorry! ¡lo siento!
sort clase f; tipo m; **a ~ of** una especie de
sour ácido(-a)
south sur m
South Africa Sudáfrica
South African *(person)* sudafricano(-a)
souvenir recuerdo m; **~ guide** catálogo m de recuerdos; **~ store** tienda f de recuerdos
spa *(spring)* manantial m; *(place to stay)* balneario m
space espacio m; *(in campsite)* parcela f
spade *(shovel)* pala f
spades *(cards)* picas fpl
Spain España
Spaniard español(a) m/f
Spanish *(adj.)* español m
spare *(extra)* de sobra; *(piece/wheel)* de repuesto
speak, to hablar; **do you speak English?** ¿habla inglés?
special rate tarifa f especial
special requirements peticiones fpl especiales
specialist especialista m/f
specimen muestra f
spectacles gafas fpl
speed limit límite m de velocidad
speed, to llevar exceso de velocidad

spell, to deletrear
spend, to *(money)* gastar; *(time)* pasar
spicy *(containing spices)* con especias; *(taste)* a especias
spin-dryer secadora f
spine columna f vertebral
sponge esponja f
spoon cuchara f
sports deportes m; **~ club** club m deportivo; **~ ground** campo m de actividades deportivas
sporting goods store tienda f de deportes
sprained, to be tener un esguince
spring manantial m; *(season)* primavera f
square cuadrado(-a)
stadium estadio m
stain mancha f
stairs escaleras fpl
stall: the engine stalls el motor se ha calado
stalls *(orchestra)* patio f de butacas
stamp sello m; **~ machine** máquina f expendedora de sellos
stand in line, to permanecer en la cola
standby ticket billete m de standby
start *(noun)* comienzo m
start, to empezar; *(car)* arrancar
starter primer plato m
stately home casa f solariega
statement *(legal)* declaración f
station estación f
stationer papelería f
statue estatua f
stay, to quedarse
steak house churrasquería f
stereo equipo m estéreo
sterilizing solution solución f esterilizante
stern *(ship)* popa f
stiff neck tortícolis f
still: I'm still waiting todavía estoy esperando
sting ardor m
stockings medias fpl

stomach estómago m; **~ache** dolor de estómago m; **~ cramps** retortijones mpl
stool *(feces)* heces fpl
stop *(bus, tram, subway)* parada f
stop, to parar; **please stop here** pare aquí, por favor
stopover parada f, escala f
store tienda f; **~ detective** detective m/f de una tienda; **~ guide** directorio m
stormy, to be tronar
straight ahead todo recto
straw *(drinking)* pajita f
strawberry *(flavor)* (de) fresa
stream arroyo m
string cuerda f
striped *(patterned)* a/de rayas
strong *(potent)* fuerte
stuck: the key's stuck la llave se ha atascado
student estudiante m/f
study, to estudiar
style estilo m
styling mousse espuma f moldeadora
subtitled, to be estar subtitulado(-a)
subway metro m
sugar azúcar m
suggest, to sugerir
suit traje m de chaqueta
suitable for apropiado(-a) para
summer verano m
sun block filtro m solar
sun lounger tumbona f
suntan cream/lotion crema f bronceadora
sunbathe, to tomar el sol
suncare protección f contra el sol
Sunday domingo m
sunglasses gafas fpl de sol
sunshade *(umbrella)* sombrilla f
sunstroke insolación
super *(gas [petrol])* súper
superb espléndido(-a)
supermarket supermercado m
supplement suplemento m
suppositories supositorios mpl
sure: are you sure? ¿estás seguro(-a)?
surfboard tabla de surf f
surgery *(doctor's office)* consulta f

surname apellido m
sweater jersey m
sweatshirt sudadera f
sweet *(taste)* dulce
sweets *(candy)* caramelos mpl
swelling hinchazón f
swim, to nadar
swimming natación f; **~ pool** piscina f;
~ trunks bañador (de hombre) m
swimsuit bañador (de mujer) m
switch interruptor m
switch off, to apagar
switch on, to encender
swollen, to be estar hinchado(-a)
symptoms síntomas mpl
synagogue sinagoga f
synthetic sintético(-a)

T

T-shirt camiseta f
table mesa f; **~ cloth** mantel m
table tennis ping-pong m
tablet comprimido m
take, to tomar; *(medicine)* tomar;
(carry) llevar; *(time)* tardar; **I'll take it**
(purchase) me lo quedo
take away, to llevar
take photographs, to hacer fotografías
take someone home, to llevar a alguien a casa
taken *(occupied)* cogido(-a) ocupado(-a)
talcum powder polvos mpl de talco
talk, to hablar
tall alto(-a)
tampons tampones mpl
tan *(color)* moreno m
tap *(faucet)* grifo m
taste sabor m
taxi taxi m; **~ driver** taxista m/f; **~ stand [rank]** parada f de taxis
tea té m; **~ bags** bolsitas fpl de té
tea towel paño m de cocina
teacher profesor(a) m/f
team equipo m

teddy bear osito m de peluche
teenager adolescente m/f
telephone teléfono m; **~ bill** cuenta f del teléfono; **~ booth** cabina f telefónica; **~ calls** llamadas fpl (telefónicas); **~ kiosk** cabina f; **~ number** número m de teléfono
telephone, to llamar por teléfono
television televisión m
telex télex m
tell, to decir; **tell me** dígame
temperature temperatura f
temporarily provisionalmente
ten diez
tendon tendón m
tennis tenis m; **~ ball** pelota f de tenis;
~ court pista f de tenis
tent tienda f; **~ pegs** estacas fpl; **~ pole** mástil m
terminus terminal f
tetanus tétano m
thank you gracias
that eso(-a), aquello(-a); **~ one** ése(-a);
that's all eso es todo
theater teatro m
theft robo m
their su
theirs suyo(-a)
them ellos; **to/for them** a/para ellos(-as)
theme park parque temático m
then *(time)* entonces, luego
there allí; **~ is ...** hay ...
thermometer termómetro m
thermos bottle termo m
these estos(-as)
they ellos(-as)
thick grueso(-a)
thief ladrón(a) m/f
thigh cadera f
thin fino(-a), delgado(-a)
think: I think that ... creo que ...
think about it, to pensár(se)lo
third tercero(-a); **a ~** un tercio
thirsty: I am ~ tengo sed
thirteen trece
thirty treinta
this one éste(-a)

those esos(-as), aquel(lla)

thousand mil

thread hilo m

three tres

throat garganta f

throat lozenges pastillas fpl para la garganta

through a través de/por

thumb pulgar m

thunder, to tronar

Thursday jueves m

ticket billete m; entrada f; ~ **agency** agencia f de venta de entradas; ~ **office** despacho m de billetes

tie corbata f

tight *(clothing)* apretado(-a); estrecho(-a)

tights medias fpl

till receipt recibo m de caja

time hora f; **on ~** puntual; **free ~** tiempo m libre

timetable horario m

tin lata f; ~ **opener** abrelatas m

tin foil papel m de aluminio

tint, to teñir

tinted (glass/lens) con un tinte

tip propina f

tipping dar propina

tire [tyre] neumático m

tired, to be estar cansado(-a)

tissues pañuelos mpl de papel

to *(place)* a

toaster tostador m

tobacco tabaco m

tobacconist estanco m

today hoy

toe dedo del pie

together junto(-a)

toilet servicio m

toilet paper papel m higiénico

toilets servicios mpl; aseos mpl

tomorrow mañana

tongue lengua f

tonic water tónica f

tonight esta noche; **for ~** para esta noche

tonsillitis amigdalitis f

tonsils amígdala f

too demasiado; *(also)* también

tooth diente m; ~**ache** dolor m de muelas; ~**brush** cepillo m de dientes; ~**paste** pasta f de dientes

top *(mountain)* cima f

top floor planta f/piso m de arriba

torn, to be *(muscle)* estar desgarrado(-a)

totally totalmente

tough *(food)* duro(-a)

tour visita f turística.; ~ **guide** guía m/f turístico(-a); ~ **operator** operador(a) turístico(-a) m/f; ~ **representative** representante m/f turístico(-a)

tourist turista m/f

tourist office oficina f de turismo

tow rope cuerda f de remolque

tow, to remolcar

tow truck camión m de reparto

toward hacia

towel toalla f

toweling felpa f

tower torre f

town *(small)* pueblo m; *(large)* ciudad f; ~ **hall** ayuntamiento m

toy juguete m

toy and game store juguetería f

track sendero m

tracksuit chándal m

traditional tradicional

traffic tráfico m; ~ **circle** rotonda f; ~ **jam** atasco m (de tráfico); **traffic violation [offence]** violación/infracción f del código de circulación

tragedy tragedia f

trail sendero m

trailer roulotte f; ~ **park** cámping m para roulottes

train tren m; ~ **station** estación f de trenes; ~ **times** horarios mpl de trenes

training shoes zapatillas fpl de deporte

tram tranvía m

transfer *(bank)* transferencia f; *(transport)* trasbordo m

transit, in en tránsito

translate, to traducir
translation traducción f
translator traductor(a) m/f
trash basura f; ~ can la papelera fpl
travel agency agencia f de viajes
travel iron plancha f (de viaje)
travel sickness mareo m
travel, to viajar
traveler's check cheque m de viaje
tray bandeja f
tree árbol m
tremendous (good) formidable
trip (excursion) excursión f; (journey)
viaje m
trouble: I'm having trouble with
tengo problemas con
trousers pantalones mpl
true: that's not true eso no es verdad
try on, to (clothing) probarse
Tuesday martes m
tumor tumor m
tunnel túnel m
turn, to torcer; ~ down (volume,
heat) bajar; ~ off apagar; ~ on
encender; ~ up (volume, heat) subir
turning desvío m
TV televisión f; ~ room sala f de la
televisión
TV-listings (magazine) guía f de
televisión
twelve doce
twenty veinte
twice dos veces
twin bed dos fpl camas
twist: I've twisted my ankle
me he torcido el tobillo
two dos
type tipo m
tyre neumático m
typical típico(-a)

ugly feo(-a)
United Kingdom Reino Unido
umbrella (sun) sombrilla; (rain)
paraguas m
uncle tío m

unconscious, to be estar inconsciente
under (place) debajo de
underdone (adj.) crudo
(-a)
underpants calzoncillos mpl
underpass pasaje m subterráneo
understand, to entender; do you
understand? ¿entiende?;
I don't understand no entiendo
undress, to desvestirse
unfortunately desgraciadamente
uniform uniforme m
unit unidad f
United States los Estados Unidos
unleaded gasoline gasolina f sin
plomo
unlimited mileage kilometraje m
ilimitado
unlock, to abrir
until hasta
upper berth litera f de arriba
upset stomach dolor m de estómago
upstairs arriba, en el piso de arriba
up to hasta
urgent urgente
us: (for/with) (para/con) nosotros(-as)
use, to usar
useful útil
utensils (cutlery) cubiertos mpl

vacancy habitación/plaza f libre
vacant libre
vacation vacaciones fpl
vaccination vacuna f
vaginal infection infección f vaginal
valet service servicio m de planchado
valid válido(-a)
validate, to (ticket) picar
valley valle m
valuable de valor
value valor m
valve llave f de paso
vanilla (flavor) (de) vainilla
VAT (sales tax) IVA m; ~ receipt recibo m con el IVA

vegan, to be ser vegetariano(-a) estricto(-a); **suitable for vegans** apropiado(-a) para vegetarianos estrictos; **~ dishes** platos para vegetarianos estrictos mpl

vegetable store verdulería f

vegetables verduras fpl

vegetarian *(noun/adj.)* vegetariano(-a) m/f; **to be ~** ser vegetariano(-a)

vehicle vehículo m; **~ registration document** documento de registro del vehículo m

vein vena f

very muy

vest chaleco m

video vídeo m; **~ game** videojuego m; **~ recorder** aparato de vídeo m

view: with a view of the sea con vistas al mar

viewpoint/viewing point mirador m

village pueblo m

vineyard/winery viñedo m

visa visa f

visit, to ver; visitar; *(hospital)* hacer una visitar a

visiting hours horas fpl de visita

vitamin pills vitaminas fpl en comprimidos

voice voz f

vomit, to vomitar

W

wait (for), to esperar (a); **wait!** ¡espere(n)!

waiter! ¡camarero!

waiting room sala f de espera

waitress! ¡camarera!

wake, to *(self)* despertarse; *(someone else)* despertar a

wake-up call llamada-despertador f

Wales Gales

walk, to go for a ir de paseo

walking boots botas fpl de montaña

walking gear equipo m de senderismo

wallet cartera f

want, to querer

ward *(hospital)* sala f

warm caliente; *(weather)* caluroso(-a)

warm, to calentar

wash, to lavar

washbasin lavabo m

washer *(for tap/faucet)* junta f

washing machine lavadora f

watch reloj m (de pulsera)

watch TV, to ver la televisión

water agua f; **~ bottle** bolsa de agua caliente; **~ carrier** garrafa para el agua f; **~fall** catarata f; **~ heater** calentador m; **~ skis** esquís acuáticos mpl

waterproof impermeable; **~ jacket** chubasquero m

waterskiing esquí m acuático

wave ola f

waxing depilación f a la cera

way *(direction)* camino m; **I've lost my ~** me he perdido; **on the ~** de camino

we nosotros(-as)

weak *(coffee)* poco cargado

wear, to vestir/llevar puesto(-a)

weather tiempo m; **~ forecast** pronóstico m del tiempo

wedding boda f; **~ ring** anillo m de boda

Wednesday miércoles m

week semana f

weekend fin de semana m; **during [at] the ~** el fin de semana; **~ rate** tarifa f de fin de semana

weekly ticket tarjeta f para una semana

weight: my weight is … peso …

welcome to … bienvenido(-a) a …

well-done *(steak)* bien hecho(-a)

Welsh *(noun/adj.)* galés(a) m/f

west oeste m

wetsuit traje m de neopremo

what? ¿qué?

what kind of…? ¿qué clase de…?

what time? ¿a qué hora?

what's the time? ¿qué hora es?

wheelchair silla f de ruedas

when?

where? ¿dónde?; **~ are you from?** ¿de dónde es?; **~ is …?** ¿dónde está …?; **~ can we …?** ¿dónde podemos …?

which? ¿cuál?; **~ stop?** ¿qué parada?

while mientras

white blanco(-a); **~ wine** vino m blanco

who? ¿quién?

whole: the whole day el día entero

whose? ¿de quién(es) ?

why? ¿por qué?

wide ancho(-a)

wife mujer f

wildlife flora f y fauna f

windbreaker chubasquero m

window ventana f; (shop) escaparate m; **~ seat** asiento m de ventanilla

windshield [windscreen] parabrisas m

windy, to be hacer viento

wine vino m; **~ list** carta f de vinos

winter invierno m

wishes: best wishes to … saludos a …

with con

with long/short sleeves de manga larga/corta

with v-/round neck de cuello de pico/a la caja

without sin

witness testigo m/f

wood (forest) bosque m; (material) madera f

wool lana f

work, to trabajar; (function) funcionar; **it doesn't ~** no funciona

worry: I'm worried estoy preocupado(-a)

worse peor; **it's gotten [got] ~** ha empeorado(-a)

worth: is it worth seeing? ¿merece la pena guardarlo?

wound (injury) herida f

write, to escribir; **~ soon!** ¡escriba pronto!

write down, to escribir

writing pad cuaderno m

wrong mal; equivocado(-a); **~ number** número m equivocado; **there's something ~ with…** hay algo que está mal en…; **what's ~?** ¿qué pasa?

x-ray radiografía f

yacht yate m

year año m

yellow amarillo m

yes sí

yesterday ayer

yogurt yogurt m

you tú (singular, familiar); vosotros(-as) (plural); usted(es) (formal, singular); ustedes (formal, plural)

young joven

your su/tu/vuestro(-a)

yours suyo(-a)/tuyo(-a)/vuestro(-a)

youth hostel albergue m juvenil

zebra crossing paso m de cebra

zero cero m

zip(per) cremallera f

zone zona f

zoo zoológico m

zoology zoología f

DICTIONARY
SPANISH-ENGLISH

This Spanish-English Dictionary covers all the areas where you may need to decode written Spanish: hotels, public buildings, restaurants, stores, ticket offices, and transportation. It will also help with understanding forms, maps, product labels, road signs and operating instuctions (for telephones, parking meters, etc.).

If you can't locate the exact item, you may find key words or terms listed separately.

A

a descontar de su próxima compra … off your next purchase
a estrenar brand new
a la tarjeta de crédito charge your credit card
a su elección at your choice
abierto open
abierto de … a … y de … a … opening hours
abril April
abrir aquí cut here/open here
abróchense los cinturones fasten your seat belt
acantilado cliff
acceso al garaje prohibido durante la travesía no access to car decks during crossing
accesorios de baño bathroom accessories
accesorios de cocina kitchen equipment
aceite oil
acero steel
acto event
actuación gig
actualizado updated
acueducto aqueduct
administración de lotería lottery
admisiones admissions
adultos adults

aerodeslizador hydrofoil
aeropuerto airport
agencia de viajes travel agent
agencia inmobiliaria real estate agent
agítese bien antes de usar shake well before use
agosto August
agua potable drinking water
al aire libre open-air/outdoor
al recibir respuesta introduzca las monedas on reply, insert coins
albergue de carretera motel
alerta L storm warning
algo que declarar goods to declare
algodón cotton
alimentos dietéticos health foods
almacén de muebles furniture warehouse
almacenes de música music store
almacenes generales general store
alpinismo mountaineering
alquiler de coches car rental
alta tensión high voltage
altitud altitude
altura máxima headroom/maximum height
altura sobre el nivel del mar height above sea level
aluminio aluminum [aluminium]
amarre prohibido no docking
andén platform
anfiteatro circle
animales de compañía pet store
antes de entrar, dejen salir let passengers off first
antes de las comidas before meals
anticuario antiques store
antigüedades antiques
Año Nuevo New Year's Day
apague el motor turn off engine
aparcamiento parking lot [car park]
aparcamiento autorizado parking permitted
aparcamiento de clientes customer parking [car park]
aparcamiento de residentes residents only
aparcamiento gratuito free parking

aparcamiento no vigilado parking at your own risk
apartadero way side [lay-by]
apellido name
apellido de la esposa wife's name
aperitivo aperitif
apto para cocción en horno microondas microwaveable
apto para regímenes vegetarianos suitable for vegetarians
apuestas deportivas betting shop/bookmaker
arca de agua water tower
arcén blando soft shoulder
arcén duro hard shoulder
área de servicio service area
arenas movedizas quicksand
aroma flavoring
arroyo stream
arte art
artículos de regalo gifts
ascensor elevator [lift]
asiento de pasillo aisle seat
asiento de ventanilla window seat
asiento número seat number
asiento reservado para personas que merecen especial atención please give up this seat to the old or infirm
atención al cliente customer service
atletismo athletics
atracción para turistas tourist attraction
auténtico genuine
autobús bus
autocar (de línea) long-distance bus [coach]
autocine drive-in
autopista highway [motorway]
autoservicio self-service
autovía expressway [dual carriageway]
avenida avenue
avión airplane
avisamos cepo/grúa unauthorized vehicles will be booted/clamped/towed away
aviso warning

aviso de tempestad gale warning
ayuntamiento town hall
azúcar sugar

B

bahía bay
bailador dancer
baile dance
bajar to go down
bajo su responsabilidad at your own risk
baloncesto basketball
balonmano handball
balonvolea volleyball
banco bank
baños baths
barbacoa barbecue
barca de remos rowboat
barco ship
bebidas incluidas drinks included
bebidas sin alcohol soft drinks
béisbol baseball
bicicleta bicycle
bienvenido welcome
billar snooker
billete de abono season ticket
bodega vineyard/winery
bolera bowling
bomberos fire department [fire brigade]
bosque forest/wood
botas de esquí ski boots
bote salvavidas lifeboat
botiquín medicine box
bufet buffet
bulevar boulevard
butaca stalls

C

caballeros gentlemen *(toilets)*
cada ... horas every ... hours
caduca el ... valid until ...
café coffee
caja checkout
caja de ahorros savings bank
caja rápida express checkout
cajero automático automated teller (ATM) [cash machine]

...ajero fuera de servicio teller out of ...der
...ajeros cashiers
...ala creek
...lcio calcium
calle road/street
calle cortada road closed
calle de sentido único one-way street
calle mayor main [high] street
calle sin salida no throughway/ road closed
callejón lane
callejón sin salida cul-de-sac
calorías calories
calzada en mal estado poor road surface
camarotes cabins
cambie (a otra línea de metro) change lines *(subway/metro)*
cambie en ... change at ...
camino nature trail
camión truck
cámping con hierba grass campsite
cámping de piso de arena sand campsite
cámping de piso de piedra stone campsite
campo countryside; field/pitch/ground
campo de batalla battle site
campo de deporte(s) playing field [sports ground]
campo para meriendas picnic area
camposanto churchyard
cancelado cancelled
canoa canoe
canónigo canon
caña de pescar fishing rod
cañón canyon
capilla chapel
cápsulas capsules
caravana trailer [caravan]
carga máxima load limit
carnaval carnival
carne meat
carnicería butcher
carretera de peaje toll road

carretera en construcción road under construction
carretera estrecha narrow road
carretera helada icy road
carretera secundaria secondary road
carretera sin pavimentar unpaved road
carril bici bicycle path/lane
carril bus bus lane
carritos carts [trolleys]
carta menu
casa house
casa de huéspedes guest house
casa solariega stately home
cascada waterfall
casco protector crash helmet
castillo castle
cata de vinos wine tasting
catedral cathedral
ceda el paso yield [give way]
cementerio cemetery
céntimo cent
centro antiguo old town
centro ciudad downtown area
centro comercial business distict; shopping mall [arcade]
centro de jardinería garden center
cepo en rueda booting [wheel clamping]
cerrado al tráfico road closed
cerrado closed
cerrado hasta el ... closed until ...
cerrado por descanso semanal day off/closed
cerrado por reformas closed for repairs
cerramos al mediodía closed for lunch
cerveza beer
chaleco salvavidas lifejackets
charcutería delicatessen
ciclismo cycling
cierren la puerta close the door
cine movie theater [cinema]
circo circus
circuito de carrera racetrack
circulación en ambos sentidos two-way traffic

circulación prohibida closed to traffic
circulen por la derecha/izquierda keep to the right/left
circunvalación bypass
ciudad city
ciudades de vacaciones vacation [holiday] village
clínica de salud health clinic
clínica oftalmológica eye infirmary
clínica pediátrica pediatric ward
club de campo country club
coche car *(automobile)*; car [coach] *(train)*
cocina cookery
cocinar sin descongelar cook from frozen, do not defrost
colina hill
coloque el tíquet detrás del parabrisas place ticket on windshield
colores sólidos colorfast
comedia comedy
comedor dining room
comedor para desayunos breakfast room
comestibles groceries
comida para llevar take-out
comienza a las … (de la mañana/tarde) commencing/begins at … (in the morning/afternoon)
comisaría de policía police station
compact disc CD
competición contest
completo full
compra-venta de … we buy and sell …
comprimido tablet/pill
con baño with ensuite bathroom
con cocina self-catering
con las comidas with meals
con plomo leaded
con recargo extra charge/supplement
con suplemento extra charge/supplement
con vistas al mar with sea view
concierto de música pop pop concert
confitería confectioner
congelado frozen
congelados frozen foods

congestión delays likely
conservantes preservatives
conservar en lugar fresco keep in a cool place
conservar en refrigerador keep refrigerated
conservas preserves
conserve su billete please retain your ticket
consigna baggage check [left-luggage office]
consulta del doctor doctor's office [surgery]
consulte con su médico antes de usar consult your doctor before use
consultorio consulting room
consumir antes de … best before …
contador de luz (electricidad) electric meter
contenedor para botellas bottle bank
contorno contour
control de aduana customs control
control de inmigración immigration control
control de pasaportes passport control
convento convent
correduría de seguros insurance agent
correos post office
costa coast
cristal reciclado recycled glass
cruce crossing; interchange [junction]
cruce de autopista highway [motorway] junction
cruceros cruises
cruceros en barco steam cruises
cruceros en el río river trips
cubierta cabin deck
cubierta de sol sun deck
cubierta superior upper deck
cuero leather
cuidado con el perro beware of the dog
cuidados intensivos intensive care
cumbre peak
curvas peligrosas dangerous bend

D

dársena docks
de etiqueta formal wear

203

de fácil acceso al mar within easy reach of the sea
de gira on tour
de la mañana/madrugada a.m.
de la tarde/noche p.m.
de ... a ... horas from ... to ...
deje su coche con la 1º marcha leave your car in first gear
dejen libre keep clear
dejen sus bolsos aquí please leave your bags here
deporte sport
deportes (la tienda de ...) sporting goods store
derecho straight ahead
derecha right
desayuno breakfast
desconectado disconnected
descuentos discounts
deshechable disposable
desierto desert
desprendimientos falling rocks
después de las comidas after meals
destinación destination
desvío alternative route; detour [diversion]
desvío para camiones alternative truck route
devolución del depósito refund
devuelve cambio returns
día festivo national holiday
día y noche 24-hour service
diciembre December
diócesis diocese
dirección manager
directo direct; direct service
director (de orquesta) conductor
distancia entre tren y andén mind the gap *(subway/metro)*
disuélvase en agua dissolve in water
divisas compra currency bought at
divisas venta currency sold at
doblada dubbed
domicilio habitual home address
domingo Sunday
Domingo de Ramos Palm Sunday
Domingo de Resurección Easter Sunday

dosis dose
droguería pharmacy [chemist]
duchas showers
duna dune
durante ... días for ... days

E

€ euro
edificio público public building
el chef recomienda ... the chef suggests ...
electricidad electricity
electrodomésticos electrical household appliances
embajada embassy
embarque boarding now
emergencia emergency (services)
embutidos sausages
empieza a las ... commencing ...
empujar push
en ayunas on an empty stomach
en caso de avería llamar al ... in case of breakdown, phone/contact ...
en caso de emergencia rompa el cristal break glass in case of emergency
en construcción under construction
en el acto while you wait
en sala indoor
en temporada in season
encienda luces de carretera switch on headlights
enero January
enfermería sickbay
enfermos de ambulatorio outpatients
ensanche para adelantar passing bay
entrada entrance/way in
entrada de autopista highway [motorway] entrance
entrada libre free admission
entrada por la puerta delantera enter by the front door
entrada sólo para residentes residents only
entradas tickets
equipo de buceo scuba diving equipment
escalera mecánica escalator
escarpa escarpment

escuela school
especialidad de la casa/del chef
speciality of the house/chef
espectáculo floor show
espectadores spectators
espera de ... mins. wait ... mins.
espere aquí (detrás de este punto)
stand behind this point
espere detrás de la valla please wait
behind barrier
espere la luz verde wait for
green light
espere respuesta wait for a reply
espere su turno wait your turn
espere tono wait for tone
esquí de fondo cross-country skiing
esquí naútico waterskiing
esquiar skiing
esquís skis
esta máquina no da cambio
no change given
está prohibido forbidden
esta tarde this evening
estación de ferrocarril train station
estación de servicio service station
estación de metro subway station
estadio stadium
estanco cigarette kiosk/tobacconist
estatua statue
estreno first night/première
extintor fire extinguisher

F

fábrica factory
factor 8 (de protección solar) factor
8 (sun lotion)
farmacia pharmacy [chemist]
faro lighthouse
febrero February
**fecha de caducidad de la tarjeta de
crédito** credit card expiration date
fecha de nacimiento date of birth
feria fair
ferrocarril railroad
festival festival
fibra artificial man-made fiber
ficción fiction
fila row/tier

fin de autopista end of highway
[motorway]
fin de desvío end of detour
[diversion]
fin de obras end of construction
fin del trayecto/servicio terminus
firma signature
firme en mal estado uneven road
surface
flash prohibido no flash
floristería florist
flotador rubber ring
fotocopias copying
fotografía (la tienda de ...) camera
store; photography
frágil ... cristal fragile ... glass
franquicia de equipaje baggage
allowance
freno de emergencia emergency brake
fresco fresh
frontera border crossing
frutas fruit
frutos secos nuts
fuegos artificiales fireworks
fuente fountain
fuera de servicio out of order
fuerte fortress
fumadores smoking
funicular cable car
funicular aéreo cable car/gondola
fútbol soccer [football]
fútbol americano American football

G

gabinete dental dentist
galería shopping mall/arcade
galería de arte art gallery; art store
galería superior balcony
galletas cookies [biscuits]
ganga bargain
garaje garage/car deck
garaje subterráneo underground
garage
garganta gorge
gasa de seda chiffon
gasolina gas
gasolina normal two-star gas
gasolina sin plomo lead-free gas

gasolinera gas station
gastos bancarios bank charges
giro postal postal orders
giros money orders
giros y transferencias drafts and transfers
glutamato monosódico monosodium glutamate
gorro de baño obligatorio bathing caps must be worn
gotas drops
grada tier
gragea pills
grandes almacenes department store
granja farm
gratis free
gravilla loose gravel
grifo faucet [tap]
grúa breakdown services
grupos bienvenidos parties welcome
gruta cave
guardarropa coatroom
guía directory
guía del almacén store guide

H

habitaciones rooms (breakfast not usually included)
habitaciones libres rooms to let/ vacancies
hacer la habitación this room needs making up
hasta 8 artículos 8 items or less
hay refrescos refreshments available
hecho a medida made to measure
herido casualty
hielo ice
hierro iron
hilo linen
hípica horseback riding
hipódromo racetrack [course]
hockey sobre hielo ice hockey
homeopático homeopath
horario de invierno winter timetable
horario de verano summer timetable
horario de visitas visiting hours
horarios timetables
horas de oficina business hours

horas de recogida times of collection
horas de visita visiting hours
hospicio hospice
hostal de juventud youth hostel
hoy today

I

ida single
ida y vuelta round trip [return]
idiomas languages
iglesia church
importe exacto exact change/fare
imprenta printing
impuestos sales tax [VAT]
incluido included in the price/ inclusive
incluye primera consumición includes one complimentary drink
inflamable inflammable
información directory enquiries
información al cliente customer information
información nutricional nutritional information
ingredientes ingredients
inserte monedas y pulse botón del producto elegido insert coins, then push botton of selected item
intersección intersection
introduzca su tarjeta insert your credit card
introduzca una moneda insert coin
introduzca una tarjeta de crédito insert credit card
invierno winter
Islas Baleares Balearic Islands
Islas Canarias Canary Islands
I.V.A. (incluido) sales tax [VAT] (included)
izquierda left

J

jardín garden
jardines botánicos botanical garden
joyería jeweler
jueves Thursday
juguetería toy store
julio July

junio June
juzgado courthouse

K

kiosko newsstand [newsagent]

L

la dirección declina toda responsabilidad en caso de robo o daños the owners can accept no responsibility for any damage or theft
laborables weekdays *(only)*
lago lake
lana wool
lavabos bathrooms [toilets]
lavado car wash
lavandería laundromat [laundrette]
lavar a máquina machine washable
leche milk
lechería dairy
legumbres legumes
lentamente slow
levante el auricular lift receiver
libre for rent/vacant
librería bookstore
lino linen
lite diet
literas sleeping car [sleeper] *(train)*
liquidación por cierre closing down sale
llamada gratuita toll free number
llame al timbre please ring the bell
llegadas arrivals
lluvia rain
lo mismo servido con ... the same served with ...
local equipado con sistemas de vigilancia surveillance system in operation
luces lights
lugar site/venue
lugar de nacimiento place of birth
lunes Monday
Lunes de Pascua Easter Monday
luz de carretera use headlights

M

madera wood
manantial spring

manténgase congelado keep frozen
mantener fuera del alcance de los niños keep out of reach of children
mantenga esta puerta cerrada keep gate shut
mantequería dairy
mañana tomorrow
mar sea
marisma swamp
marque el número dial the number
marque ... para obtener línea dial ... for an outside line
marque ... para recepción dial ... for reception
martes Tuesday
marzo March
materia grasa fat content
maternidad maternity
matrícula (número de ...) license plate [registration] (number)
mayo May
mayores de ... no children under ...
media pensión half board
mejorado(-a) improved
memorial memorial
menú del día set menu
menú turístico tourist menu
mercado market
mercado cubierto covered market
mercancía libre de impuestos duty-free goods
merendero picnic site
mermeladas jams and marmelades
mesas arriba seats upstairs
metro subway [metro]
miércoles Wednesday
mina mine
mínimo ... minimum ...
mirador viewpoint
modo de empleo instructions for use
molino mill
molino de viento windmill
monasterio abbey; monastery
moneda extranjera foreign currency
montaña mountain
montañismo rock climbing
monumento monument

onumento histórico ancient
onument
ostrador (para registrarse)
eck-in counter
ostrador de información
information desk
moto de agua jetski
mountain bike mountain bike
muebles furniture
multi cine multiplex movie theater
[cinema]
muralla wall
murallas de la ciudad city wall
museo museum
música clásica classical music
música de baile dance music
música de órgano organ music
música en directo live music
música ligera easy-listening music
música regional folk music
muy despacio dead slow

N

nacionalidad nationality
nada que declarar nothing to declare
natación swimming
navegar sailing
Navidad Christmas
nieve snow
niebla fog
nieve helada icy snow
nieve húmeda wet snow
nieve pesada heavy snow
nieve polvo powdery snow
nilón nylon
niños children
**niños sólo acompañados por un
adulto** no unaccompanied children
no abandone su equipaje do not
leave baggage unattended
no acercarse keep clear
no administrar por vía oral not to be
taken orally
no aparcar no parking
no apoyarse sobre la puerta do not
lean against door
no asomarse a la ventana do not
lean out of windows

no adelantar no passing
no contiene azúcar sugar-free
no da cambio no change given
no daña películas film-safe
no dejar desperdicios: multa de ...
no littering: fine ...
no deje objetos de valor en el coche
do not leave valuables in your car
no devuelve monedas no change
given
no echar basura don't dump rubbish
no fumadores non-smoking
no hay descuentos no discounts
no hay entradas sold out
no hay entreactos no intermission
no incluido exclusive
no ingerir not for internal
consumption
**no introducir monedas hasta
obtener respuesta** do not insert
money until answer received
no molestar do not disturb
no pega non-stick
no pisar el césped keep off the grass
no planchar do not iron
no retornable non-returnable
no se aceptan cambios goods cannot
be exchanged
no se aceptan devoluciones no
refunds
no se aceptan talones no checks
[cheques]
no se aceptan tarjetas de crédito no
credit cards
no se admite durante las misas no
entry during services/mass
no se deforma will not lose its shape
**no se permite la entrada una vez
iniciada la función** no entry once the
performance has begun
**no se permiten alimentos en la
habitación** no food in the room
no tirar al fuego do not burn
no tirar basura do not litter
no tocar do not touch
no verter escombros no dumping
no-retornable non-returnable
noche night

Nochebuena Christmas Eve
Nochevieja New Year's Eve
noviembre November
nuevas normas de circulación new traffic system in operation
número de la cartilla de la seguridad social social security number
número de la tarjeta de crédito credit card number
número de vuelo flight number
número del pasaporte passport number

O

obispo bishop
objetos perdidos lost-and-found [lost property]
obra de teatro play
obras a ... mts construction (... meters) ahead
obsequio free gift
octubre October
ocupado occupied/engaged
odontólogo dentist
oferta especial special offer
oficina de cambio (de moneda) currency exchange office [bureau de change]
oficina de información information office
ojo con los rateros beware pickpockets
ojo con los ladrones thieves about
operadora operator
óptica optician's
oraciones prayers
orilla river bank
oro gold
orquesta sinfónica symphony orchestra
ortodoncista orthodontist
osteópata osteopath
otoño fall [autumn]
otros pasaportes non-EU citizens

P

pabellón pavilion
páginas amarillas yellow pages

pagos payments
pagos y cobros payments and receivables
pague 2 lleve 3 buy 2 get 1 free
pague antes de repostar please pay for gas/petrol before filling car
pague aquí please pay here
palacio palace
palcos boxes
palos de esquí ski poles/sticks
pan bread
panadería bakery
panorama panorama
pantano bog/marsh; reservoir
pantomima pantomime
papel reciclado recycled paper
papelería stationery store
paquetes packages
para cabello graso for oily hair
para cabello normal for normal hair
para cabello seco for dry hair
para dos personas for two
paracaidismo parachuting
parada de ambulancias ambulance station
parada de autobús bus stop
parada de taxi(s) taxi stand [rank]
parada discrecional request stop
parada solicitada bus stopping
paraíso superior balcony
pare el motor turn off your engine
pared wall
parlamento parliament building
parque park
parque de atracciones amusement park
parque nacional country park; national park
parque reserva nature reserve
parque temático theme park
párroco fr. (Father)
parroquia parish
particular private
partido match
pasaje alley
paseo walk
paseo peatonal walkway
paso units

aso a nivel grade [level] crossing
aso de peatones pedestrian crossing
aso exclusivo para peatones
edestrians only
aso subterráneo underground
passage
pastelería pastry shop
patín pedallo
patinage sobre hielo ice skating
patines skates
peaje toll
peatón pedestrians
peligro danger
peligro de avalancha avalanche danger
peligroso dangerous
peluquería hairdresser/barber
multa por viajar sin billete penalty
for traveling without a ticket
pendiente gradient
pendiente peligrosa dangerous slope
pensión completa full board
permiso de circulación y ficha
técnica registration papers
pesca con caña angling
pesca con licencia obligatoria
fishing by permit only
pesca prohibida no fishing
pescadería fish store [fishmonger]
PGC guardia civil highway police
piel leather
píldora pill
piragüismo canoeing
piscina swimming pool
piscina para salto de trampolín
diving pool
piso en alquiler apartment for rent
pista cerrada ski trail [piste] closed
pista de bicicletas cycle track
pista para principiantes for
beginners *(ski trail)*
pista track
planeo gliding
plata silver
platea orchestra
plato del día dish of the day
plato regional local specialties
platos preparados precooked meals
playa beach

playa de nudistas nudist beach
plaza square
plaza redonda roundabout
podólogo chiropodist
policía police
policía de tráfico traffic police
polideportivo sports center
poliéster polyester
pomada ointment
porcelana china
portero de noche night porter
postres desserts
pozo (water) well
precaución drive carefully; caution
precio de la habitación room rate
precio por litro price per liter
precipicio cliff
prefijo territorial area code
prepare importe exacto please have
exact change ready
presa dam
presente en estante hasta ...
sell by ...
primavera spring
primer piso first floor [U.K. ground
floor]
primera clase first class
principal dress circle
privado staff only
probador(es) fitting room(s)
prohibida la entrada keep out/no
entry
prohibido a menores de 18 años
under-18 not allowed
prohibido a vehículos pesados
closed to heavy vehicles
prohibido acampar no camping
prohibido adelantar no passing
[overtaking]
prohibido bañarse no
swimming/bathing
prohibido consumir alimentos
adquiridos en el exterior no food
purchased elsewhere allowed on the
premises
prohibido correr no running
prohibido detenerse entre ... y ...
no stopping (between ... and ...)

prohibido esquiar fuera de las pistas no trail skiing
prohibido estacionar no waiting
prohibido fotografiar no photography
prohibido fumar en el garaje no smoking on car decks
prohibido hablar al conductor do not talk to the driver
prohibido encender fuego no fires/barbeques
prohibido juegos de pelota no ball playing
prohibido la entrada/el paso no entry
prohibido la salida/el paso no exit
prohibido usar el claxon use of horn prohibited
prohibido viajar de pie no standing
protéjase de la luz do not expose to sunlight
próxima visita a las … next tour at …
psiquiatra psychiatrist
pueblo village
puente bajo low bridge
puente bridge
puente inferior lower deck
puente levadizo drawbridge
puerta (de embarque) (boarding) gate
puerta corta-fuegos fire door
puerta door/gate
puertas automáticas automatic doors
puerto cerrado (mountain) pass closed
puerto deportivo marina
puerto dock; harbor
puesto de pescado fishstall
pujar to go up
punto de embarque embarkation point
punto de encuentro meeting point

queso cheese
quien rompe, paga all breakages must be paid for
quirófano operating theater

radiología x-ray
rambla avenue
rampa ramp
rápido express train
rápidos rapids
raqueta racket
rasgar aquí tear here
rayos X x-ray
rebajado bargain
rebajas clearance [sale]
recambios y accesorios del automóvil car accessory [spares] store
recepción reception
recibimos paid
recién pintado wet paint
recital de poesías poetry reading
recogida de equipajes baggage reclaim
recogidas a … next collection at …
reduzca la velocidad slow down
referencia reference
regalos gifts
remitente sender
remo rowing
reparación del calzado shoe repair
reserva de entradas/plazas ticket reservation
reservada reserved
respete su carril stay [get] in lane
respeten este lugar de culto please respect this place of worship
retirar dinero withdrawals
retire el billete take ticket
retornable returnable
retraso/retrasado delayed
revisado(-a) revised
revista review/variety show
revistas magazines
rezos prayers
río river
ronda ring road
ropa de caballero menswear
ropa de niños childrenwear
ropa de señoras ladieswear
ropa interior femenina lingerie
rugby rugby
ruinas ruins

ruta de autobús bus route
ruta del ferry ferry route
ruta opcional alternative route
ruta turística scenic route

sábado Saturday
sal salt
sala ward
sala de conciertos concert hall
sala de conferencias conference room
sala de curas treatment room
sala de espera passenger lounge/waiting room
sala de juegos game room
sala de máquinas fitness room
salida exit/way out
salida de autopista highway [motorway] exit
salida de camiones truck exit
salida de emergencia emergency exit
salida de incendio fire exit
salida por la puerta trasera exit by the rear door
salidas departures
salón lounge
salón de convenciones convention hall
salón de televisor television room
salsas sauces
salvavidas life preserver [lifebelt]
se aceptan tarjetas de crédito we accept credit cards
se alquila for rent
se envían fax faxes sent
se habla inglés English spoken
se procederá contra el hurto shoplifting will be prosecuted
se procederá contra los intrusos trespassers will be prosecuted
se requiere un documento de identidad proof of identity required
se ruega mostrar su bolso a la salida please show your bags before leaving
se ruega pagar en caja please pay at counter

se ruega un donativo please make a contribution
secador de pelo hairdryer
sector para familias family section
seda silk
según mercado subject to availability
segunda clase second class
segundo piso third floor [U.K. second floor]
seguridad security
selecciones destino select destination/zone
sellos de correo stamps
semáforo provisional temporary traffic lights
Semana Santa Easter
sendero footpath/path
sentido único one-way street
señas address
señoras ladies *(toilets)*
septiembre (setiembre) September
sepultura grave
servicio service charge
servicio de ampliación enlargement service
servicio de habitaciones room service
servicio incluido service included
servicio no incluido service not included
servicio nocturno night service
servicios bathrooms/restrooms [toilets]
sesión continua continuous performance
sesión de noche evening performance
sesión de tarde matinée
si es correcto pulse continuar if correct press "continuar" (continue)
si no pulse cancelar otherwise press "cancelar" (cancel)
si no queda satisfecho de su compra le devolvemos su dinero satisfaction or your money back (money-back guarantee)
si persisten los síntomas, consulte su médico if symptoms persist, consult your doctor

sierra mountain range
silencio durante las oraciones quiet, service in progress
sin grasa fat-free
sin salida para peatones no thoroughfare for pedestrians
sírvase frío serve chilled
sobre pedido made to order
solicite parada stopping service *(bus)*
solicite vendedor please ask for assistance
sólo abonados permit-holders/ticket holders only
sólo bus buses only
sólo domingos Sundays only
sólo en efectivo cash only
sólo entrada only access
sólo hombres men only
sólo laborables weekdays only
sólo lavado a mano hand wash only
sólo mercancías freight only
sólo mujeres women only
sólo para máquina de afeitar razors [shavers] only
sólo para uso externo for external use only
sólo personal de la empresa staff only
sólo residentes residents only
sólo vehículos autorizados unauthorized parking prohibited
sombrilla umbrella [sunshade]
sopas soups
subtitulada subtitled
submarinismo diving
sugerencias para servir serving suggestion
súper premium [super] *(gasoline/petrol)*
surtidor pump *(gasoline/petrol)*

T

tabla de surf surfboard
tabla de windsurf sailboard
tableta tablet
talla única one size fits all
taller mecánico car repairs
taquilla box/ticket office

tarifa rate
tarjeta de emba... card ...mbarkation
tarjeta mensual ...
tarjeta semanal ...icket
tarjeta de teléfono...ket ...ard
té tea
teatro theater
teclee su número pe... your PIN number ...e in
teleférico cable car/go...
teléfono con tarjeta ca...
teléfono de emergencia... telephone
teléfono público public t...
telesilla chairlift
templo chapel/church *(non...*
tenis de mesa table tennis
termine el tratamiento fini... course *(treatment)*
terraplén embankment
terraza balcony
tienda de regalos gift shop
tienda libre de impuestos duty... shop
tintorería dry-cleaner
tipo de cambio exchange rate
tirad/tirar pull
tire de la palanca pull the handle
todos con guarnición de ... all the above are served with ...
tolerada universal *(film classification)*
torre tower
tráfico de frente traffic from the opposite direction
tráfico lento slow traffic
tragar entera swallow whole
traje de calle informal wear
tranvía streetcar [tram]
transbordador ferry
transbordador de pasajeros passenger ferry
tren train
tren con literas sleeper (train)
tren de cercanías local train
tribuna para espectadores viewing gallery
tribuna stand/grandstand

trolebús tr...
tumba to...air...
tumbona...
túnel tu... **en todas las**
TV (po...satellite) TV in every
habit...
room...

U

...ada a las ... last entry

...solinera antes de la
... last gas [petrol] station
...e highway [motorway]
...dad university
...ias accident and emergency
...bligatorio de cadenas o
...áticos de nieve use chains or
...tires
...está aquí you are here

V

...ado permanente keep clear/do not
block entrance
vagón de (no) fumadores
(non-)smoking compartment
vagón restaurante dining car
válido para zonas ...
valid for zones ...
valle valley
vapor steamer
veces al día ... times a day
vehículo pesado heavy vehicles
vehículos lentos slow vehicles
velero sailboat
velocidad máxima maximum speed
velódromo cycle track
veneno poison/poisonous
venta anticipada advance bookings
venta de billetes ticket office
venta inmediata tickets for today
verano summer
verdulería greengrocer
verduras a elegir choice of vegetables
verduras vegetables
vereda layaway
verificación de pasaportes passport
check/control

verifique su cambio please check
your change
vestuario changing rooms
vía preferente main road/principal
highway
vía segundaria minor road
viaje travel
viernes Friday
vino wine
vinos y licores wines and spirits
visitas con guía guided tours
vísperas evensong
vista panorámica panoramic view
viveros garden center
vuelos internacionales international
flights
vuelos nacionales domestic flights

Y

yate yacht
yogurt yogurt

Z

zapatería shoe store
zapatillas de deporte obligatorias
white soles only
zapatos shoes
zona comercial shopping area
zona de aparcamiento regulado
"ORA" "pay and display" parking
zona de carga loading bay
zona de carga y descarga deliveries
only
zona de descanso rest area
zona de no fumadores non-smoking
zona peatonal pedestrian zone
[precinct]
zona residencial residential zone
zona urbana urban [built-up] area
zoológico zoo
zumos de fruta fruit juices

REFERENCE

GRAMMAR

Regular verbs and their tenses

There are three verb types which follow a regular pattern, their infinitives ending in -**ar**, -**er**, and -**ir**, e.g. *to speak* **hablar**, *to eat* **comer**, *to live* **vivir**. Here the most commonly used present, past and future forms.

	PRESENT	PAST	FUTURE
yo *I*	hablo	hablé	hablaré
tú *you* (informal)	hablas	hablaste	hablarás
él/ella/Ud. *he/she/you* (form.)	habla	habló	hablará
nosotros *we*	hablamos	hablamos	hablaremos
vosotros *you* (pl. inform.)	habláis	hablasteis	hablaréis
ellos/ellas/Uds. *they/you* (form.)	hablan	hablaron	hablarán
yo *I*	como	comí	comeré
tú *you* (informal)	comes	comiste	comerás
él/ella/Ud. *he/she/you* (form.)	come	comió	comerá
nosotros *we*	comemos	comimos	comeremos
vosotros *you* (pl. inform.)	coméis	comisteis	comeréis
ellos/ellas/Uds. *they/you* (form.)	comen	comieron	comerán
yo *I*	vivo	viví	viviré
tú *you* (informal)	vives	viviste	vivirás
él/ella/Ud. *he/she/you* (form.)	vive	vivió	vivirá
nosotros *we*	vivimos	vivimos	viviremos
vosotros *you* (pl. inform.)	vivís	vivisteis	viviréis
ellos/ellas/Uds. *they/you* (form.)	viven	vivieron	vivirán

Very often, people omit the pronoun, using only the verb form.

Examples: **Vivo en Madrid.** *I live in Madrid.*
   ¿**Habla español?** *Do you speak Spanish?*

There are many irregular verbs whose forms differ considerably.

To be – ser and estar

Spanish has two verbs for *to be*, **ser** and **estar**. Their usage is complex, and we can give you only some general guidelines.

	PRESENT	PAST	FUTURE
yo	soy/estoy	fui/estuve	seré/estaré
tú	eres/estás	fuiste/estuviste	serás/estarás
él/ella/Ud.	es/está	fue/estuvo	será/estará
nosotros	somos/estamos	fuimos/estuvimos	seremos/estaramos
vosotros	sois/estáis	fuisteis/estuvisteis	seréis/estaréis
ellos/as/Uds.	son/están	fueron/estuvieron	serán/estarán

Ser is used to identify people or objects, to <u>describe their basic and natural characteristics</u>, also to <u>tell time and dates.</u>

Examples: **¡Fue caro!** *That was expensive!*
             Somos médicos. *We're doctors.*
             Son las dos. *It's 2 o'clock.*

Estar is used when the <u>state of a person or object is changeable</u> and to <u>indicate locations.</u>

Examples: **Estoy cansado.** *I'm tired.*
             ¿Dónde estuvo? *Where was he?*
             Estarán en Roma. *They'll be in Rome.*

Nouns and articles

Generally nouns ending in **-o** are masculine, those ending in **-a** are feminine. Their indefinite articles are **el** (masc) and **la** (fem). In the plural (**los**) the endings are **-s** or **-es** when the singular form ends with a consonant.

Examples: Singular <u>**el** tren</u> *the train*   Plural <u>**los** trenes</u> *the trains*
                      <u>**la** mesa</u> *the table*   <u>**las** mesas</u> *the tables*

The definite articles also indicate their gender: **un** (masculine), **una** (feminine), **unos** (plural masculine), **unas** (plural feminine).

Examples: Singular <u>**un** libro</u> *a book*   Plural <u>**unos** libros</u> *books*
                      <u>**una** casa</u> *a house*   <u>**unas** casas</u> *houses*

Possessive articles relate to the gender of the noun that follows:

	SINGULAR	PLURAL
my	**mi**	**mis**
your (informal)	**tu**	**tus**
his/her/its/your (formal)	**su**	**sus**
our	**nuestro/a**	**nuestros/as**
your (plural, informal)	**vuestro/a**	**vuestros/as**
their/your (plural, formal)	**su**	**sus**

Examples: **¿Dónde está <u>su</u> billete?** *Where is your ticket?*

<u>Vuestro</u> tren sale a las 8. *Your train leaves at 8.*

Busco <u>mis</u> maletas. *I'm looking for my suitcases.*

Word order

The conjugated verb comes after the subject.

Example: **Yo trabajo en Madrid.** *I work in Madrid.*

Questions are formed by reversing the order of subject and verb, changing the intonation of the affirmative sentence, or using key question words like *when* **cuándo**.

Examples: **¿Tiene Ud. mapas?** *Do you have maps?*

¿Cuándo cerrará el banco? *When will the bank close?*

Negations

Negative sentences are formed by adding *not* **no** to that part of the sentence which is to be negated.

Examples: **No fumamos.** *We don't smoke.*

No es nuevo. *It's not new.*

El autobús no llegó. *The bus didn't arrive.*

¿Por qué no escuchas? *Why don't you listen?*

Imperatives (command form)

Imperative sentences are formed by using the stem of the verb with the appropriate ending.

Example:

tú *you* (informal)	**¡Habla!** *Speak!*	[no hab**les**]
Ud. *you* (formal)	**¡Hable!** *Speak!*	
nosotros *we*	**¡Hablemos!** *Let's speak!*	
vosotros *you* (inf. pl.)	**¡Hablad!** *Speak!*	[no habl**éis**]
Uds. *you* (form. pl.)	**¡Hablen!** *Speak!*	

Comparative and superlative

Comparative and superlative are formed by adding *more* **más**/*the most* **lo más**, or *less* **menos**/*the least* **lo menos** before the adjective or noun.

ADJECTIVE	COMPARATIVE	SUPERLATIVE
grande	**más grande**	**lo más grande**
big, large	*bigger*	*the biggest*
costoso	**menos costoso**	**lo menos costoso**
expensive	*less expensive*	*the least expensive*

Example: **Estas tarjetas son las más baratas.** *These postcards are the cheapest.*

Pepe tiene menos dinero que Juan. *Pepe has less money than Juan.*

Posessive pronouns

Pronouns serve as substitutes and relate to the gender.

	SINGULAR	PLURAL
mine	**mío/a**	**míos/as**
yours (informal singular)	**tuyo/a**	**tuyos/as**
yours (formal)	**suyo/a**	**suyos/as**
his/her/its	**suyo/a**	**suyos/as**
ours	**nuestro/a**	**nuestros/as**
yours (plural, informal)	**vuestro/a**	**vuestros/as**
theirs	**suyo/a**	**suyos/as**

Examples: **Sus hijos y los míos.** *Your children and mine.*

¿Es tuyo este café? *Is this coffee yours?*

Adjectives

Adjectives describe nouns. They agree with the noun in gender and number.
Masculine forms end in **-o**, feminine forms end in **-a**. Generally adjectives
come after the noun. The feminine form is generally the same if the masculine form ends in **-e** or with a consonant.

Examples: **Tenemos un coche vie<u>jo</u>.** *We have an old car.*

Mi jefa es simpátic<u>a</u> . *My boss is nice.*

El mar / La flor es azul. *The ocean / The flower is blue.*

Most adjectives form their plurals the same way as nouns:

Example: **una casa ro<u>ja</u>**   **unas cas<u>as</u> ro<u>jas</u>**
          a red house   *red houses*

Adverbs and adverbial expressions

Adverbs describe verbs. They are formed by adding **-mente** to the feminine
form of the adjective if it differs from the masculine. Otherwise add **-mente**
to the masculine form.

Examples: **María conduce lentamente.** *Linda drives very slowly.*

Roberto conduce rápidamente. *Robert drives fast.*

Ud. habla español bien. *You speak Spanish well.*

Some common adverbial time expressions:

actualmente *presently* **todavía no** *not yet*

todavía *still*   **ya no** *not anymore*

NUMBERS

Larger numbers are built up using the components below:

Example: 3 456 789   **tres millones, cuatrocientos cincuenta y seis mil, setecientos ochenta y nueve.**

Note that from 31 to 99, **y** (and) is used between tens and units, but never between hundreds and tens.

0	**cero** _thero_		40	**cuarenta** _kwarenta_
1	**uno** _oono_		50	**cincuenta** _theenkwenta_
2	**dos** _dos_		60	**sesenta** _sesenta_
3	**tres** _tres_		70	**setenta** _setenta_
4	**cuatro** _kwatro_		80	**ochenta** _ochenta_
5	**cinco** _theenko_		90	**noventa** _nobenta_
6	**seis** _says_		100	**cien** _theeyen_
7	**siete** _seeyeteh_		101	**ciento uno** _theeyento oono_
8	**ocho** _ocho_		200	**doscientos** _dostheeyentos_
9	**nueve** _nwebeh_		500	**quinientos** _keeneeyentos_
10	**diez** _deeyeth_			
11	**once** _ontheh_		1 000	**mil** _meel_
12	**doce** _dotheh_		10 000	**diez mil** _deeyeth meel_
13	**trece** _tretheh_		1 000 000	**un millón** _oon meel-yon_
14	**catorce** _katortheh_			
15	**quince** _keentheh_		first	**primer(a)** _preemer(a)_
16	**dieciséis** _deeyetheesays_		second	**segundo (-a)** _segoondo(-a)_
17	**diecisiete** _deeyetheeseeyeteh_		third	**tercero(-a)** _terthero(-a)_
18	**dieciocho** _deeyetheeocho_		fourth	**cuarto(-a)** _kwarto(-a)_
19	**diecinueve** _deeyetheenwebeh_		fifth	**quinto(-a)** _keento(-a)_
20	**veinte** _baynteh_		once	**una vez** _oona beth_
21	**veintiuno** _baynteeyoono_		twice	**dos veces** _dos bethes_
22	**veintidós** _baynteedos_		three times	**tres veces** _tres bethes_
30	**treinta** _traynta_			
31	**treinta y uno** _traynta ee oono_			

one half	**la mitad**	_la meetath_
half an hour	**media hora**	_medeeya ora_
a quarter	**un cuarto**	_oon kwarto_
a third	**un tercio**	_oon tertheeyo_
a pair of ...	**un par de ...**	_oon par deh_
a dozen ...	**una docena de ...**	_oona dothena deh_

DAYS

Monday	**lunes** _loones_
Tuesday	**martes** _martes_
Wednesday	**miércoles** _meeyerkoles_
Thursday	**jueves** _khwebes_
Friday	**viernes** _beeyernes_
Saturday	**sábado** _sabado_
Sunday	**domingo** _domeengo_

MONTHS

January	**enero** _enero_
February	**febrero** _febrero_
March	**marzo** _martho_
April	**abril** _abreel_
May	**mayo** _mayo_
June	**junio** _khooneeyo_
July	**julio** _khooleeyo_
August	**agosto** _agosto_
September	**septiembre** _septeeyembreh_
October	**octubre** _oktoobreh_
November	**noviembre** _nobeeyembreh_
December	**diciembre** _deetheeyembreh_

DATES

It's …	**Estamos a …** _estamos a_
July 10	**diez de julio** _deeyeth deh khooleeyo_
Tuesday, March 1	**martes, uno de marzo** _martes oono deh martho_
yesterday	**ayer** _eye-yer_
today	**hoy** _oy_
tomorrow	**mañana** _mañana_
this month	**este mes** _esteh mes_
last week	**la semana pasada** _la semana pasada_
next/every year	**el año que viene/todos los años** _el año keh beeyeneh/todos los años_

220

SEASONS

spring	**la primavera**	*la preemabera*
summer	**el verano**	*el berano*
fall [autumn]	**el otoño**	*el otoño*
winter	**el invierno**	*el eenbeeyerno*
in spring	**en primavera**	*en preemabera*
during the summer	**durante el verano**	*dooranteh el berano*

GREETINGS

Happy birthday!	**¡Feliz cumpleaños!**	*feleeth koompleaños*
Merry Christmas!	**¡Feliz Navidad!**	*feleeth nabeedath*
Happy New Year!	**¡Feliz Año Nuevo!**	*feleeth año nwebo*
Congratulations!	**¡Enhorabuena!/¡Felicidades!**	*en'orabwena/eleetheedades*
Good luck!/All the best!	**¡Buena suerte!**	*bwena swerteh*
Have a good trip!	**¡Que tenga un buen viaje!**	*keh tenga oon bwen beeyakheh*

PUBLIC HOLIDAYS

January 1	Año Nuevo	New Year's Day
January 6	Epifanía	Epiphany
March 19	San José	St Joseph's Day
May 1	Día del Trabajo	Labor Day
July 25	Santiago Apóstol	St James's Day
August 15	Asunción	Assumption Day
October 12	Día de la Hispanidad	Columbus Day
November 1	Todos los Santos	All Saints' Day
December 6	Día de la Constitución	Constitution Day
December 8	Immaculada Concepción	Immaculate Conception Day
December 25	Navidad	Christmas Day
Movable dates:	Viernes Santo	Good Friday
	Lunes de Pascua	Easter Monday (Catalonia only)

Note: There are many local variations.

Excuse me. Can you tell me the time?	**Disculpe. ¿Puede decirme la hora?** *deeskoolpeh pwedeh detheermeh la ora*
It's five past one.	**Es la una y cinco.** *es la oona ee theenko*
It's …	**Son las …** *son las …*
ten past two	**dos y diez** *dos ee deeyeth*
a quarter past three	**tres y cuarto** *tres ee kwarto*
twenty past four	**cuatro y veinte** *kwatro ee baynteh*
twenty-five past five	**cinco y veinticinco** *theenko ee baynteetheenko*
half past six	**seis y media** *says ee medeeya*
twenty-five to seven	**siete menos veinticinco** *seeyeteh menos baynteetheenko*
twenty to eight	**ocho menos veinte** *ocho menos baynteh*
a quarter to nine	**nueve menos cuarto** *nwebeh menos kwarto*
ten to ten	**diez menos diez** *deeyeth menos deeyeth*
five to eleven	**once menos cinco** *ontheh menos theenko*
twelve o'clock (noon/midnight)	**doce en punto (del mediodía/de la noche)** *dotheh en poonto (del mehdeeohdeeah/ deh la nocheh)*
at dawn	**al amanecer** *al amanether*
in the morning	**por la mañana** *por la mañana*

during the day	**durante el día** *dooranteh el deeya*
before lunch	**antes de comer** *antes de komer*
after lunch	**después de comer** *despwes de komer*
in the afternoon	**por la tarde** *por la tardeh*
in the evening/at night	**por la noche** *por la nocheh*
I'll be ready in five minutes.	**Estaré listo(-a) en cinco minutos.** *estareh leesto(-a) en theenko meenootos*
He'll be back in a quarter of an hour.	**Volverá dentro de un cuarto de hora.** *bolbera dentro deh oon kwarto deh ora*
She arrived half an hour ago.	**Llegó hace media hora.** *l-yego atheh medeeya ora*
The train leaves at …	**El tren sale a las …** *el tren saleh a las*
13:04	**trece horas y cuatro minutos** *trethe oras ee kwatro meenootos*
0:40	**cero horas cuarenta minutos** *thero oras kwarenta meenootos*
10 minutes late/early	**diez minutos más tarde/diez minutos antes** *deeyeth meenootos mas tardeh/ deeyeth meenootos antes*
5 minutes fast/slow	**cinco minutos adelantado/atrasado** *theenko meenootos adelantado/atrasado*
from 9:00 to 5:00	**de nueve a cinco** *deh nwebeh a theenko*
between 8:00 and 2:00	**entre las ocho y las dos** *entreh las ocho ee las dos*
I'll be leaving by …	**Me iré antes de las …** *meh eereh antes deh las*
Will you be back before …?	**¿Estará de vuelta antes de …?** *estara deh bwelta antes deh*
We'll be here until …	**Estaremos aquí hasta …** *estaremos akee asta*

Océano Atlántico

La Coruña

Mar Cantábrico

Bilbao

FRANCE

PORTUGAL

Pamplona

Salamanca

Zaragoza

Madrid

Barcelona

ESPAÑA

Toledo

ISLAS BALEARES

Valencia

Mallorca

Men

Cordoba

Ibiza

Sevilla

Granada

Cartagena

Cádiz

Málaga

Gibraltar (UK)

Mar Méditerráneo

MOROCCO

ALGERIA

ISLAS CANARIAS

Santa Cruz

Océano Atlántico

Las Palmas de
Gran Canarias